The Kitchen Counter Cooking School

The Kitchen Counter Cooking School

*How a Few Simple Lessons
Transformed Nine Culinary Novices into
Fearless Home Cooks*

Kathleen Flinn

VIKING

VIKING
Published by the Penguin Group
Penguin Group (USA) Inc., 375 Hudson Street, New York, New York 10014, U.S.A. • Penguin Group (Canada), 90 Eglinton Avenue East, Suite 700, Toronto, Ontario, Canada M4P 2Y3 (a division of Pearson Penguin Canada Inc.) • Penguin Books Ltd, 80 Strand, London WC2R 0RL, England • Penguin Ireland, 25 St. Stephen's Green, Dublin 2, Ireland (a division of Penguin Books Ltd) • Penguin Books Australia Ltd, 250 Camberwell Road, Camberwell, Victoria 3124, Australia (a division of Pearson Australia Group Pty Ltd) • Penguin Books India Pvt Ltd, 11 Community Centre, Panchsheel Park, New Delhi – 110 017, India • Penguin Group (NZ), 67 Apollo Drive, Rosedale, Auckland 0632, New Zealand (a division of Pearson New Zealand Ltd) • Penguin Books (South Africa) (Pty) Ltd, 24 Sturdee Avenue, Rosebank, Johannesburg 2196, South Africa

Penguin Books Ltd, Registered Offices: 80 Strand, London WC2R 0RL, England

First published in 2011 by Viking Penguin, a member of Penguin Group (USA) Inc.

10   9   8   7   6   5   4   3   2   1

Names and identifying characteristics have been changed to protect the privacy of certain individuals.

Photograph credits
Page 5: Maggie Savarino; 125: Kathleen Flinn; 183: Jeff Maness

LIBRARY OF CONGRESS CATALOGING IN PUBLICATION DATA
Flinn, Kathleen.
    The kitchen counter cooking school : how a few simple lessons transformed nine culinary novices into fearless home cooks/Kathleen Flinn.
        p.   cm.
        Includes bibliographical references and index.
    ISBN 978-0-670-02300-4 (hardback)
    1. Cooking—Study and teaching—Anecdotes. 2. Flinn, Kathleen—Anecdotes. 3. Cook books. I. Title.
    TX661.F57 2011
    641.507—dc23   2011016222

Printed in the United States of America
Designed by Carla Bolte

For my mother, Irene

For encouraging me to find joy in everything, not just cooking

Contents

PART III

SEAFOOD, SOUP, AND THE IMPORTANCE OF LEFTOVERS

Author's Note

~~

In theory, the story presented herein represents a year of my life teaching one round of lessons to nine volunteer students. In reality, it's the result of numerous additional kitchen visits, scores of interviews with cooks, researchers, and cooking teachers, plus my own teaching experiences in the year since the project ended.

I recorded every home interview and most of the original classes, resulting in about fifty hours of video and two hundred pages of handwritten notes. I've done my best to portray events accurately, but consolidated or shifted events and comments in some situations. In a few scenes, the dialogue in classes was built from memory. The names of some of the volunteers and their children have been changed to protect their privacy.

When it comes to the techniques taught here, ardent foodies or culinary professionals may debate the "right" method to roast a chicken or some other technique. I might even look back on these lessons to find that I have changed the way I teach the same recipes. That's one of the great things about cooking; there's more than one way to skin a fish. As long as an approach yields good, nourishing food, it isn't "wrong."

The Kitchen Counter Cooking School

෨෧

The Woman with the Chicken

"You teach best what you most need to learn."
—Richard Bach, *Illusions: The Adventures of a Reluctant Messiah*

෨ Normally, I do not stalk people in grocery stores.

I confess to the occasional practice of supermarket voyeurism. But who doesn't sometimes notice the curious collections of fellow shoppers, then contemplate what they may reveal about them?

What goes on in the home of a hunched, graying woman with nineteen cans of cat food, iceberg lettuce, a family pack of steaks, and a copy of *In Style* magazine? Or a young woman in full stage makeup oblivious to the world outside her headphones, a pack of tofu hot dogs among the contents of a hand basket nestled in the crook of her tattoo-littered arm? Or an elegant man with a perfect manicure who lingers over the imported cheese counter, his cart filled with organic greens, expensive olives, and four bottles of champagne? Every grocery cart tells a story.

Late on an otherwise average Tuesday afternoon, a sight near the canned tuna stopped me dead in my tracks. The cart sat as if abandoned in the middle of the aisle. It contained two dozen haphazardly piled boxes of dehydrated mixes for pasta, casseroles, rice, and stuffing and dubious jars of gravy. Despite being half full, the cart contained no *real* food. As I stood contemplating its contents, a heavyset woman in her late thirties, casually attired in an eggplant-colored fleece, claimed the cart. Her preteen daughter twirled impatiently around her, quietly singing a Lady Gaga song under her breath.

Would it be wrong if I followed her to find out what else she might buy?

Small basket in hand, I trailed behind her to stealthily observe. I feigned interest in various items along the aisles as she stocked up on packaged waffles and pizza pretzel bites, a collection of frozen dinners, chicken potpies, and a family-style package of pot roast with mashed potatoes and gravy.

By the time we hit the meat department, I suspected she was onto me. Hugging my shoulders against the damp chill and trying to avoid inhaling the vague smell of chlorine, I clumsily relied upon my peripheral vision to spy her selecting a heavy family-sized pack of ground hamburger at the other end of the case. She pushed her cart in my direction. I pretended to peruse the plastic-wrapped turkey options. "Can you believe how expensive chicken breasts are these days? Crazy," she said out loud, to no one in particular. She reluctantly tossed a package into her cart.

I seized the opportunity to say something. "Whole chickens are on sale," I said. "Ninety-nine cents a pound, I think."

She chuckled. "Thanks, but I would have *no* idea what to do with a whole chicken."

It hit me. After a year deboning chickens and stuffing meat with other meats at a famous Paris cooking school, I had information this woman needed. For some reason, at that moment, I felt compelled to give it to her. "Come with me. I'll get someone to show you how to cut up a chicken."

"Ah, no, thanks," she said. A reasonable response given that I was a complete stranger who had followed her for twenty minutes through the maze of grocery store aisles.

Somehow I assured her that I was not trying to sell a time-share in front of the turkey kielbasa. She shrugged and said, "Okay, why not?" We headed over to the butcher.

"Sure, I'm happy to show you how to cut it up, no problem," the butcher said as I handed him the chicken. The woman peered over the glass case to his thick white cutting board as he sectioned the bird deliberately. He stopped to show her how each cut was done. As he finished, he crackled fresh butcher paper around the pieces.

"So just how much is that whole chicken?" she asked.

He looked at the tag. "Let's see, it's on sale, so $5.20."

"How much would that go for if you sold me the pieces all cut up and packaged, like those breasts over there?" She waved toward the meat case.

He looked up, mumbled abstractly under his breath, counting on his fingers. "Well, breasts are out at $5.99 a pound, the thighs at $2.29, so I'd say about $10 or so."

"Get out!" she exclaimed. "So I pay twice the price to buy it as separate pieces? Well, who knew that!" She smiled broadly.

He winked and passed her the freshly wrapped chicken. It landed heavy in her hand. She looked thoughtful. "What is it?" I asked.

She looked around, leaned forward, and whispered in a conspiratorial tone, "I don't know what to do with the other parts of the chicken. I only know how to cook the breasts." She shrugged, embarrassed. "But thanks for your help."

As she pushed her cart away, her daughter in tow, I stopped her. I could not let this woman go without knowing what to do with the rest of her chicken. By chance, this supermarket happened to be carrying the paperback of my first book. I fetched a copy. I flipped to a recipe for braised chicken thighs with mustard and then to one for stock.

At first, she didn't believe it was my book. I showed her my driver's license. "I'm not trying to sell you a book," I assured her. "I'm happy to buy it for you. I can't explain it, but I just really want to help you."

For the next hour, I led her around the store, making notes in the margins and writing new recipes in the notepad that I always carry in my purse. We discussed why she bought so many boxes and cans, and as we did, I slowly convinced her to clear out most of them from her cart and replace them with the real food that the boxed versions attempted to replicate. A three-pound beef roast replaced four shelf-stable individual pot roast dinners. When rounded out with inexpensive vegetables, the roast would yield a dozen servings for the same price.

"You know, I can't thank you enough for all this," she said earnestly as we made our way to the checkout, where, as promised, I bought her the book. "At first, I thought you were some crazy person. But this feels like Wonder Woman stopping to help fix a flat tire." She and her daughter waved an enthusiastic good-bye. I didn't even get her name.

That afternoon stayed with me. It awakened a curiosity that I hadn't realized I had. Somehow, I knew this chance encounter was going to change my life.

PART I

Changing Courses

"For most people, the only real stumbling block is fear of failure. In cooking you've got to have a what-the-hell attitude."

—Julia Child

Terri, Trish, Shannon, and Sabra
practice knife skills

CHAPTER 1

ઝ

We'll Always Have Paris

"They say that time changes things but you actually have to change them yourself."

—Andy Warhol, pop art icon

ઝ Standing on the stage delivering the graduation speech at Le Cordon Bleu in Paris is not the optimal time for an existential crisis.

Yet there I stood in my simple black dress, speech in hand, dwarfed by the vaulted gilded ceilings of the opulent ballroom in Le Club du Cercle just off the Champs-Élysées. Two years earlier, I had awaited my diploma sitting right where this year's graduates were now.

The school knew that I would be in Paris to lead a culinary tour and asked if I would speak. I'd said yes, flattered, before thinking the whole thing through. The applause at my introduction drifted away during the eternity it took to walk to the podium. I silently surveyed the rows of the immaculately dressed audience. In the front sat two of the many young Japanese women in full celebration kimonos, their small hands carefully folded in their laps. Behind me, a dozen instructor chefs in tall toques spanned the width of the stage in a single row, waiting. I hid my panic behind a manic smile.

What was I doing here? What words of wisdom could I possibly offer when I wasn't sure what to do next with my *own* life? At age thirty-seven, I had realized my lifelong dream to graduate from the world's most famous cooking school. But what was I supposed to do now?

I kept hearing two questions again and again, often from the same people. "You graduated from culinary school, where is your restaurant?" and "When are you two having kids?" I had no answer for either.

A lot had happened since I'd left school. I'd settled into married life in Seattle while my husband, Mike, had joined a start-up company. We'd experienced the usual stuff of life as it marched unrelentingly onward; friends and relatives got married, others divorced, a few had children, and a couple got sick. I dealt with the curious, feast-and-famine life of authorship. Two days after I read to a packed crowd at the James Beard House in New York, I stood before an audience of three at a bookstore event in San Francisco, and *that* included two of the store employees. The next week in Milwaukee, a quirky woman wearing her sweater inside out asked me to sign a book—to her cats. I wrote, "Dear Mr. Hinkel and Winkie Pie, I hope you enjoy the book, especially the parts about the fish."

About three weeks before this trip to Paris, Mike had a strange premonition. "I'm going to join my dad on his vacation in Mexico after all. I can't explain it, but I feel that if I don't go, I'll never see him again."

Within minutes of Mike's arrival at his dad's time-share, something went wrong. His dad, Floyd, pawed awkwardly against the dresser and suddenly fell heavily forward. Mike caught him and they tumbled to the floor. A doctor arrived on the scene and said Floyd had suffered a small stroke. A standard procedure to break up the stroke-causing clot led to a massive brain hemorrhage, sending Floyd into a coma. Mike arranged for an airlift to a Miami hospital for possible surgery. After an agonizing thirty-six-hour wait, doctors declared that nothing could be done. Over the next week, we watched helplessly as Floyd slipped away.

On a clear May afternoon, Mike broke down as he delivered the eulogy at a packed church in Spokane, Washington. "He was my best friend . . . the best man at my wedding and . . ." Mike stopped, fighting back tears. His sister came up and took his hand. "I always wanted to grow up to be just like him."

We left for Paris three days after the funeral. When the seat belt light dinged, we finally exhaled. We felt a strange sense of relief, as if leaving the grief and stress behind.

Standing at the podium with all this fresh in my mind, I cleared my throat as I surveyed the audience sitting in quiet expectation. I unfolded my speech. The sharp crinkling of paper echoed loudly in the vast room. I looked at Mike just offstage, proudly gripping a video camera. He tipped his head forward in a nod of encouragement. I folded my speech back up.

"So, today you've earned your culinary degree. What are you going to do with it?" I asked. "How many of you know? Raise your hands." A small group held their arms aloft.

"Here's what some of my classmates did with theirs." I talked about the friends I'd met at Le Cordon Bleu. Sharon had labored at Internet start-up companies, but now resided as a chef and kosher caterer in her hometown of Tel Aviv. Lely had traded corporate marketing to run a cooking school in Jakarta. Jose had left his job selling shoes to attend Le Cordon Bleu and was now an apprentice in a Michelin-starred restaurant in Madrid. Isabella, a former psychologist, had worked as the private chef for a Russian paper baron and later moved to Los Angeles, where she taught cooking classes in French to Hollywood celebrities' kids. Chinese-born and British-bred LP had been an attorney in London, but she now managed a French wine import business in Shanghai. Another friend had returned to work as a management consultant, but did pro bono work analyzing food distribution issues to combat hunger in places such as Mozambique.

"People ask, 'What can you do with a culinary degree?' The reality is that you can go anywhere and do anything," I continued. "You're only limited by your passion and your imagination. Be open to the possibilities, take chances. Your career doesn't have to be traditional. It doesn't even have to be in a restaurant or even in a kitchen.

"For some reason, your passion for cooking and your desire to nourish people led you to this moment and place in time. Consider for a moment what success looks like when passion enters the equation. Is it money? Is it fame? Or is it having the strength to follow that passion? To have the will to go down a path you never thought you'd venture?"

I looked at the students' faces. Most were impossibly young. "No matter what, remember that life is short, shorter than you think." I looked at Mike again. I thought back to our final moment in the Miami hospital with his father, to the last time I saw my own dad when I was thirteen, and the tear-filled interviews that I conducted writing obits in my early twenties. "It can be gone just like that," I continued, and snapped my fingers in front of the microphone. The sound echoed like a stone dropping into a well. "You think you'll figure it out someday, only to find that someday never comes." My throat caught on the words. "One thing that I hope you'll do is try not to focus on what other people expect from you. At one point in my life I was so concerned about the next rung on the corporate ladder, and only later realized I missed the entire point of the climb. Find something *you* believe in. Then, just do it. That's what matters."

The crowd applauded, but the toques rustled behind me. *"Où est la traduction?"* Where is the translation? I heard a chef ask. Between the funeral and being unsure of what to say, I'd turned in the speech too late for an official translation. Everyone agreed that if I did it on the fly in my paltry French, we'd be there all night. For once, most of the chefs couldn't understand *me*.

At the reception, as I was clutching my champagne, a radiant young woman approached. Her silky yellow-orange robes and sequined headdress perched atop her jet-black hair reminded me of an extra from the Elizabeth Taylor version of *Cleopatra*. Hessa hailed from Bahrain, but she spoke English in an accent more befitting a midwestern college sorority sister with a twinge of Valley Girl. "I, like, really identified with your speech. I'm such a question mark. How do people figure out what they want to do? What are you doing? Do you have a restaurant?"

Before I could answer, the fabulously suave Chef Savard arrived at my side. He had changed from his chef's whites into a tan suede blazer and black turtleneck to striking effect. After kissing me on both cheeks, he asked, "So, *chérie,* tell me, what are *you* doing with your culinary training? Are you and Mike going to have any children?"

I downed my champagne.

Despite our emotionally fragile states, the trip started well. Fresh from our flight, Mike dropped our bags in the tidy rental apartment near Rue Moufftard in the 5th arrondissement and immediately went downstairs. He returned with a pair of warm, fresh baguettes and a small bag of goods from a nearby *alimentation,* the Parisian equivalent of a convenience store. We ripped greedily at the still-warm bread, slathering it with sweet French butter and finishing each bite with a sip of cold, bracing Chablis.

Jet-lagged, we napped mightily until dinnertime. We awoke, disoriented, to the sticky summer heat and crimson twilight, the distinct wail of French ambulances drifting through the open shutters. Half awake, we slipped outside to experience the city as if in a dream. The wide sidewalks reflected the heat of the day as we reacquainted ourselves with the marvels of seventeenth-century architecture and the brazen yet sophisticated female nudity of modern French advertising. We saw Parisians sitting at small round tables, sipping tiny espressos or glasses of wine. We walked the streets to the Seine, drew in deep breaths of its earthy scent, and looked out over the late summer sunset. We felt strangely at home.

The speech occurred at the start of our trip, but our primary reason for being there was to lead a vacation tour organized by the American Automobile Association. It was billed as a "culinary tour of Paris"; Mike and I agreed to take a group of Americans through an abbreviated version of our life in the city. The week the tour started, we met Sabine, the tour operator in Paris. "It is a small group, yes, but the people here have all read your book and are very excited to meet you both." The group was a diverse mix that ranged from a paralegal to a flight attendant to a wealthy Florida homemaker who wielded a diamond ring the size of a baby food jar.

To kick off the tour, Mike and I led a walking tour of our former neighborhood near Les Halles. Among a smattering of meals and sightseeing, the itinerary included a tour of the wholesale food market Rungis, followed by a lunch buffet of impeccably fresh fish delivered only hours earlier to the massive seafood hangar across from the restaurant. The next day, we headed north in minibuses to Rouen, best known as the place where Joan of Arc was imprisoned by the English, then burned at the stake. Our visit was for dinner at an equally important landmark, at least for me: La Couronne, the restaurant where Julia Child ate her first meal in France. Julia Child is my longtime hero. After earning her diploma, she threw herself into writing *Mastering the Art of French Cooking,* an effort that turned into a decade-long project that defined the later part of her life. I met Julia at the edge of an earlier existential crisis when I was twenty-three years old, shortly after I first began longing to study at Le Cordon Bleu but kept my desire secret. She was among the first people to whom I revealed what seemed like an impossible dream then: to study cooking in Paris.

Each evening after dinner, the weeklong agenda descended into the "where will Mike and Kathleen take us drinking?" tour. If there's one bright spot in my French-speaking skills, it's my ability to navigate the delicate rigors of ordering a round of beverages. One evening Mike led an impromptu "Introduction to Calvados" lesson at the hotel bar. Another night, we familiarized our group with French beers and martini blancos at a place near the Palais Royal.

We enjoyed the group so much that we organized a dinner with them on the one free evening on the itinerary. As we dined on the patio of a small bistro on Rue Moufftard, we began to notice workers carrying fake hams and rubber lamb shanks passing by our table. Our waiter told us that scenes from the film version of *Julie & Julia* would be shot on the street the next day.

By the next morning, a small army of prop designers and carpenters finished transforming the corner into a street market from the 1950s. Workers installed brand-new signs designed to appear weathered above the doors. They brought in aging handcarts, dozens of barrels, antique cash registers, and even a 1940s-era delivery truck. A few extras walked around in 1950s garb, smoking and talking on their cell phones, careful to avoid the thick tangle of cables that led to a massive camera and lighting setup choking the small street's intersection.

Mike and I watched Meryl Streep, dressed as Julia, wandering the market during Julia's early days learning to cook in Paris as a student at Le Cordon Bleu. Even from a distance, we could see a radiant smile as "Julia" took it all in with delight.

By chance, the tour ended the next day with its advertised highlight: a private class at Le Cordon Bleu. As we entered the familiar glass doors, I felt pangs of stress, as if I were still a student, a living version of an anxiety dream from which I'll probably never awaken. Just as I began a brief tour, one of my toughest teachers, the Gray Chef, appeared from around the corner. He had once scolded me mercilessly for a too-sweet duck à l'orange sauce, prompting me to flee the kitchen in tears. I introduced him, first in stuttering English and then in clumsy French. Recognizing his name from the book, the group descended as a hungry pack on the man—who now seemed much shorter than I remembered—circling for a photo. I offered to take it. Suddenly, the once-imposing Gray Chef looked vulnerable and intimidated. I felt overwhelming tenderness for him. *"Êtes-vous célèbre maintenant?"* he asked gingerly. Are you famous now?

"Non, chef, vous êtes," I told him sweetly. No, you are. He smiled broadly and then spread his arms around the group, confident again. I clicked the photo.

After the rest of the group departed the next morning, one person remained for an extra day. Holly was an affable silver-haired flight attendant from Orlando in her early sixties. Holly had come to Paris with a secret mission. As we stood on the historic Pont Neuf bridge, she confessed that she had been discreetly leaving bits of her late sister's ashes on the trip.

"She wanted to visit Paris all her life, but she always found reasons not to do it," Holly said. My mind went to Floyd. We'd invited Mike's dad to visit us when we lived in Paris and even offered to buy him a spot on the AAA tour. He always declined, although he promised he'd visit "someday." Just then, as the Eiffel Tower erupted in a sparkling display of strobe lights, Holly reached into her pocket, pulled out a small bag, and emptied it into the Seine. "Now she finally got to come here, and stay," Holly said. Just before her sister died, they watched the movie *Something's Gotta Give,* starring Diane Keaton, whose character visits Paris every year on her birthday to dine on roast chicken at a bistro called Le Grand Colbert. "She was going through chemo, and she kept saying, 'I'm going to get through this because I want to eat at that restaurant in Paris.' The idea of that meal and coming to Paris got her through all of it, at least mentally. But finally, her body just gave up."

That night, the three of us dined at Le Grand Colbert. As we bid farewell to the gilded decor, Holly deposited a bit of her sister in a potted fern near the bar.

Mike and I had arranged a week to ourselves in Paris after the tour group ended. We thought that we'd be relieved to have the time alone, but Mike and I missed the enthusiasm of the group. Spurred on by that dinner with Holly, to make up for their absence and to avoid thinking of Mike's dad, we ate.

We began by haunting our favorite bistros. Curiously, a disproportionate number of their names contain *cochon,* the French word for "pig." At Au Pied de Cochon at Les Halles, we ordered steaming bowls of arguably the best French onion soup in Paris. We made a game of digging into the hot crust of Gruyère and pulling the oozing, salty cheese with our forks a foot off the table as the pungent-yet-sweet aroma of onion-scented beef stock wafted around the room like a heavy cloud. At Aux Trois Petits Cochons, we started dinner with thick slabs of foie gras, spreading it like the smoothest butter onto crisp toasts. Au Cochon de Lait in the 19th arrondissement, a nondescript yet welcoming place that once served the workers of the slaughtering trade that operated nearby, had the aroma of grilled steaks, campfire, and stale red wine. The only foreigners in a sea of regulars, we ordered their specialty, l'Onglet Villette, a wickedly tender hanger steak topped with a buttery heap of caramelized onions splashed with red wine and a side of knife-cut crisp fries. We both closed our eyes to chew, and opened them to find our waitress automatically refilling our *pichet* of red wine with a knowing smile.

"I wish that my dad had come to Paris, at least once. He would have loved this," Mike said. Neither of us wanted to talk about the empty place in our hearts that would greet us when we left the distractions of Paris.

On our last night in the city, in lieu of a standard author reading at a bookstore, I presented a knife skills demonstration at WHSmith, a splendid English-language bookstore at Place de la Concorde, the intersection of the grand boulevards and the former site of the ghastly guillotines of the French Revolution. Being in a city most famous for its food, I worried that my demonstration on basic cuts would be too remedial, but the crowd stood transfixed.

"I've always thought that if I could hold a knife properly, it would change my whole life," a South African woman in the crowd commented. "I feel like I just never really learned. I always assumed that I'm doing it wrong."

I had four chef's knives with me. I gathered everyone into groups and taught the fundamentals of holding a knife and drilled them on the basics of dicing, slicing, and julienne. Simple stuff, but then I realized that I'd learned the same fundamentals only a couple of years earlier. As the crowd disbanded, the South African woman pumped my hand in thanks. "I know this sounds totally stupid, but I don't cook at all and you've just inspired me to learn. I thought this whole knife thing was so much more complicated. I feel like I've had a complete epiphany! Have you ever thought of teaching?"

CHAPTER 2

৩৩

What Would Julia Do?

"You have to give yourself that dream assignment. No one is going to give it to you."

—Penny de los Santos, photographer

৩ How quickly we shifted back into our regular lives in Seattle. Still, after that moment on the stage, what *was* my regular life? The notion weighed heavily on me. So did my weight. In France, we ate as if training for an Olympic eating event. Yet I returned weighing a few pounds less. So did Mike. Less than a month back in the United States I gained nearly ten pounds. How? Sure, we walked more in Paris. But what was it about being back in the States that led us to gain weight?

The French eat less in general and lean toward more fresh food and few snacks. As in other European cities, Parisians shop more often for groceries. Some of it is cultural, but most of it is practical. When I first moved to London in 1999, I had to completely shift my thinking about grocery shopping thanks to the dorm-room-sized fridge in my minuscule kitchen. I couldn't "stock up"; I had no physical space. My freezer was only slightly larger than the size of a paperback novel. Plus, I knew that I had to carry home with me whatever I bought. Since I shopped frequently, I chose mostly fresh food and prepared it that night. In Paris, we did the same thanks to the easily accessible street markets. Even so, I saw a lot of shoppers buying frozen quiche Lorraine in Parisian supermarkets, not to mention the customers who flocked to American-style fast-food outlets.

While it might once have been true that French women don't get fat, more recent surveys show that as the French adopt more American-inspired habits of eating, notably consuming long-shelf-life products, their national weight steadily increases.

Contemplating all this not long after we returned from Paris, I wandered over to my local supermarket, a vast sixty-thousand-square-foot store that's open twenty-four hours a day in the urban Capitol Hill neighborhood of Seattle. When it comes to diversity and cart voyeurism, it's hard to beat the collection at my local grocery.

That was the day I met the woman and her daughter, the one with the cart full of boxed and frozen ultraprocessed food products. She was shopping in a store with a bakery, a full-service deli, a sushi bar, a large meat department with trained butchers, a seafood counter replete with water tanks featuring live crabs and lobsters, plus signs bragging that the store carried 129 different varieties of produce, a third of them organic. With all those options, why did she actively select mostly food in boxes and cans?

We started talking after the butcher demonstrated how to cut up a chicken. "When I make stuff from a box, it always turns out right," she explained. "I never really learned to cook. Mom made dinner when we were young, but by the time I was in high school, she worked a lot, so my brother and I ate a lot of frozen dinners."

She picked up one box of pasta, the kind that makes a side dish in a few minutes. "I know that Alfredo sauce is made with cream, but I would have no idea how to make it."

I spent a year in culinary school learning endless variations on cream sauce. I explained a simple technique—boil cream until it reduces and then extend it with a bit of the cloudy water left over from cooking pasta. "That's it? Oh, wow, I thought it was a lot more complicated."

She agreed that if I wrote down the recipe, she'd give it a try. Out went the nine boxes, and in went two packages of whole wheat pasta, a quart of cream, and a small wedge of Parmesan cheese—for roughly the same amount of money yet enough to make twice as many servings.

This result made her curious about what else we could replace from her cart. Boxes of Hamburger Helper were swapped for ingredients to make simple skillet dishes—onions, garlic, peppers, canned tomatoes, and a block of Cheddar cheese. We visited the bulk herbs and spices area and stocked up on several, including a Cajun blend, chili powder, mixed herbs, oregano, thyme, and red pepper flakes. Her daughter, initially bored by our conversation, took over filling and labeling the plastic bags of spices and herbs. "This is fun, Mama," she said as she sealed one bag. "We should do this every time we shop."

Real potatoes picked out by her daughter (along with a pink peeler) replaced the dehydrated variety. As we stood in the produce section, the woman looked around feebly. "I know that I don't make vegetables enough," she said. "I'm not very good at figuring out what to do with them. I kind of avoid anything that requires a lot of cutting something up. I see those chefs on TV and it looks so easy. I guess I'm not very good at it, and it always feels like it takes a long time." We bought a few bags of a precut broccoli and cauliflower mixture on sale that day, a bottle of olive oil, and some lemons. I wrote down instructions for how to steam and roast the vegetables, then top them with some lemon or a bit of her new herbs and spices.

I couldn't stop thinking about that afternoon. I was certain I had overwhelmed her with information. She seemed like a smart woman and a good mom, but when we talked about cooking, she was discouraged, frustrated, and convinced that shortcuts remained the only path she had the time or skill to navigate.

"I don't mind boxed mashed potatoes" was not the sort of comment that crept into my usual conversations. As a food writer, I'd slipped into what I call "the foodie bubble," a magical place where everyone talks about ramps,* perfect local peaches, and smoked duck prosciutto. People casually name-drop obscure chefs and discuss how many recipes they've tried from *The French Laundry*

---

*Also known as wild leeks, a trendy vegetable among the foraging and farmers' market set.

Cookbook. Don't get me wrong: Life is *great* in the bubble. It's just that most people don't reside there. Normal people live and shop in the center aisles of the grocery store, just like the woman I met. That afternoon, I decided it was time to abandon the bubble.

I stumbled upon a TV interview with English chef Jamie Oliver a few days later in which he talked about why the United Kingdom had been gripped by an onset of obesity. "The thing, I think, is that as people stop cooking, they get less healthy, yeah? People are going by the chippie* to pick up dinner, but chips† aren't dinner." Without realizing it, Jamie got animated, even upset, his adorable East London accent growing even more pronounced. "If there was one thing that I could do, one thing that I could change, it would be to get people to just realize that cooking isn't that tough. It's a walk."

His words rang in my head. The woman and her cart of boxed food . . . the idea that cooking is too difficult . . . the refrain from the woman in Paris about knife skills. Ever the reporter, I started to conduct research on how they all related. Several studies back up Jamie's assertions that the less a person cooks real food, the more they rely on processed or convenience foods, whether at home or in the fast-food line, and the more weight-related health problems they experience. To a large extent, the more you cook, the less you weigh.

What intrigued me was that the woman I met felt that she *was* cooking. To her, opening a box and doing something with it was creating a meal. I disagree. Yet neither of us is right or wrong. Researchers can't even seem to agree on the definition of *cooking*. While a lot of food writers bemoan the loss of home cooking, I found surprisingly little research into the matter. Sure, various studies examined the amount of time people spend cooking, such as one led by a Harvard team that found people spend about twenty-seven minutes a day preparing food, about half the time spent in the 1960s.

*A small shop that sells inexpensive fried fish and fries.
†French fries.

"There's this notion that there is some kind of decline in cooking and that people aren't doing it anymore. But that's not so clear. It's just that there are so many other choices on what they can do to get food," said Dr. Amy Trubek of the University of Vermont, a food historian and researcher who has spent more than a decade studying how people cook. "People aspire to cook what they believe is good, healthy food. But then they find the food environment very complex. There's also a strong sense of 'time poverty' in the American culture, this sense that you don't have time. Cooking is a thing many people perceive they don't have time to do." She equated it with going to the gym. "Everyone knows that you should exercise, so they say that they will go five days a week, but when it comes down to it, they don't."

The woman in the supermarket lacked confidence and skill when it came to cooking. She wasn't sure how to turn whole foods into dinner, and as a result, she found her choices were limited. But that's the issue. If you can't cook, you put yourself at the mercy of companies whose interests are overwhelmingly financial.

Frances Short, the author of *Kitchen Secrets: The Meaning of Cooking in Everyday Life,* says that while consumers may want to eat healthy and even actively seek out this information, it doesn't have much effect if they can't act on it. "Advice to, say, grill or steam food can only be followed if you know how to grill or steam," Short noted.

Trubek told me that what I probably gave to the woman in the supermarket was awareness, a good start. "But awareness is no good unless you have repetition associated with it. That's how knowledge becomes practice and practice becomes habit."

One reason that Julia Child made such a formidable impact was her unique ability to inspire people to get off their couches and go into their kitchens. While viewers watched her make *potage parmentier,* they often took a crucial step—they made it themselves. They searched out leeks, chopped potatoes, and maybe even crafted their own chicken stock. But somewhere along the line, people stopped getting off the couch. Cooking turned into a spectator sport. While

Julia demonstrated how to fillet a fish or wrestle the bones out of a roast, most modern cooking shows fall into what industry experts refer to as "dump and stir" shows or reality-based competitions such as *Iron Chef.* While some viewers may follow along, even executives for the network admit that they focus more on entertainment and less on instruction.

"I watch Wimbledon but it has no relationship to my ability as a tennis player," Trubek said. "It's beautiful and aesthetic, but practice is the only thing that is going to help my backhand."

Back in the 1960s, Julia battled the idea that adding some ingredients to a box or heating something up somehow constituted cooking. Mike's late mother, pressed for time while working the night shift as a telephone operator on a military base, relied heavily on convenience foods. In fact, when we first married, he waxed so fond about something called Noodles Romanoff that in my dizzy honeymoon state, I spent three full days trying to track down either a box or a recipe for it. It turns out Betty Crocker ceased selling Noodles Romanoff in May 1994. I'm sure it's a coincidence, but that's the same month the FDA required manufacturers to include nutritional labels on food products. (I ended my quest when I learned that faithful replication of Noodles Romanoff required a portion of an orange flavoring packet from Kraft macaroni and cheese and commercial powdered mayonnaise.)

We live in a world where experts and the government preach that we should all eat leafy green vegetables, but then we're bombarded with messages that sugar-laden cereals are part of a "nutritious breakfast," and commercials present Subway sandwiches as the holy grail to weight loss. TV cooking show host Sandra Lee cheerfully suggests that "gravy is too hard to make, so just buy jars of gravy" and advises viewers to buy jars of garlic because "mincing garlic just takes too long."

To be fair, I think her voice is just one in a cathedral-worthy chorus shilling the idea that convenience is the *most* important asset when it comes to eating. No wonder we've forgotten that the most essential thing we do is to feed ourselves and the people we care about. When I saw the stuff the woman had in her basket, it struck me as *antinourishment.*

Consider the ingredient list for a brand-name box of a pasta Parmesan side dish. The goal of the product, a company spokesperson told me, is to approximate the flavor of pasta tossed with a bit of Parmesan cheese and olive oil. In order to do it, they used the following:

refined bleached wheat flour, partially hydrogenated palm oil, salt, whey, reduced lactose whey, corn syrup, natural flavors, palm oil, monosodium glutamate, cultured nonfat buttermilk, Parmesan cheese (cow's milk, cheese cultures, salt, enzymes), sodium caseinate,* modified corn starch, freeze-dried parsley, nonfat milk, onions, spices, lactic acid, ferrous sulfate, niacin, soy lecithin, yellow 5, yellow 6 lake, yellow 6, thiamin mononitrate, riboflavin, folic acid

That's twenty-seven ingredients, mostly chemicals, in place of three real items. To make this palatable, it's loaded with corn and so much monosodium glutamate† and cholesterol-agitating palm oil‡ that they had to list all three at least twice. All this to simulate the flavor of three ingredients: pasta, olive oil, and Parmesan cheese.

I believe that everyone has it within them to boil pasta, add olive oil, and grate a little fresh Parmesan cheese over it. I believe that anyone can learn to chop up garlic in less than a minute. So how do companies get consumers to buy a box filled with chemicals, dehydrated milk, and pasta fused with deeply fattening oils so that it will cook

---

*Sodium caseinate is another name for monosodium glutamate (MSG).

†MSG is a chemical derived from the monosodium salt of the amino acid glutamic acid. It's made by processing fermented starch, corn, sugar beets, sugar cane, or molasses. Like aspartame, it's an excitotoxin that stimulates the neural system's "pleasure" cells, resulting in increased appetite. When researchers studying obesity need to fatten up lab rats, they dose the animals' food with MSG.

‡Partially hydrogenated palm oil is on the hit list of many nutritionists; although cheap, it's considered a major artery clogger by several food scientists.

two minutes faster? Or to buy products that are little more than dressed-up military rations? They do this by convincing people that making pasta tossed with some olive oil and cheese falls beyond their culinary grasp.

Decades of savvy marketing conspired to make the woman I met at the supermarket believe that a simple cream sauce fell outside her abilities, and who could blame her?

"As a culture, there's a lack of balancing cost as opposed to actual value," Trubek said. "We surrender our best interests for the sake of seeming convenience. By failing to understand what's involved in certain kinds of basic food preparations, American consumers have been duped."

All of this thinking converged when I stumbled on the show *What Not to Wear* on cable TV one night. The immaculately coiffed host and hostess went through the weekly guest's wardrobe, critiqued her normal choices, and then tutored her on what to wear. That week, they transformed a frumpy housewife into a smartly turned-out woman with a chic haircut with particularly striking blond highlights. They visited her two months later to see if she'd stuck to her new look. She had, plus she'd lost her "last ten pounds" and radiated enthusiasm. "You just gave me a push, the confidence I needed to make the changes that I knew I should make for myself. I feel proud of myself."

I bolted upright on the couch.

Armed with a yellow notepad, I interrupted Mike in the other room as he worked on a kitchen redesign for one of our rental apartments.

"I have this crazy idea . . ." I started.

"Oh, no. Not another one," he joked. He put his pencil down. "You hungry?"

We talked as I sat on a stool while he made dinner, his specialty, chicken and vegetable Thai curry with brown rice. I gave him the rundown.

"I want to try to understand what could motivate people to cook more often. I want to give people different cooking lessons and see which of the things they learn might stick with them." But before we started, I told him, I needed to educate myself on what people had to work with at home and get a sense of the choices they had already made. So I would go into homes and look into fridges, freezers, and cupboards—the culinary equivalent of auditing their closets. "I'll have them make a dish they usually make, so I can see how they cook. Then I'll put together some lessons around the skills I think they're missing. Afterward, we'll follow up and see how they're doing." He poured the coconut milk into the curry. "Well, what do you think?"

"Exactly where are you going to find people willing to let a stranger come into their house?" Mike asked.

"Well, I don't know. I haven't figured that part out yet. I thought of this just now."

The smells of coconut and curry filled the kitchen, now so quiet that I could hear the metal spoon dinging around the bottom of the wok as he stirred.

"Our kitchen is too small for lessons," he said, concentrating on his dish. "What about the commercial kitchen your friend Ace is using?"

"So you think it's a good idea?" I asked, relieved.

"Well, it's an admirable notion, anyway. You can't force people to cook differently. It's like that old joke, How many therapists does it take to change a lightbulb?"

"One," I answered. "But the lightbulb has to *want* to change."

"Exactly. If you approach this as a way to encourage people and give them a few skills, maybe it could motivate them. But remember that everyone's life is different and complicated, and people are smart enough to know if they are willing to change." I nodded. He handed me a bowl of red curry chicken and brown rice. "Now eat."

As part of my author duties, I was scheduled to be a guest on a long-running local radio show hosted by Seattle celebrity chefs Tom Douglas and Thierry Rautureau. I've known both since my days as a restaurant critic in the 1990s. The owner of a group of popular restaurants and an *Iron Chef America* winner, Tom balances the titles of culinary icon and astute businessman, yet for all his success he's remarkably down-to-earth. Thierry reminds me of my chefs in France. He started as a classic apprentice in French restaurants at age fourteen and worked his way up. He now owns the impeccable French restaurants Rover's and Luc, plus hosted a radio segment on NPR called *What's in the Fridge?* Listeners called in and described ingredients in their pantries and refrigerators, and he'd coach them on the possibilities. They both have won the James Beard award for Best Chef in the Northwest, plus seemingly every other culinary award possible. If that's not enough, they've both appeared on *Top Chef.**

As I pulled on headphones in the pleasant, cluttered studio, Chef Thierry offered me a glass of a nice French red he had brought in to sip during the show. I told them about the woman in the supermarket and what I'd been learning about home cooking. Tom and Thierry were intrigued.

"This is a person you just met out of the blue?" Thierry asked.

"She went along with you, in this cold call in the grocery store?" Tom asked incredulously.

I threw in a few statistics that I'd picked up. Americans waste about a third of the food they purchase, for instance. I told them about the project and that I wanted to include some of their listeners.

"How long do you think it would take to find a person who can't boil an egg and change them into a person who can open up a fridge door and figure out how to make something from what they find inside?" Thierry asked.

---

*Tom was a judge on season six of *Top Chef,* while Thierry was a cheftestant on *Top Chef Masters.*

"I don't know, I guess we'll find out," I said.

Tom nodded behind the tangle of microphones. "Also, maybe they can realize that cooking can be fun, and a good way to spend your time."

Then we took a call. "I used to listen to these radio shows and the old-time commercials were thrown in," the caller said. "I remember there was one for what to make with evaporated milk. That woman must have rattled off various recipes in a minute or so. It struck me that no one could understand those recipes today. No one would even understand the vocabulary. We've moved into a place where people don't understand basics of cooking and food."

Tom thanked the caller. Then he looked at me. "How do you plan to address this lack of knowledge?"

"That's an interesting point," I said. "You know, recipe writers don't use certain words anymore, like *braise*. Instead, they write, 'Cover and simmer in the oven,' because people don't know what *braise* means. There's a loss of language specific to the kitchen, and it's evaporated just like that milk."

"But it's not just *braise*," Tom said. "I mean, people are uncomfortable with the idea of a pinch of salt. What's a pinch?"

We talked about the demise of home economics in public schools and the notion that many Americans are two generations away from knowing how to cook.

"I think you can trace a lot of those skills back to Madison Avenue and the ad agencies," Tom said. "They're the ones who sold us the idea that you didn't need to cook, you could simply buy products instead." He looked at the clock on the wall. "Well, thanks for coming on the show. I'm excited to see how it goes. And you know what? In a funny way, I'm interested to see what you get out of it."

When I got home from the show, I found two dozen messages waiting in my e-mail inbox. More streamed in over the weekend.

As I read through them, I realized that the conversation on the air had appeared to touch a nerve. I glimpsed moments of guilt, embarrassment, and downright melancholy.

"When I was nineteen, I was asked to make the salad at my boy-friend's parents' for Thanksgiving. I didn't know where to start, and they all made fun of me. It made me never want to try to cook anything ever again," wrote one woman.

"I rely on boxed products because it's easy, but I don't want to. I have NO idea how to butcher anything. I can't fillet a fish, cut up a chicken, etc. When I look at an artichoke . . . well, I just walk right on by," wrote Cheryl, a thirty-three-year-old mother of two young sons. "I'd like to learn how to make 'real' food, more food from scratch and what I have on hand, rather than pulling out a frozen pizza for my family."

"My mother never let me in the kitchen; she thought I was in the way," wrote Shannon, thirty-two, also a mother of two. "When I read about little girls cooking side by side with their mothers . . . it makes me so sad for what I missed."

Another wrote, "I grew up with a grandmother that could make a meal out of nothing and make it taste as good as any five-star menu. I've lived for years on frozen dinners and anything that is easy or fast." She considered herself "addicted" to cooking shows. She watched them all—*Top Chef, Iron Chef, The Next Food Network Star,* Alton Brown, Giada, Emeril. "But then I am totally lost when it comes to knowing what to do when I try to fix anything. I've watched Gordon Ramsey while eating Tuna Helper. I'm so ashamed."

In the end, I selected ten people for what I began to refer to simply as "The Project."* They shared little in common in terms of background, except that they all identified themselves as a "poor cook" or an "aspiring cook" who relied regularly on processed or fast foods. I told them little about what to expect, other than a few dates and times. I wasn't trying to be mysterious. I didn't really have a plan.

In retrospect, I'm not sure what I was thinking. I'm not an academic type or a researcher; I had taught only a couple of informal

---

*I originally selected nine women and one man, but the token male dropped out before the first class.

cooking classes. My thoughts on what lessons I'd teach were murky. I would have to make it all up as I went along.

The first stop was a generic apartment building in the rustic former logging town of Granite Falls, Washington. After three hours, I climbed back into our Mini Cooper and leaned my head against the steering wheel. "What did I get myself into?"

CHAPTER 3

☙☜

The Secret Language of Kitchens

☙ LESSON HIGHLIGHTS:
What Really Lurks in Cupboards, Fridges, and Freezers

SABRA

"This is what you call White Trash Garlic Bread," announced Sabra, a lovely, fair-haired twenty-three-year-old young woman clad in a skin-tight blue shirt and strategically ripped jeans. "This is one of the few things that I learned about cooking from my mother." She slathered one-half of a soft hamburger bun with Gold 'n Soft margarine, added a few hearty shakes of generic garlic salt, and topped it with dried Parmesan cheese from a can. After repeating the process with a half dozen buns, she slid the baking sheet into her immaculate white oven.

Sabra was the first volunteer I met. She shared an apartment in a basic but pleasant complex with her boyfriend in a sleepy former lumber town an hour north of Seattle. Her standard-issue kitchen was small but tidy. In the living room, a tiny kitten she had rescued the day before took halting steps on the black leather sectional, her occasional mewing competing with the big flat-screen TV tuned to a poker tournament that Sabra wasn't watching.

While the buns lingered under the broiler, Sabra alternated between sips of Red Bull and peach schnapps mixed together in an orange plastic tumbler while waxing poetic about her favorite food.

"I *love* Gold 'n Soft," she said, holding up the half-full one-pound plastic tub of margarine. "If it had Gold 'n Soft in it, that's what my mother and I ate growing up. Now pretty much everything I eat has Gold 'n Soft in it. Anything else, especially butter, just doesn't taste right."

The "garlic bread," combined with Stouffer's five-cheese lasagna, straight from thirteen minutes in the microwave, constituted her lunch. As the microwave counted down, she and I finished the inventory of her cabinets, freezer, and fridge. Among the goods: nine varieties of Stouffer's frozen dinners, six boxes of Hamburger Helper, a five-pack of mac and cheese, half a case of Cup Noodles, and the remainder of a case of Red Bull, all of it from a recent warehouse-store haul. Sabra and her boyfriend dedicated the rest of the pantry to an impressive liquor assortment that featured thirty-eight bottles, everything from bitters to vodka and five varieties of schnapps.

In the fridge, newly purchased bundles of broccoli and cauliflower filled the crisper drawers to capacity, a change for her. A recent pap test found precancerous cells, curable but a worrying sign that she inherited a familial propensity for cancer. A doctor suggested Sabra overhaul her diet to include more fruits and vegetables. "We found a fruit stand near here, and it's cheap. We got three pounds of cauliflower for three dollars," she said. "I couldn't get Cheetos that cheap."

Sabra was nominated for the project by her stepmother, my friend Lisa, a culinary school graduate, a part-time chef, and the kind of woman who routinely makes her own mayonnaise. Back in 2006, I decided to hire someone to help test recipes for my first book. I put an ad on Craigslist describing appalling pay and erratic hours. Within twenty-four hours, eighty-five people had applied. Many sent résumés and long pleas for the position. Lisa had assumed that I was a man and responded with a snarky "Is this a dream job or are you looking for a date?" When we met, the intense, briny smell of cheese preceded her. She walked into my office and handed me a bag. "My mom owns a cheese shop. If you hire me, there's more where this came from."

Lisa quickly became one of my best friends. She tested recipes, helped me organize various events, and Mike insisted she play Clinton Kelly from *What Not to Wear* when I went shopping for clothes to wear on book tours. ("You want jewel tones, no pencil skirts, and at least two pairs of Spanx.") When I told her about the project she said, "That sounds like a ton of work. If you're really going to do it, I'm all in."

Over the years as we worked together, Lisa relayed stories of frustration in terms of food as it related to her relationship with Sabra. When she married her husband in her early twenties, he had primary custody of Sabra, then six years old. When Sabra was a child, Lisa would make dinner, such as roast chicken with vegetables and a salad. Sabra would sit back in her chair with her little arms crossed over her chest and refuse to touch it. After rejecting dinner, Sabra would run from the table to call her mother, who lived less than a mile away. Lisa would overhear the litany of complaints about the fare Sabra said she'd been served. Invariably, they'd hear a honk from the driveway minutes later—it was Sabra's mother, there to take her to McDonald's.

After a couple of years of this, Lisa bought a case of ramen noodles. If Sabra didn't want what she made for dinner, fine. But no more McDonald's, not for dinner. Sabra could eat ramen instead, which she liked, but she had to make it herself. After four nights of noodles, Sabra started eating dinner with them again.

I asked Sabra about all of this, and she nodded, taking another long pull on her drink. "Oh, yeah, I *love* McDonald's. When I was a kid, that's how my parents showed me they loved me after they were divorced. Who took me to McDonald's the most? That's who loved me the most."

I pondered this as Sabra checked on her garlic bread. How much of this was about the food? Or did that trip to McDonald's mean time alone with her parent, forced to focus only on her as she swung, slid, and ran around the colorful play area?

As part of the kitchen visit, I asked each volunteer to prepare a lunch or dinner, something that they routinely ate, so I could get a sense of their kitchen skills and eating habits. Could they hold a knife? Did they taste as they cooked? What kind of portions did they serve up? Frozen dinners were Sabra's go-to dinners. Breakfast involved toaster pastries and half a can of Red Bull. "That's because I don't drink coffee," she explained. The Cup Noodles was her mid-morning snack. She hit McDonald's for lunch. Throughout the day, she consumed a few soft drinks. "And there's the constant grazing on a lot of chips and popcorn. There's always a bowl of something on my desk," she added.

Red Bull for breakfast isn't as unusual as you'd think for someone her age. It has roughly 70 percent of the energy-drink market, a narrow but influential wedge of consumers between ages fifteen and thirty. At age sixteen, Mike's niece, Michelle, lived primarily on various energy drinks for three months. The caffeine gave her energy, while the high sugar content—roughly equivalent to a glazed doughnut—kept her from feeling hungry. She drank several every day. Her doctor commanded her to quit. "You're not getting any nutrients," he said. "You're starving yourself."

Sabra offered some bright spots. The guy at her liquor store introduced her to a woman who supplied fresh eggs from a nearby farm. As a downside, Sabra warned me that she didn't want to spend more than twenty minutes making dinner. "If it takes longer than that, I'll just get fast food." Plus, there was her devotion to Gold 'n Soft.

We sat down for lunch. To me, the lasagna had a vaguely sweet tomato flavor. The "garlic bread" was an exercise in blandness. I asked her how she liked the lasagna. "Well, this brand has really good deals, like, you can get four for ten bucks sometimes," she started.

"No, what I mean is, do you like its taste? The flavor, I mean."

She thought about it. "I don't know. I like it better than some of the other frozen lasagnas."

"But how does it compare to homemade lasagna?"

She tilted her head to one side. "I don't know. I've never thought about it. I like it, but I mainly buy it because it's cheaper than the other ones."

Later, I calculated that over the course of a typical day, Sabra consumed a cup and a half of sugar. Sabra's food choices were motivated by money, ease, and that refreshing live-forever mentality that grips so many of us in our twenties. Who has to worry about their diet when they're so young? Isn't youth enough to overcome a high-sugar, high-fat, high-salt diet? She represented the dark side of "taste memory" that comes from the early adoption of unhealthy foods such as fast foods. Everyone has their comfort food, that flavor that harkens back to a time in childhood that they felt safe and loved. This explained her fondness for Gold 'n Soft and McDonald's. But it was clear that she put more thought into creating cocktails than into developing dinner.

TRISH

Our next stop offered insight into a whole different generation. Trish was a sixty-one-year-old psychologist living in a modest condo on the edge of the affluent Madison Park neighborhood. She fretted when Mike and I showed up with a small video camera in hand to record the proceedings.

"I'm sure that I'm going to be doing everything wrong," she said, a tinge of defeat in her voice. She literally wrung her hands. Mike kept the camera low, out of her face, and joked with her to keep her talking as she gave us a tour of her comfortably modern apartment dominated by obviously inherited antique furniture, dark yet luminous with a patina developed through many decades of careful polishing. Trish wanted to feel like she belonged in the kitchen. "I want to feel at ease. I want to feel like I can make meals for my friends who are good cooks." She pounded her fist into her palm. "I want to like cooking!"

Trish grew up outside Washington, D.C., in what she describes as a "fairly typical" 1950s suburban family. Her grandmother played an important role in their lives. She taught Trish and her siblings to bake, read "old-fashioned" cookbooks, and lent a formal but friendly note to the family dinners and conversations. In Trish's house, dinner was served at six o'clock sharp on a table set with silver and china. Despite her grandmother's baking prowess, her mother wasn't much of a cook; she relied on *The Compleat I Hate to Cook Book*. Dinners starred a meat, supported by some kind of potato and at least one canned or frozen vegetable cooked to the point of gray. Her mother's star turn was fried chicken.

"I remember some truly awful stuff, such as spaghetti sauce made from tomato soup!" Trish said, laughing. "I guess I was kind of a picky eater. I loved the mahogany furniture, the chandelier, the silver and china, but I never cared about eating."

Trish's cabinets and fridge offered a striking contrast to Sabra's, with baking supplies, cans of beans, tomatoes, tuna, salmon, and chicken, boxes of organic soup and broth, jars of pasta sauce, salsa, pickles, jams, salad dressings, and artichokes, oils and vinegars, dry pasta, spices and herbs. "For a meal, we usually open a can, a box, or a jar," she said. But most of it was real food, just preserved. She had the same kinds of stuff in her cupboard that I had in mine at home.

She climbed on a stool and pulled down three flat silver boxes. As she opened one, a strong smell of curry mingled with cinnamon escaped. Inside she kept carefully marked small flat disks filled with spices and dried herbs. "I got these storage things somewhere years ago," she said. She shrugged while looking at them. "I wish that I knew how to use all these spices better." She closed the box and put it back up on the shelf.

"I guess I can cook, but I'm not very pleased with the results. I've never learned to cut or chop things properly. Lots of times I try a new recipe but the results are disappointing. It's hard to get enthusiastic about cooking a meal that's going to take more than thirty minutes to make and it doesn't usually turn out well."

When I asked about recipes, Trish took us over to her well-ordered bookcase. She pulled out volume after volume of excruciatingly organized recipes, categorized and neatly maintained in a series of white binders, another marvel of organization. I gazed in wonder. A protective plastic sheath housed each clipping. As a Gemini and a creative type who can barely keep track of bills, I could never imagine having done such a thing.

She pulled out a binder labeled "Entrees." She flipped through it. "Yeah, this turned out sort of bland. And this one, I did something wrong, the chicken was tough." She flipped a few more pages. "Oh, this one, it came out all right. I was kind of surprised."

As I looked through the recipes she'd clipped from magazines, I recognized the names of a couple of food writer friends, including the dish she referred to as bland. I later talked to the author about it. "Oh, I know the recipe she's talking about," she said with a sigh. "I was only allowed to include six ingredients in the list. So I cut out at least four from my original version. Plus, I had fresh basil in the dish, and that really made it work. But my story got bumped from August to November, and since basil isn't seasonal then, the food editor cut the basil. It's funny, home cooks think recipes turn out bland because it's their fault. The reality is that there is so much pressure to make recipes short that food writers have to cut out steps or ingredients to make them look simpler, or, in the case of the basil, less expensive."

For lunch, Trish made ratatouille. She chopped an eggplant in a curious moment of butchery with a blunt paring knife. "Knife skills," I wrote on my notepad. Next she opened a couple of cans of tomatoes. As it cooked, she talked. Mike kept filming her discreetly. She and her husband avoided fast food, red meat, and pork for health reasons. Trader Joe's was their main stop for groceries. "We don't have a budget for food, but, then, we don't have extravagant tastes either. We're coming close to retirement age, and, like most everyone else, there is less money now." She broiled the occasional fish fillet in the toaster oven or baked sweet potatoes. Her husband made the nightly salad. She bought a lot of bottled salad dressings. I made another note on my pad: "Teach vinaigrette."

"In terms of seasonings, they're basic. I sprinkle a little balsamic vinegar on green vegetables, lemon on the fish, and butter and salt on potatoes. That's what I know how to do."

As we sat down for lunch, she fussed, setting the table with expensive antique dishes, embroidered white cloth napkins, and real silver. Her ratatouille was good, just a little undersalted, which made sense as Trish seemed absolutely terrified of salt.

All this made me curious as to how a smart, organized woman who possessed the basic building blocks of cooking had ended up so tentative. When asked a question, she'd invariably answer, "I don't know, is that right?" Yet she's a psychologist, a professional paid for thoughtful commentary and insight into others' lives. She had so much emotional baggage wrapped up in cooking that I kept stifling my urge to say, "And Trish, how does that make you feel?"

SHANNON

The next day, Lisa and I pulled up to a classic 1960s-era ranch house with a white picket fence in a quiet working-class neighborhood. Toys in various states of repair languished on torn-up sod in the front yard. Shannon was a thirty-two-year-old stay-at-home mom with two kids. She had recently purchased a couple of chickens to keep in her backyard and grew a small patch of vegetables. Shannon subscribed to food magazines and combed Internet sites for recipes. None of it made her feel what she called "kitchen confident."

Her mother answered the door. "I don't know what you're going to teach her," she said dismissively to Lisa and me, turning away as soon as we entered. "She burns everything." Shannon appeared behind her, a trim, pretty brunette with an easy smile and a pixie haircut, a lean baby girl balanced on her hip. Visibly irritated by her mother's remark, she let it pass. Shannon handed her the baby and took us into her kitchen, a large sunny space with pale Formica countertops and a classic suite of nondescript white appliances. She kept a row of cookbooks on one shelf, something of a rarity in the kitchens we visited.

Shannon has an easygoing way about her, occasionally punctuating sentences with flinging arms or wide-eyed expressions or a curious rolling-winking of one eye, an endearing tic. "I'd describe my cooking skills as pretty basic," she started. "I can bake pretty well but cooking has always kind of escaped me. I can read a recipe and follow it, but most stuff turns out pretty bland. I make a lot of casserole-type dishes, which aren't very popular in my house." Cue eye-rolling tic.

Unlike the other cooks I would meet in the project, Shannon did try to plan meals before she hit a grocery store. "My problem is when I'm making up the menu for the week. I just run out of ideas and end up cheating by filling up two days with burritos and spaghetti." By "spaghetti" she meant a jar of sauce. "Oh, yeah, that's it. I've never made it from scratch. Sauces, that kind of thing, it's all just kind of beyond me. I buy those or get a seasoning packet."

Otherwise, a meal to her included a meat-plus-veggie-plus-starch combination. "I'm not very good at cooking meat. I'm scared to death of uncooked chicken so it's usually super overdone." Pork chops are pretty easy, she said, but she usually did the same seasoning every single time, a mix of salt, garlic powder, and pepper. "I try to fit in fish once a week, but it is always a boring night because I really don't know what to do with fish."

She budgeted about seven hundred dollars a month for groceries and meals out. Given they're a family of five, restaurant trips were a rarity. Her big splurge was a sushi place near her house. "At the beginning of the month, things are good. By the end, the meals get increasingly basic as I try to stick to the budget."

I asked about her mother's remark. "Oh, my mom." Her cheeks

flushed, a wince flashed across her face. "My mother started every single meal with a can of soup. She cooked but she never really wanted me in the kitchen, so I didn't learn much. I want to teach my kids to cook when they're older, but since I don't really feel like I know what I'm doing, what am I going to pass on?" Shannon would occasionally make variations on the stuff her mother had served her, such as Parmesan chicken, sweet and sour beef with egg noodles, and tuna casserole, even though she now considered it "old lady food."

"I am so interested in cooking, but I find it frustrating. I can't look at a recipe and conceptualize how it will taste. I can't figure out what is necessary in a recipe and what can be left out. I wish that I were one of those people who could look at my cupboards and my fridge and just improvise something. Or go to a restaurant and eat something I like and then replicate it at home. I don't feel like I have the skills to do that, you know?"

Shannon had the desire, motivation, and time to cook but felt she lacked the core competencies. Like so many people, she didn't learn to cook from her mother, nor did she learn any cooking skills in school. By contrast, women of her mother's generation had multiple opportunities to learn—from their own mothers and in high school back in the days when home economics enjoyed a more robust place in the curriculum. She struck me as similar to a frustrated aspiring musician who just wanted to get the scales down so that one day she could riff.

DRI

"Welcome to the hood," Dri said, spreading her arms wide in a welcome as we walked up the neat path to her well-tended apartment building in the city's Central District. In theory, this is the "rough" part of town, but in recent years much of it has been undergoing serious gentrification. When there's a Starbucks on a nearby corner, it's tough to think you're in a ghetto, even in Seattle.

Vivacious and good-natured, Dri had the air of a nervous comic about her. She kept a smile fixed on her face for almost the entire visit. Dri planned to move soon into a condo she had bought in another part of town. "Good-bye, eight-by-six-foot kitchen!"

Dri was dressed entirely in black, possibly an effort to hide the extra fifty-plus pounds she carried on her tall, sturdy frame. She had recently started hitting the gym. "But the whole food piece is just kind of missing," she told Lisa and me as she started to empty the contents of her cupboard. Her kitchen was so small, only she could fit in it; I stood in the doorway and watched.

She was as delighted as a kid at Christmas by the first thing she dug out—a caked packet of spices. "Oh, here's the magic herb mix that they gave me [at the food co-op] to make pot roast one time. Once. I only did it once. How sad." She dropped it dramatically on the counter. Dri pulled down aging jars of paprika and curry, a bulk jar of peppercorns, catering-sized jugs of olive oil and balsamic vinegar. "Every time I make a real meal I seem to buy new spices. I usually buy them in bulk, so, hello"—she pulled down another quart container. "Give a hearty Dri's Kitchen–style welcome to another stupidly large container of cinnamon!"

Although she lived alone, Dri bought a lot of her food at a warehouse store. It's a habit she adopted from growing up in a family with seven kids. Her kitchen seemed so small yet food kept coming out of the cupboards like clowns from a circus car. At one point, she produced industrial-sized boxes filled with granola bars and instant oatmeal. "For breakfast," she said. "Oh, here's five pounds of cheap not-very-good-for-the-world kind of rice."

Dri described her "vicious circle," one that will likely resonate with a lot of people.

"Okay, so I go to the grocery store and I have all these great intentions. I think, Okay, I'm going to make my lunch every day this week! I see all these great greens and I stock up on them. But then it's late when I get home, I'm tired. I promise myself that I'll eat them the next day. By then, I'm back in my routine that doesn't involve a lot of food preparation." Eventually, she finds a big, wilted, green stain at the bottom of the drawer. "So I throw away a LOT of food. It's tragic how much I waste." A statement she followed up by noting that she has a degree in environmental studies; she now works in urban planning. "I try to buy organic because sustainability is important to me, as a life choice."

Her fridge was nearly empty. I suspected that she'd cleaned it out for my visit, but she insisted that wasn't it; she was going out of town the next day. On first inspection, it appeared immaculate save a few organic condiments, a half dozen eggs, and a solitary green pepper.

In a dairy drawer, she had the remnants of a large package of feta cheese. She sniffed. "Ewww. Okay, this cheese is probably bad. That's the problem with bulk, right? It's cheaper to get a big thing than it is to buy a small one at the co-op. So I get it, eat part of it, and then the rest goes bad." She closed the fridge door and shook her head. For a moment, her permanent smile faded. "It makes me feel terrible."

"Hey, you know, food waste is really common," I said. "They say that people waste a third of what they bring home."

Dri pulled her mouth to one side. "It's not very sustainable behavior, is it?" she said flatly. She spent a quiet moment in self-judgment. Then she brightened. "Want to see the freezer?"

She pointed out artichoke hearts purchased months ago for a recipe that she never made. "I'm not sure what to do with them now," she mused. She had organic hamburger as well as individual chicken breasts wrapped in plastic sleeves and several bags of random food that she didn't recognize. As with other people we visited, the freezer often became The Land of Food That Time Forgot. "I like leftovers for one day but I don't want them on day two. So I think, I'll freeze them. And then they just sit in there until I move or the next millennium rolls around."

We moved on to a cupboard featuring what she referred to as her meager baking supply area. "I bake so infrequently that I forget that I have stuff and buy it again." As if to prove her point, she uncovered fifteen pounds of white sugar.

For dinner, she decided to make a staple meal: spaghetti with a jar of tomato sauce. That's what she ate at least a couple of nights each week. As she waited for the water to boil, she explained that while growing up, her mom's cooking repertoire had relied heavily on pot roast and taco salad. "We ate a LOT of taco salad," Dri said. "We often had fend-for-yourself kinds of nights. Dad was a contractor, so we had very irregular hours."

It wasn't until she moved away from home that Dri realized her mother's food was, well, boring. "If she went crazy, she used a bit of Lawry's seasoning salt. She doesn't believe in garlic, which I now believe is critical to life. Depending on where our family was financially, she would use stuff like powdered milk. I remember there would be times when she canned fruit and cooked much more from scratch. But there were a lot of frozen things in our lives."

Dri put the pasta into a bowl, a portion large enough for at least three people. "You know, I fall back on pasta because, well, it doesn't take long, I can't screw it up, and I don't have to plan for it. But I want to have more options. I want to feel like I'm an adult who can feed herself. Sometimes I still feel like a kid in the kitchen; I'm just not sure what I'm doing. I mean, what am I going to do with those artichoke hearts in my freezer?"

To me, Dri represented someone who was relying on old behaviors (shopping at a warehouse store when she lived alone) and couldn't stick to new ones that she wanted to adopt (eating more vegetables, cooking more often). There's nothing wrong with either, but how could she find strategies to do both and still fit in with her personal philosophies around sustainable food? I wondered.

JODI

A cute Japanese American with a quick laugh and a dimpled smile, Jodi lived in a comfortable split-entry house on a quiet suburban cul de sac. Her house was among the more upscale I visited, with expensive overstuffed furniture and a kitchen equipped with marble countertops and stainless steel appliances. At five feet two inches, she weighed about 135 pounds. "I could probably stand to lose fifteen or twenty pounds," she admitted. "It's funny, in America, I look pretty normal. But I went to Japan to visit my relatives recently. They all say"—she did a fairly pathetic Japanese accent here—"'You so fat! You just sooooo faaaat!'" They took her shopping and nothing fit. The shopkeepers looked at her and shook their heads. "She too fat."

Jodi purposely never learned to cook. "My mother has spent her life basically being my father's slave. It's part of Asian culture. So I figured that if I couldn't cook, then I couldn't be forced into that role." Jodi grew up with wildly conflicting maternal advice. The expectation cycle went something like this: Study hard, get good grades, get a good job, then get married. Wait, now you're married, why are you still working? My grandson is in day care? You're a horrible mother! You should quit your job.

Jodi married a good-looking, strikingly tall Thai American man with a flair for cooking. From the very start of their relationship, he cooked most of their weekend meals and dinner once a week. The rest of the time, they ate out or ordered takeout, an arrangement that satisfied them both—until she was laid off from her job with a high-tech firm. Suddenly, they had half the income, plus a fussy three-year-old who refused to eat much of anything. Newly unemployed, tight for cash, and at home all day, she felt that the least she could do was to cook her husband dinner and feed her kid. They had long shopped at warehouse stores for food, where the savings held huge appeal. As a result, they bought a second fridge for their garage.

"All this food takes up so much space!" she lamented, as food items fell out of her freezer when she opened the door. We pulled it all out: a vertical stack of twenty-plus breaded chicken cutlets, steaks of multiple shapes and sizes, a vacuum-packed whole beef tenderloin, dozens of individually wrapped boneless chicken breasts, and catering-sized bags of frozen vegetables.

A closer inspection told an interesting tale. This penchant for bulk buying was not a new habit; a few steaks were four years old, and the chicken breasts had a sell-by date of two years prior. As she dug farther, she found whole salmon fillets and ribs bought for a camping trip three years earlier. "Oh, wow, I forgot we had these!"

Jodi and her husband infrequently made anything from the freezer, yet they kept buying food to put into it. Only two items had a good rotation: fish sticks and breaded chicken cutlets, both items her son would eat, and she could cook them easily on a tray in the oven. Their fridge was similarly packed. They purchased most condiments in industrial-sized jars. The mayonnaise in a hearty gallon jug had a sell-by date of a year earlier. "I hate to throw it out, though, there's so much left. I guess we don't really eat that much mayonnaise."

The crisper drawer had three browning heads of iceberg lettuce. "Oh, I hate it when this happens," she said. "We always throw out lettuce. It's hard to go through it. They come five to a pack where we shop." Then she led us to the pantry, a closet larger than the kitchen of either Dri or Sabra, and we found it stuffed floor to ceiling with enough boxes and cans to last through the start of a nuclear winter: cases of soup, canned vegetables, boxed pasta dishes, instant ramen noodles ("kid food"), microwavable cups of mac and cheese, and a twenty-pound sack of white rice. "There's more in the garage, too," she said.

Many of her evening meals consisted of the "brown and stir" variety, some kind of sauce that involved adding a protein, usually chicken. For lunch, she worked up her most ambitious dish: cooked strips of chicken and chopped-up onion and red pepper in a skillet, flavored by adding a cube of "golden curry" seasoning. "This is a Japanese household standby," she said, showing off the shimmering brown, gelatinous cube before she dropped it into the pan. She added water and stirred. Like a miracle, it thickened and created a thick, shiny brown sauce. She boiled water for Minute rice. "I'm such a bad Asian! But our rice cooker has been broken for ages," she confessed.

"So how often do you eat rice?" I asked.

Jodi cocked her head to one side, stirring her dish. "Pretty much every day," she said thoughtfully. Then she laughed. "I guess we should fix it, huh?"

I looked at the golden curry package. One serving, a mere quarter cup, contained 41 percent of the recommended sodium intake. The cube's flavor came primarily from monosodium glutamate. I told her it affects many people like a toxin. "It's funny, now that you mention it, I always get a headache after I eat this stuff," she said. Although the package claimed five servings, Jodi said that she and her husband usually split a package—each eating two and a half servings. Or 120 percent of the recommended daily sodium intake and 60 percent of the recommended daily fat intake, which didn't include the oil needed to stir-fry the chicken and vegetables. As she sat at the table, she fell into her chair with a heavy sigh.

"I didn't know all that. I guess I shouldn't make it anymore." But what would happen to the six packages in her pantry? Plus the curry remained one of the few things that her son, Koji, would eat. "He will eat a little of the chicken and sauce sometimes, but not the rice and definitely none of the vegetables," she said. Like many toddlers, Koji was a wildly fussy eater. He eschewed vegetables. Unpleasant scenarios occurred when they tried to force him to eat anything other than chicken nuggets, pizza, fish sticks, or mac and cheese. "It all started with day care. That's what they feed him there. Now he won't eat anything else. I worry about him. I mean, that can't be healthy, right?"

Research studies have found that an increasing number of American children may get enough food to eat yet remain undernourished due to overreliance on foods that are high in fat, salt, and sugar yet lack the fundamental nutrients. A 2004 study found that nearly a third of the calories in a typical American child's diet came from junk foods, defined as ultraprocessed foods with little nutrition.

It's hard to blame kids, according to Dr. David A. Kessler, the author of *The End of Overeating: Taking Control of the Insatiable American Appetite*. Many of the foods on the common kid-food list— chicken nuggets, powder-based mac and cheese, fish sticks—have been engineered to stimulate pleasure centers in the brain. Studies found that as a result, rats can become addicted to junk food in the same way that they do to cocaine or heroin. Just as with drug addictions, rats often reject their standard "rat chow" and starve to death when denied junk food. That may explain the difficulty—or sometimes impossibility—of trying to force broccoli into a four-year-old in place of dinosaur-shaped pizza bites.

An acquaintance of mine took her fussy, plump toddler to the doctor when she noticed he had become grumpy and started to gain weight. The doctor described his condition as "a sort of starving." He was dehydrated, an unsurprising fact given that he shunned water and insisted on sugar-spiked fruit juices or flavored milk. When she tallied up his collective meals from day care and at home, she was horrified to realize that he was subsisting on juice boxes, chicken nuggets, cheeseburgers, French fries, and hot dogs. She couldn't place the last time she had been able to make him eat a vegetable. I told Jodi that story.

"It's not like she was a bad mother," I said. "She started realizing that wherever they went, the children's menu invariably included mac and cheese, fries, pizza, hot dogs, and hamburgers. It gives people the message that that's how kids should eat."

The normally bubbly Jodi stared at the counter. "That pretty much describes what Koji eats, too." She stared into her coffee. "I'm the one who is supposed to take care of him. I know that I shouldn't give him that kind of stuff. Sometimes, though, I come home and I think, I will make him eat a healthy dinner. I look in the cupboards and the fridge and pull out some vegetables and think, I don't even know how to actually cook these. Do you boil them?" She appeared suddenly defeated. The golden curry had seemed like a good option because at least it wasn't breaded or fried. "I never even thought to look at the label. Is that something you could make without a cube?"

TERRI

Terri was a soft-faced, strawberry-blond-haired forty-six-year-old who had ditched a law career in the wake of a crumbled marriage and battles with alcoholism a dozen years ago. She managed a small tourism business from her one-bedroom condo. Due to the sedentary nature of her work, plus a recent broken ankle, she figured she was forty pounds overweight. She was battling high blood pressure, among other health problems.

Accumulated papers, brochures, magazines, newspapers, bills, and unopened junk mail rose like a small mountain off her dining room table, with a portion of the pile cascading like a glacier into a puddle on the floor. Her kitchen remained pristine. "That's because I don't use it that much!" she said, laughing nervously.

Terri struggled to find the motivation to cook for herself. Dinner tended to be takeout oriented. "I rely on Chinese food and baguette sandwiches from a local bakery," she said. "I make far too many runs to McDonald's and Jack in the Box for burgers, shakes, that sort of thing." Most weeks, she ordered a large pizza and ate it over the course of two or three days.

"The thing is that I like vegetables, but I don't feel like I cook them very well. I also tend to go overboard at the farmers' market and then I find all this stuff dead in my fridge." The previous summer, she had signed up for a Community Supported Agriculture (CSA) basket filled with fresh produce direct from a farmer. "Even though I got it every other week, it was still too much for one person. I felt even worse when that went bad."

Her fridge was a graveyard of expired condiments, a heavy vine of aging grapes, and a container of Greek yogurt with an eight-month-old expiration date. She pointed to a few jars with unidentifiable goo in them. "Attempts at making vinaigrette," she said, nodding. "I make too much so it stays in there forever."

The freezer was equally stark; one of its few contents was a four-year-old turkey dinner. "That's from a Thanksgiving when I decided I couldn't deal with my family," she said, then laughed nervously again. On Thanksgiving, she went to McDonald's. She looked a bit sad at the memory as she shut the door on the frozen-food tour.

Her shelves were nods to healthy eating and falls from grace of it. Next to the quinoa (unopened) there was a shelf-stable microwavable meatloaf dinner and cracked bulgur next to fried onions ("for green bean casserole," she interjected).

For her meal, she boiled whole wheat pasta and tossed it with olive oil. "I would have no idea how to make pasta sauce," she said, grinding sea salt onto her pasta. "I'm feeling kind of virtuous today because I'm not using Hamburger Helper or a jarred sauce." She'd been relying on them less after she learned that she had high blood pressure. As she sat down with her pasta in a beige La-Z-Boy chair in her living room, she talked wistfully about the days when, as a newlywed, she tried her hand at cooking. She made holiday roasts and even hosted dinner parties.

"I lost interest in cooking after I stopped drinking," she said honestly. "But I'm realizing now that by not cooking I'm hurting myself, probably more than I realize. I want to be excited by it again," she said. "I don't want to be on a diet. I just want to change the way I eat. But I don't know where to start or how to sustain that, you know?"

Terri struck me as a tough case. For high blood pressure, the best step she could take would be to cook more often. The vast majority of average Americans' sodium intake—nearly 80 percent—comes from fast food or ultraprocessed fare. By comparison, only 5 percent of sodium comes from home cooking. She mentioned time as an issue, but then talked about a lot of trips to physically pick up food and eat out, time that she might use to make dinner instead. I feared that what she wanted wasn't cooking lessons, but a magic bullet.

DONNA

In Tacoma, we met Donna, a shy, sweet-faced twenty-six-year-old newlywed who resided in a row of modest starter homes. Her hair reminded me of Shirley Temple's, dark and spiraling down just above her shoulders. In a tinny, little-girl voice she asked, "Do you want any iced tea? I have some in the garage."

Donna was gosh-darned adorable. She and her husband had purchased the house two years earlier the week before they got married, a symbol of their mutual gung-ho commitment. Her pleasant kitchen looked as if it came directly out of a scene from *Mad Men,* replete with canary-colored retro appliances. The fridge sported an extra door, presumably child-sized, built into the front. "Isn't this weird? It's kind of a midget door or something. We want to redo it," Donna trilled brightly. "But it's so darned expensive. Sure you don't want any tea?"

"Do you have any vodka?" I asked, only partly in jest.

Donna laughed. "Of course not, silly!"

Donna worked long hours in communications for an international aid organization that helps families in Africa. "We should have two people to do my job, but of course it's a nonprofit so they just work you to the bone. But it's very rewarding."

When Donna and her husband married, they agreed that he would cook and do dishes and she would do all the laundry. "But now I realize that I can't rely on my husband to cook, or that what he makes will be healthy," she said. "He goes back and forth about eating healthy, but when it comes down to it, he just eats what he wants. He says that he'll be more interested in it as I lose more weight, but right now he's not much of a good sport."

Although Donna dutifully attended Weight Watchers for months, she'd lost only five of the fifty pounds she wanted to lose. She can cite the program's "points"* for anything. But she finds they're not helpful when eating out, and lately they've been eating out—a lot.

"My husband and I fight to the death about this. He doesn't eat all day or all afternoon. So he's supposed to be the cook in the family,

---

*The Weight Watchers points system uses predetermined scores for food based on its nutritional value to help members avoid overeating.

but then by the time we're driving home together, he's starving. He stops and gets fast food or he wants to go out. Then he snacks all night. He thinks this is supposed to help him lose weight?"

She revealed that just before they got married two years ago, he'd lost ninety pounds. Since then, he'd gained it all back.

"I guess back then he had to find a girl to impress," she said wryly. "One reason that I want to learn to cook is because I can cut down on calories all day, but I when I get home from work, it's like a free-for-all. I don't know how to cook; it's not my element, so I am kind of at the mercy of whatever he wants to do."

She recently learned she's allergic to soy, and has long had an unusual reaction to raw vegetables. In the first cupboard, we hit abandoned cans of Slim-Fast. "Oh, right, I forgot about those," she said sheepishly. "It's got soy in it, so it's going to have to go."

From the next one, she pulled out boxes for a hamburger-based skillet casserole. "I grew up eating it, so I bought those when we were first married, but my husband hates it because he didn't grow up on it," she said. "These might even be expired. I don't know, does Hamburger Helper have an expiration date?" She examined the box. "November 2008. Funny, I wonder what's in it that could expire?"

In the same cupboard she found dehydrated mashed potatoes, boxes of Jell-O, and a block of Velveeta cheese. "This I use for a dip when guests come over. You mix it with a can of chili." She dug in and pulled out an assortment of spices, many of them duplicates. "Oh, we have three or four of the same kinds of spices. When we find a recipe we buy all the ingredients, not realizing that we already have the same herb or spice until we get home."

On a higher shelf, she had multiple bags full of flour, sugar, and other baking goods. "I'd like to think that I do a lot of baking, but I don't. I think most of the stuff in this cupboard we haven't touched in more than a year."

She moved on. Condensed soup, cans of black olives, kits to make Mexican food, tins of tuna, a jar of pineapple chunks. "We bought these for shish kebabs for camping," she said. As she pulled out more cans, she made a discovery. "Here's the pineapple chunks from last year." She found many cans of turkey chili. "We put them on Fritos or things like that for a snack."

From another cupboard, she set out eight boxes of cornbread mix. "You just add water, it's easy." I asked why she had so many boxes of the same items.

"We spend so much at this one warehouse store that they told us to upgrade to the business level because we would save money." Another cupboard revealed cases of granola bars and microwavable brown rice, an echo to Dri's shopping habits. A low drawer had a cache of hundred-calorie snacks. She picked up a small puffy bag of Cheez-Its and handled it disdainfully. "Yeah, I was into these but they don't work for me. I'm kind of an addictive personality so I can't have just one. I can't think of anything else until I have another bag." She dropped it back into the drawer and quickly slammed it shut.

Without a word, she moved on to the fridge. A gallon of some pink drink dominated the top shelf. "Yeah, my husband bought this. I didn't want to throw it away, so I've been drinking it." She looked at the label. "I mean, this looks bad. I know anything that ends in -*ose* is probably bad, or if the additive has an *x* in it." She put it back.

"This is why I want to be educated, so that I can make better decisions." She bought books on nutrition, but rarely made it past the first couple of chapters. "I buy a lot of cookbooks but I never really use them." She's made only one recipe from a book, a chicken dish from *Fresh Food Fast* by *Cooking Light* magazine. "I was disappointed that it was so bland. My chicken was too dry, and I don't know why."

In the rest of the fridge, we found bricks of butter and a drawer devoted to an array of low-fat cheeses. A food chemist once described the process of making fat-free cheese as a complicated puzzle, one that typically required a lot of chemicals, gums, sugars, and added salt to solve. "Do you ever wonder what they do to make them low-fat?" I asked.

She cocked her head to one side. "No, I guess I've never thought about it."

We moved on. There was a lot of packaged fruit, including some in small clear plastic containers. "Oh, yeah, I stopped eating the grapefruit since it doesn't expire until next year. That kind of scared me. Isn't fruit supposed to expire?"*

When she opened a crisper drawer, a putrid, vinegar-like odor escaped. She'd purchased a dozen apples in bulk, and half of them sat rotting in the bin. "I totally forgot about those." Polite Donna looked visibly mortified. "My husband thinks that if you can get it cheaper in bulk, you should buy it even if you throw half of it away."

"But you look upset," Lisa said, training the small video camera on her.

"I don't have an opinion on it," she replied. But then the color rose in her cheeks. She continued with the fridge tour. We discussed expired condiments and a rainbow of diet sodas. Then she discovered two browning heads of lettuce in another drawer. She clenched her jaw. She picked one up and examined it, not unlike Hamlet contemplating Yorick's skull.

"You know, I grew up not having much food in our house," she said, talking more to the head of lettuce than to us. "We went to a lot of food banks as a kid. For me to throw away food, that's kind of sacrilegious. And, well, I work with starving kids in Africa." Her voice ratcheted up an octave. She dropped the lettuce back into the bin. "So, yeah, it does bug me that we're throwing food away as if it's not important. That we're wasting anything."

Lisa and I looked at each other. We'd tapped something deep. "You know, Donna, earlier you said that you didn't have an opinion," I said gently.

She started to drum her fingers against the door, avoiding our gaze. "Apparently, I do have an opinion." She banged the door shut.

---

*I learned later they're plastic cans, a miracle of modern packaging science. The contents do not need to be refrigerated, but to make the product feel "fresh," the marketers sell it that way.

She paused and purposefully slowed her breathing. Then she opened the freezer door.

Big bags of frozen fried snacks dominated the freezer. Among them was a family-sized bag of Any'tizers, differently shaped and stuffed fried chicken products from Tyson. "Those are my husband's." I asked Donna how many they normally eat at once. "Oh, he'll make half the package for us to eat as a snack after dinner while we watch television." That's six servings, or 1,280 calories and 66 grams of fat.

She moved quickly on to the many bags of frozen vegetables, but they never used them because they didn't cook with vegetables. "I know that I don't get enough fruit and vegetables in my diet. I don't know how to make them taste good."

Part of the appeal of frozen vegetables is that they come precut. "My husband makes fun of me when I cut things. Whenever I cook, I screw everything up and then I lose my courage." Her brother used to tease her if she helped in the kitchen. "He'd say, 'Oh, you're not going to cook, are you? You're going to do it wrong and we're all going to die.' It wasn't actually all that funny."

She went quiet for a bit, organizing the elements of the meal she planned to cook. When she spoke, it was almost as if she were simply saying her thoughts aloud. "I think it could be fun to cook. When I watch people cook, I get inspired. When I do it myself, I just get really freaked out. I panic. I don't want to cook for anyone. I used to lack confidence in everything in my life, and now I think I have confidence about everything else except cooking."

For her meal, she decided on "El Paso Casserole," a menu staple she learned from her mother that featured canned tomato soup, canned turkey chili, canned cream-style corn, and shredded Cheddar cheese. As she used the can opener to open the chili, I noticed her hands shaking. Sweet Donna. This must have been so hard for her, to have not one but two people come into her kitchen, ask nosy questions, and film her while asking about the one thing she felt she didn't do well.

"Hey, I screw things up and I went to culinary school," I said, approaching her. I gave her a quick hug around the shoulder. "I burned toast this morning. I overcooked a steak the other night. I mean, it happens. Even Julia Child screwed up sauces and dropped potatoes, right on TV."

She smiled at me thankfully and offered a polite laugh, but then went quiet as she started to brown a pound of hamburger. I decided to shift the conversation to how she would remodel her kitchen. Her mood lightened. As she topped the layered casserole with Cheddar cheese, she offered some final thoughts.

"I have friends who say, 'Oh, cooking is so easy, let me show you.' But to me, it's so intimidating. My friend comes over, and she's an amazing cook, she makes it all look so fun. But when she comes over and wants me to cook, I say, Let's go out. I'm too self-conscious."

She thinks some of it stemmed from growing up in a household where cooking was looked on as a chore rather than a rewarding act of creation and sharing. "We go to my in-laws' house and you can tell that the women in his family love to cook. Everything my mother-in-law makes is wonderful and tastes great. But at my house, my mom and my grandmother, they don't really cook. Everything is very bland and heavy. Kind of unhealthy and artificial." She looked down at the dish she had just put together. "Well, just like this casserole." She shoved it into her canary-colored retro wall oven.

"More than anything, I wish that cooking could become natural to me. I've come to realize that it's important for me to find options around food that I don't feel I have right now. If I'm going to eat right, I have to finally learn to do it myself."

Cooking seemed like a minefield to Donna, in terms of both her own relationship to food and the power struggle she felt in her relationship with her husband. He could cook, she couldn't, and that unfortunate balance led her to a place where she felt uncomfortable and out of control in the heart of her own home. She described it as "his kitchen" and commented that she didn't even know where to find some utensils and pans. She worked fifty-hour weeks trying to help feed kids in Africa, and her husband's buying decisions meant that she ended up wasting a lot of food. Yet she had clearly hit a point in her young life where she realized that she needed to make a change. Of all the people I visited, I felt that Donna had both the most to gain and potentially the most to lose.

ANDRA

"I'm sorry, it's going to be so hot!" Andra apologized repeatedly as she walked us up the stairs to her apartment. Edging toward the nineties, it was unseasonably hot for early June. "I have no AC, so I hope you don't mind, but it's just too hot to wear a bra."

The life of Andra, a forty-three-year-old paralegal, had clearly taken some curious turns. Raised in an affluent family, she lived in what she called "a sort of a slum," a complex of low-slung apartments that offered subsidized housing adjacent to the airport. In the wake of the economic meltdown of 2008, her firm slashed both her hourly rate and her hours during a major round of cost cutting. On a good week she took home $180 after taxes. For the past four months she'd been using food stamps for the first time in her life, a fact she kept secret from her colleagues and from her parents living nearby in an upscale suburb. "They have a personal chef now," she said, an edge of what could have been either jealously or dismay in her voice. She hadn't seen them in three weeks, not since she sold her ten-year-old Honda Civic to keep up with her rent and cover her daily living expenses.

Large furniture overwhelmed the small apartment. A curious collection of knickknacks gave the impression that she had moved here from much larger quarters, and that perhaps not all of her decor originated from the same place. Expensive handmade Venetian masks hung on one wall, while pink-cheeked sweet Hummel characters and Franklin Mint–style woodland critters cluttered shelves not far from items emblazoned with Harley-Davidson logos. Crescent moons and astrological symbols decorated everything from pillows to a faux wall tapestry, and an inflatable celestial globe hovered in the corner of her dining room. On her coffee table, there was an inexpensive plaster cast of a bald eagle clutching a struggling fish in its claws. The beaded curtain separating the living room and kitchen somehow did not seem out of place.

Andra apologized for not having much on hand. "It's the end of the month, and my food stamps don't kick in until the first." She had visited the food bank in the past week, where they had given her a package of frozen boneless chicken thighs. "I'm really not sure what to do with those," she said, thumping the hard pack with her wrists.

In stark contrast to Jodi, she had absolutely nothing in most of her cupboards. In one, she had just four items—a bottle of dried Italian herbs, a small jar of mustard, a bottle of Wesson oil, and half a package of dried egg noodles. In another, she had just two cans, cream of celery soup and beef ravioli in sauce, both marked with bright orange "Damaged—Half Off!" stickers. Equally lacking, her fridge had only a few items, mostly condiments and a head of iceberg lettuce. For dinner, she planned to make the only other item in her freezer: miniature frozen pizzas that she had purchased at a supermarket outlet store. "They have good deals there, but it's sort of a long time to get there by bus," she said.

As she placed the hard disks on a cookie sheet, Andra said that she believed people can eat well inexpensively but she hadn't yet figured out how. "I used to have enough money that I never had to think about what to eat. That's changed dramatically. My options are much more limited. It's especially true now that I don't have a car. There's nothing near here in terms of food shopping, really."

She evaded questions about her past, but alluded to having lived a much different lifestyle not that long ago. "I used to have money, but no time. Now I have time, but no money. When you have the funds, it's a lot easier if you don't know how to cook. You can go out to dinner, or you can get good takeout. But when you're strapped for cash like me, you end up eating Domino's pizza or stuff like that. It's cheaper to eat badly, or at least it seems that way, especially if you're a poor cook like me."

Most people don't realize that the average food stamp recipient receives about a dollar per meal, roughly twenty-seven dollars per week. Andra's assessment of her situation struck me as accurate. Knowing how to cook does stretch food dollars. For the price of pizza delivery (at least ten dollars), it's possible to make a whole roasted chicken with mashed potatoes and a side of vegetables. But it requires access to a grocery store, plus enough knowledge to improvise dishes, take advantage of sales, and avoid wasting leftovers.

The speed with which Andra's lifestyle had collapsed was striking. Economists say that many Americans are only two paychecks away from being homeless. Andra had a roof over her head, but little more. She was willing to do what it took to weather the economic storm and hope for a better horizon.

CHERYL

By the time we met the final two volunteers, strong themes had come through. Most volunteers were terrified of raw chicken and bemoaned their inability to make palatable vegetables. Bulk shopping and overzealous trips to the produce section or farmers' markets led to a lot of wasted food when combined with a lack of insight or inspiration for what to do with leftovers.

Cheryl, thirty-two, was the mother of a four-year-old boy and an infant son. She lived in an upscale home on the edge of a bay with commanding water and mountain views in a town well north of Seattle. Cheryl was a quiet, rail-thin woman with large, expressive brown eyes who hailed from a remote town in Canada. She focused on buying organic food and made a point to drive forty-five minutes to a local co-op.

Yet on the day we met her, she made herself a can of soup in her large, well-appointed kitchen with wide granite countertops and stainless steel appliances. When I asked if she'd ever tried to make soup, she smirked. "No. Well, okay, once, but it didn't go well so I never tried it again."

GENEVIEVE

The final volunteer, Genevieve, was a pretty twenty-five-year-old brunette who lived with three roommates in a spacious house in the city. Among them was John, who had become her boyfriend. She made one of the few dishes she knew, a combination of store-bought Asian slaw combined with a bottle of teriyaki sauce. Gen wanted to learn to cook in advance of a big life transition—she and John were planning to move into a place of their own. "I have friends who cook. It's like they belong to a sorority and I somehow never got asked to pledge, and now they seem to be guarding their secrets, you know?"

Both Cheryl and Gen came from homes in which their mothers cooked, yet neither learned much before leaving home. "It's so easy not to cook," Cheryl said. "You can always pull out a frozen pizza. But I don't want to do that. I want to feel like I'm nourishing my family, not just giving them food to subsist on."

Gen echoed her comments. "I guess I never felt compelled to learn because it feels like you could go your whole life without learning to cook. But as I've gotten older, I've just started to realize that seems like the least healthy way to go through life. I want to be able to control what I'm eating. You really just don't know what's in stuff anymore."

The goal for both of them, and for all the volunteers, was something that felt remarkably elusive. Cheryl articulated it well. "I want to be one of those people who can open up the fridge, look inside it, and come up with a meal. I simply cannot do that now. It's like some kind of magic to be able to do that."

I thought about what I had learned in the course of the week. It wasn't what I had anticipated, although, admittedly, I hadn't been sure what to expect. But I could not have predicted the residue and damage that a lack of cooking skills had on people's daily lives. Among the boxes and cans, I found a larger story of perceived failure that left them struggling with guilt, frustration, and a stinging lack of confidence.

The themes that I found in these kitchens were echoed in the others we visited. The women were so different in terms of age, background, and socioeconomic status, but they struggled with similar issues. A lot of them struggled with their weight. Lack of planning led them to rely on processed food or to stop for fast food. Some purchased too much and the wasted food made them feel bad. All of them talked about their mother, spouse, or grandmother and their ability or inability to cook, and how it impacted them as adults. None of them could hold a knife properly; then neither did I before culinary school.

From the moment I learned of Sabra's devotion to margarine, I worried that I'd gotten myself into something far too complicated. In Donna's home, meals were an emotional riptide that represented more than brown lettuce, but involed morals, money, and worldview. Jodi struggled with how to balance her fears of succumbing to Asian wife stereotypes and trying to feed her son something other than chicken nuggets. Andra represented those most affected by the economic breakdown in 2008, her comfortable life turned upside down by an unexpected downsizing that shifted her from a comfortable living to food stamps within less than six months through no apparent fault of her own. For all her good intentions, Dri ultimately lived on massive portions of starch while her greens suffered a slow death in her fridge.

I had started this on a whim, and it wasn't until I actually visited them that I realized how much courage it took all these women to allow a stranger into their homes, to poke and pry and play voyeur, then to sit in judgment of one the most intimate human acts. If you don't think of eating as intimate, think of those quiet moments you've stood alone in a kitchen, the wedge of light leaking from an open refrigerator door, seeking to satisfy a craving.

Consider a doughnut. Everyone knows that doughnuts aren't good for you. They're sugar and white flour fried in fat and traditionally topped with more sugar. But it's hard to deny the lure of the delicate aroma of a warm doughnut and the guilty pleasure of sinking your teeth into the mushy, powerful sweetness of a freshly glazed bear claw. Moments later, you feel the sugar rush, subconsciously knowing that it's too strong to last and that it's only a matter of time before the inevitable crash. How many of us have had relationships like that? The tug of something forbidden and giving in only to experience joy, disappointment, and, ultimately, regret.

As I looked over my notes and started to review the video of those visits, I wondered what my cupboards would reveal.

Unable to sleep, I slipped out of bed at two A.M. and conducted an inventory of my own kitchen. I found boxes of partially used pasta, mostly whole wheat. Three bags of white sugar. Really? Stacks of canned tomatoes, artichokes, olives, imported tuna, and locally packed clams hid two expired cans of foie gras and pâté from France. Damn, how did I forget they were there? Plastic bags with various grains I'd experimented with once or twice that Mike didn't like, so they remained untouched. Half jars of protein-shake mix from an ambitious gym period. A messy drawer crammed with tired spices, some labeled in foreign languages. In the cupboard, dying vinegars, Wondra gravy thickener, green peppercorns, a box of Krusteaz crust mix, and a couple of boxes of macaroni and cheese.

Condiments dominated the fridge, a curious collection that ranged from Baconnaise to fish sauce to four varieties of mustard. Two small takeout boxes of Thai food sat on the middle shelf next to plastic containers filled with duck fat, bacon fat, and expired yogurt. Despite efforts to diligently use produce, I found a moist green bag of what had been organic mesclun salad, and next to it, decomposing zucchini, and a handful of molding limes lurking in the crisper drawer under fresh bundles of Swiss chard. Tucked in the back was an abandoned year-old bag of decaf coffee bought after a fertility specialist suggested that I give up caffeine. In the freezer, bones for chicken stock mingled next to vodka-spiked ice pops, a bag of white pork fat (a gift from Lisa), ready-to-cook chicken dumplings from a place in Chinatown, half-used bags of spinach, frozen blueberries from two summers ago, and the remnants of an undated batch of chocolate chip cookie dough.

I was in a battle with myself. It seemed that I had as much to learn as any of the people I'd just visited.

ை

CHAPTER 4

It's Not About the Knife

ை LESSON HIGHLIGHTS:
   **Kitchen Tools, Basic Cuts, and Why You
   Really Need Only a Couple of Knives**

On a balmy June evening, the volunteers straggled into the kitchen one by one. To each we handed an apron, a notebook, and a cloth diaper.

"They make the best side towels," Lisa explained of the diapers to the puzzled volunteers. "The middle is padded, so it's like an oven mitt. You use it to pick up hot pans and stuff." Neither of us said it, but they're also dirt cheap.

Shannon picked one up and laughed. "I have these exact same diapers at home. I just don't picture them in a kitchen."

"I swear, these are new," I said.

"Oh, I believe you," Shannon said, worried that she'd offended. "I just think it's funny."

Diapers in hand, they wrote their names on pieces of masking tape because I had not thought to get name tags. They took it in stride and slapped the masking tape to their chests.

As Mike noted, our Seattle kitchen was too small to teach more than a couple of students at a time. If you've never tried, finding a kitchen that can accommodate a dozen students proves a bit more complicated than you might expect. Only a few days before the first class, I managed to secure the use of a kitchen owned by a catering company. I discovered the place via Anne-Catherine,* one of my fellow classmates at Le Cordon Bleu in Paris, affectionately known as "Ace." "I can't wait to move to Seattle. It's where I want to spend the rest of my life," Ace told the group while sipping *vin rouge* on a crisp fall Parisian evening out with our fellow students at a beaux arts bistro near Les Halles. My dream transported me to Paris, while hers was to settle in Seattle. Ace served as the executive chef of the catering company for a time and held a series of communal dinners in the kitchen's small dining room before she left to open her own restaurant.

The owner required a business license, insurance, and state health cards in order for us to rent her place. Lisa and I sat through a three-hour kitchen sanitation and safety class with several hundred aspiring kitchen workers. The short version: Wash your hands often for at least twenty seconds, roughly the time it takes to sing "Happy Birthday" twice, and don't defrost meat in the trunk of your car.

Everything secured, the owner handed me the first set of keys that I've ever had to a commercial kitchen. It wasn't *Top Chef*. The kitchen is housed in a 1950s storefront, most recently the site of a pizza joint. The extremely canted windows bring to mind the architectural works of Mike Brady. The trapezoid-shaped room feels as if it started life as a coin-operated laundry or perhaps a dry cleaner. The neighbors include a jumble of houses, a Chinese food joint, used-car dealerships, old-school mini-malls, and a Cuban place known for its mojitos.

Somehow, the owner made this spot work. A rugged six-burner gas stove anchored one wall, flanked by a grill and a pair of well-worn pastry ovens. A matching set of handsome stainless steel refrigerators lined the other wall to complement a six-by-eight-foot walk-in cooler. Organization reigned in the chrome industrial racks around the room, piled with the stuff you'd expect to find in a catering kitchen: stacks of plates, serving pieces, industrial-sized jars of oils,

---

*Anne-Catherine took it in stride that she was edited out of my first book. She runs A Caprice Kitchen, a restaurant in Ballard, Washington. You should give it a try.

vinegars, condiments, and spices, plastic bins, bottles, pitchers, boxes of glasses, cooking utensils, stacks of pans and bowls. It smelled vaguely of floor cleaner, residual cooking odors, and the lavender growing in the front planter box.

The owner left Post-it notes stuck throughout the kitchen. The tone varied from shrill to verge-of-hysteria warnings: "For catering use ONLY!"; "DO *NOT* FORGET TO TURN OFF LIGHTS!" Despite its quirky charm, or maybe because of it, I felt lucky to have found this place.

Their hands washed after multiple renditions of "Happy Birthday" and their diapers tucked into their white aprons, the volunteers stared nervously at the pile of knives.

Each volunteer hauled in her own knives from home as instructed. The cutlery cluttered the stainless steel tables pushed together in the center of the room. With that, the project officially began.

I toured the selection. Sabra had purchased her serrated-knife block set with five knives for twenty dollars because "they looked cool," she said. Trish had a set of Cutco knives custom made to fit into a shallow drawer in a house she no longer owned; she admitted that she used only a blunt vegetable knife for all tasks. Donna showed off a wedding present, an eleven-piece set from the Pampered Chef, kept pristine in the original protective covers. Cheryl brought in her knives, drawer and all, which featured everything from a few antique Ginsus to some classic all-carbon cleavers to her husband's assort-ment of hunting knives. Shannon had a set of expensive German knives, a wedding present from years earlier. Andra took three buses from Sea-Tac to get to the kitchen. "Sorry, I left the bigger ones at home. I didn't want to carry a big bag of knives on the bus," she said.

"Okay, show me your favorite knife, the one you use most of the time. Hold them up." They raised their knives aloft, like tentative knights at a medieval feast fearing their swords would not pass mus-ter. Most held a vegetable or a paring knife. Only one person lifted a chef's knife. I had them put their arms down. I asked why more people didn't use a chef's knife.

"That kind of knife scares me," Trish said. "It's so big."

Sabra shrugged. "What different does it make? A knife is a knife."

"Most of these knives look pretty expensive," Andra said, perusing the collection.

"Your mileage will vary," I replied. In an effort to present the spectrum, Lisa had raided a restaurant supply store and purchased several Mundial plastic-handled chef's knives, the default tool of restaurants everywhere. I had picked up a twenty-five-dollar OXO knife at Target and a ten-dollar knife at IKEA. I set them out next to my own collection of knives, a United Nations–style parade of metallurgy made by Wüsthof, Shun, Henckels, Global, and Sabatier and a ceramic number by Kyocera, among others. "Since I wrote a book with the word *knife* in it, people give me knives," I explained. "Maybe my next book title should include *diamonds, cash,* or *Learjet.*"

We went through Knife Anatomy 101, starting with the obvious. "As you can guess, the blade is the sharp part. The blunt back of the blade is a spine, just like a book. Many knives sport a raised lip edge near the handle known as a bolster.

"See this Wüsthof?" Like a hand model, I stroked the length of the knife. "This is what we call a 'full tang' because the blade extends all the way to the butt of the knife. It's held together by rivets. A bolster is heavy, designed to help balance the knife." I put it down and picked up one of the inexpensive restaurant knives. "See? I bet the tang extends about an inch into the handle. Second, no bolster. It's flat." That means that the knife has been stamped out of a sheet of metal, kind of like a cookie cutter. To make a knife with a bolster requires forging,* a more complicated process that requires human interaction, and so it's always more expensive.

"Take two key considerations into account when buying a knife. The steel and 'the feel.' You want a knife with the kind of steel that can take an edge and hold it." Not all steel is created equal. Harder

---

*Forging is a means of shaping metal to produce a piece that is stronger than an equivalent cast or machined part, generally through the use of heat and pressure. Think hammer and anvil.

steel takes an edge better, resulting in a sharper knife. But particularly hard steel can be brittle and trickier to maintain.

There's a complicated measure of hardness,* but for most retail knives the main concern is carbon content. "Carbon makes steel stronger. If you look for the phrase 'high-carbon steel,' that's a start." For instance, the knives from Victorinox, of Swiss Army knife fame, are made from high-carbon steel, and their chef's knives start at around thirty dollars.

"Marketers don't talk about steel since most consumers don't care," Lisa chimed in. "Instead, their job is to try to blind you with a lot of features. They know that people like value, so they will pack a set with all kinds of cheap knives, but the reality is that you don't need them all."

"Okay, here's what I use." I picked up an eight-inch extra-wide German knife. "I used this one throughout my training at Le Cordon Bleu. It's heavy, but I have small hands, and for some reason, the extra weight just feels good to me. How a knife fits into your hand is the 'feel.' Go to a place that has a good selection of knives, such as a cookware store, cutlery shop, and some department stores or restaurant supply places. Feel the subtle differences in the weight and the grip of the handle. A comfortable knife is a highly personal thing.

"Next, buy only the knives you'll use. Start with a good chef's knife. Supplement that with a paring knife and a bread knife." I picked up my German-made bread knife. "With care, good knives last for a long time. My mom bought me this for my birthday nearly twenty years ago. Other than my life, still arguably the best gift she ever gave me."

---

*Metallurgists measure relative hardness on the Rockwell Hardness Scale, or HRC. Most knives score in the 54 to 60 range. Japanese brands tend to be harder than European brands. So a Japanese-crafted Shun or Global knife might score 61 HRC, while a German-made Wüsthof rates 56 HRC. In addition to hardness, there's carbon content. The most common steel recipe for knives worldwide falls into grades of 440 A, B, or C. The lowest, 440A, tends to be a soft steel that dulls easily, but it's cheaper and easier to manufacture than the higher-carbon variety, so most cheap knife blocks are 440A. That explains why so many bad knives exist in the world.

Trish asked, "What about a vegetable knife?"

"Honestly, I don't know what you would do with a vegetable knife that you couldn't do with a chef's knife or a paring knife," I told her. "I use a chef's knife at least ninety percent of the time. I use a paring knife once in a while. I have a boning knife and a cleaver from my set from Le Cordon Bleu that I break out a few times a year. I haven't used my fillet knife in months. My chef friend Ted has four knives: a chef's knife, a paring knife, a bread knife, and a fillet knife. That's it. He was a professional chef for twelve years."

Dri raised an eyebrow and nodded her head. "All of this is good to know," she said. "My budget can handle getting one good knife. I was looking at three hundred dollars for a block set and thinking, There's no way."

"You can get a decent knife for thirty to fifty dollars, and that's a better deal than buying a cheap block set," I said. "But honestly, if you spend money on anything in your kitchen, invest it in the best knife that you can afford. If you take care of it, you'll have it for twenty or thirty years."

I looked at the clock. "Okay, no more looking. Find a chef's knife and pick it up. You can use any of mine, too." The women stirred, staking out a spot at the stainless steel table.

Cheryl reached for a Henckels knife close to her. She had her infant son, Liam, strapped to her bosom in a BabyBjörn. "I couldn't get a sitter," she had explained at the start of class. "Don't worry. I cook with him like this all the time." It is not every day that you see a baby next to a pile of a hundred knives. Liam reached for the shiny, pretty things. Cheryl kissed his head as she pulled his small hand back, "Oh, no, sweet pea, those are not for you."

"Show me how you hold a knife." All of them held it the way that I had before I went to culinary school, by making a fist around the handle.

"Don't strangle your knife," I said. "You want to sort of shake hands with it. Place the handle across your palm. Wrap your hand around it. With your thumb and index finger, pinch the juncture where the blade meets the handle. This will be on the bolster, if your knife has one. This should leave your other three fingers tucked around the handle."

I watched as they all tried this out, a study in collective awkwardness and furrowed brows. Lisa and I walked around the table, inspecting and adjusting holds here and there. It reminded me of my first day in the kitchen at Le Cordon Bleu, when the pleasant Chef Bruno Stihl walked through and stopped to correct my own grip on my brand-new knife. *"Non,"* he said as he gently unwrapped my fist and carefully reworked my fingers into the correct position. He held my hand in his as he demonstrated the rocking motion to use when cutting. *"Oui, comme ça. Un couteau doit être une extension de votre main,"* he said, smiling, and then walked away. Loosely, the phrase translates to 'Your knife should be one with your hand.' Once I figured out that phrase in French, I never forgot it. I never thought a knife demo could make me so nostalgic.

"How does that feel?"

"Weird," Sabra said. Other people nodded.

"It's a little bit like how you hold a golf club," Trish observed, looking at her knife as if it had somehow just become miraculously attached to her body.

"The reason you want to hold it like this is that you'll have more control over the blade," I said. "Plus, your hand won't get as fatigued. Okay, now hand your knife to the person on your right, handle first. *Carefully.*"

"This one is a lot heavier," Sabra said. She had been holding an inexpensive knife from her own block and shifted to a Japanese brand. "This is, like, well, a real knife."

"This is why it's great if you can test out a knife before you buy it. A comfortable knife will prompt you to chop more, which will encourage you to cook, and that's the whole point," I said.

Someone asked where to store knives without a block, so I pulled out a simple black plastic sheath that clipped on to the blade. "This is a knife cover. Slip it on like this"—I clicked it in place over a blade—"and voilà. It will protect your knives and your hands from the blade when fumbling around in a drawer." Magnetic strips on a wall work great. Mike ingeniously snapped powerful bar magnets from IKEA on the inside of our stainless steel stove hood. Knives snap solidly to the outside, up and out of the way. "I wash them by hand as soon as I use them, and then bang! They snap right to the magnet, high and out of the way." That brought up an important point.

"Always wash knives by hand. Never, ever, put a knife in the dishwasher. Steel is tempered with heat. The high heat from your dishwasher will damage the steel, dull the edge, and probably not do much for your handle either. Knives should never go into the dishwasher. Ever. Say it, everyone."

"Knives should never go in the dishwasher," they said in unison. "Ever."

"One more thing to remember: Knives are like dogs. They need occasional grooming. Get them sharpened at least once a year. Most cookware or cutlery stores will either offer this service or can tell you where to take them. It will set you back a few bucks per knife, but it's so worth it," I said.

"But doesn't this thing," asked Dri, holding up a honing steel, "sharpen your knife? Can't you do that at home?"

Lisa jumped in. "No, this is called a steel. When you run a blade across this, it's more like a fine-tuning by taking away bits of metal that collect on the edge. It keeps it straighter. But the metal should be a little bit magnetic to work and a lot of the steels aren't magnetized. So they're just for the finishing touch, really." It's the difference between brushing your dog and having it professionally groomed.

With that, we got down to business. We distributed thick cutting boards and settled a wet paper towel under each to keep it from slipping, a trick I learned from the French chefs. Then Lisa and I made sure each person had a proper chef's knife.

"Proper cutting technique involves sticks and cubes. That's about it." I grabbed a zucchini from the table. I cut it in half lengthwise and then cut each half into four vertical strips. "Remember that ad that said a Ronco-something-or-other could make julienne fries and you wondered what they were? Well, they're sticks. That's how you do it." Next, I took three sticks and cut them into cubes. "This is diced. The thinner the stick, the smaller the dice."

I diced another four sticks. "Notice that I'm not chopping down like a guillotine. Instead, I'm starting with the tip of the knife on the cutting board and then bringing the blade down. It should feel like a rocking motion."

Next, a stalk of celery. "It's always the same," I said, slicing it into two vertically. Then I diced it. "Always curl your fingers under to avoid cutting them. Then use the flat of your knuckles like a guide for the blade. If you get into that habit, you'll cut yourself a lot less often."

With a grunt, Lisa banged a five-gallon bucket containing thirty pounds of zucchini onto the table. The group stood back and stared in disbelief.

"Uh, that's a lot of zucchini," Jodi observed. "What do you want us to do with that?"

"I want you to practice," I said. "A lot of practice. So let's go."

Each person grabbed a zucchini and made her first tentative cuts. After a bit of chatter, the room settled into an air of quiet concentration. I saw Trish struggling to get a grip on her knife and went over to her. "Is everything okay?"

She said quietly, "I cut myself really bad when I was eight years old and so I have always been afraid of the blade. I think that's why I have always felt so unsure with a knife."

I placed the chef's knife back in her hand and held it as she made her first cuts. I could tell it was hard for her. "You know, years ago I badly cut one of my fingers trying to saw through a frozen bagel. See my scar?" I held out my finger. "I completely understand. But if you hold your knife back and keep your fingers out of the way, you're going to be fine." She nodded and grabbed a zucchini. I watched her deliberately slice it and then slowly carve sticks from one of the halves. When she diced her first batch, she looked relieved.

By her second zucchini, Trish moved more quickly. Soon, the regular thump-thump of knives filled the room like a healthy heartbeat.

"After a while it gets so much easier," Shannon said as I came around her side of the table to collect some of her diced vegetables. "I feel like I have more control over the knife."

With that, the mood shifted into one of cordial focus. The women chatted sporadically yet kept their eyes on their cutting boards. Halfway through her final zucchini, Jodi insisted that everyone look at the perfection of her dice. "I can't believe that I am doing this. People, I want you to know that I have never so much as peeled an apple in my life."

Within a half hour, the pile of zucchini disappeared, having been diced and then swept away into a massive thirty-two-quart pot on the six-burner stove. Then we handed each person two large yellow onions.

"When you cut an onion the classic way, it's easier, faster, and you cry less. But it also impresses people," I said. "First, cut the onion in half across the root so that a portion of the root stays intact on both pieces," I said. "If you cut it correctly, you should see *le cœur d'un oignon,* or the heart of the onion. It looks like a Georgia O'Keeffe painting. It's usually easier to peel onions after they've been cut." I pulled the papery skin away. "Now cut a vertical slit down the middle, but don't cut through the root. Make two more slits on either side." I picked it up. "It should look a little like a fan if you pick it up and spread the slits open. Now just slice it across at the end, the way you might normally slice an onion," and the cubes of onions tumbled onto the cutting board.

"Cool!" Sabra said. The group looked impressed. A few even golf-clapped.

Sabra, a quick study with a knife, tackled an onion first. I coached her on keeping her neon-green fingernails tucked back. "Hey, I'm totally getting this!" Sabra yelled to everyone victoriously, showing off her chopped onion. "I'm actually *good* with a knife! Who knew? This is *sooo* cool."

I watched Donna quietly study her onion at the corner of the table. She bought her vegetables frozen and precut to avoid having to chop in front of her husband, who mocked her. I walked around the table and picked up a bit of her chopped onion. "This looks great; perfect, actually." She flashed a quick, proud smile. "Nice job on your grip, too."

Most people got it. Terri struggled and reverted back to a modified choke hold; she made a clumsy knife wielder.

The nutty smell of sautéing zucchini drifted toward the worktable. Months earlier, Lisa had traveled to the south of Italy, where she had a remarkable pasta dish at a donkey farm. She went into the kitchen to pry the recipe from the woman who had cooked it, a professor of ancient studies at the university in Palermo. The woman spoke no English. Lisa's Italian is limited to what she refers to as "Tarzan Italian." The discussion went something along the lines of "Me want recipe. You give recipe?"

Eventually, she learned that the dish consisted of zucchini slow-cooked in olive oil, then paired with al dente pasta and finished with a lot of salt and pepper. As an extra bonus for that night, Lisa caramelized the chopped onions and added them to the zucchini. At the end of class, we handed out takeout boxes of the Italian-inspired zucchini pasta. Everyone seemed enthused and the volunteers left in a group, chattering excitedly.

We had reached the end of the first official cooking class, and it had gone without major slip-ups. We'd both been on our feet for at least six straight hours by the end of it, and an hour of cleanup remained. I searched one of the fridges marked with a "For Catering Use ONLY!" Post-it and dug out a bottle of pinot grigio. "You want some?" I asked Lisa. We feared breaking one of the glasses in the catering inventory, marked with a Post-it screaming, "Do NOT use any of the wineglasses except for DINNERS!" So we found a couple of small water glasses and clinked. "Do you think any of it sunk in?" I asked her.

She shrugged. "We'll find out."

It was time to wrap up. We divvied up the tasks. I pulled out the rolling mop and bucket. She resigned herself to the dish-cleaning area in the back. As part of my first job at age sixteen, I often helped mop the restaurant floors at night. Just as I started to sink into the memory, I noticed something on a side counter. Sabra had left behind her knife block set. I texted her.

"I won't be needing them," Sabra responded.

I debated what that meant. Was she not coming back to the class next week?

The next day, Sabra sent another text: "So excited! Got new chef's knife! Full tang, good steel, great feel for $45! See you Monday!"

ᐳ Rustic Italian Farmhouse Zucchini "Sauce" with Penne

This recipe is based on one developed by my friend Lisa Simpson after a meal at a picturesque Sicilian donkey farm. The slow-cooked zucchini takes on a nutty, earthy flavor and the pasta water "melts" the vegetables in a sort of thick sauce. This dish is best prepared in a stainless steel or cast iron pan to effectively caramelize the vegetables. Cook the pasta to not quite al dente so that it will finish cooking in the zucchini and absorb more flavor. Brown rice works well in place of pasta. Season the final outcome with liberal doses of coarse salt and ground black pepper. I sometimes add cooked Italian sausage, fresh basil, or pine nuts at the end of cooking. This pasta pairs well with a creamy white wine, such as Chardonnay.

SERVES 2 TO 3 AS A HEARTY MAIN DISH, 4 AS A SIDE

3 tablespoons olive oil
3 pounds zucchini, chopped into $\frac{1}{2}$-inch dice
6 ounces dried whole wheat pasta, such as penne
Coarse salt and freshly ground black pepper
1 cup caramelized onions (optional) (See note below.)

❧ In a large skillet, heat the olive oil over medium heat. Add the zucchini and toss to coat evenly. Stir frequently over medium heat. Depending on your pan, the heat level, and the size of the dice, it should take 12 to 25 minutes until the zucchini browns and starts to fall apart.

❧ Meanwhile, add the pasta to boiling salted water. Cook 2 minutes less than the package instructs. Before draining, *carefully* scoop out 3 cups of the hot pasta water. Add 1 cup to the browned zucchini. Bring to a soft boil, adjusting the heat if necessary, stirring to scrape up any browned bits. Add another half cup of water and repeat the process until the zucchini takes on a thick, almost creamy consistency.

❧ Add the cooked pasta, at least a couple of pinches of coarse salt, and plenty of freshly ground black pepper to the zucchini. Cook for a couple of minutes, until the pasta softens. If using caramelized onions, stir them in along with the pasta. After removing the skillet from the heat, taste again to see if the dish needs salt or pepper before serving.

Note: Caramelized Onions

Caramelized onions are an easy way to add a lot of flavor to a dish. I make a big batch and freeze it in 1-cup portions. A large ten-ounce onion cooks down to about a half cup, or five ounces, of caramelized onion. *Basic technique:* Thinly slice 2 onions. Add 2 tablespoons of olive oil to a large heavy-bottomed skillet over medium-high heat. Cook the onions until softened, then lower the heat to a simmer and gently brown them for about 25 minutes.

CHAPTER 5

᠗᠗

A Matter of Taste

᠗ **LESSON HIGHLIGHTS:**
Why You Must Taste, Taste, Taste

"This tastes weird, like a chemical," Jodi said, rolling her tongue around her mouth. The rest of the students nodded, murmuring agreement. The subject? Iodized table salt. "Gosh, it never occurred to me that salt could taste different from one another."

I planned to focus on vegetables for the second class, a major culinary blind spot for the volunteers. Yet I could not shake the ongoing references to bland recipes and the sense of inadequacy that I'd heard in regard to their palates. The simple phrase "Season to taste" was greeted with the enthusiasm of a tax audit.

"I hate it when a recipe says that," Shannon said when we visited her. "What does that mean? Whose taste? Mine? How do I know what tastes right?"

"I find it daunting," Trish said of the equally vague standard recipe phrase "Check seasonings." "Check for what? I don't know what I'm trying to make it taste like, you know? What if my palate is just way off?"

One of the most crucial lessons at Le Cordon Bleu—and for any cook—is the concept of taste, taste, taste. The chefs admonished us to taste or sniff every ingredient *before* we added it to a dish, and then to taste the dish during the cooking process, and then to taste it yet again before serving. "How can you tell how your dish will turn out if you don't taste the ingredients you're putting into it?" a chef would say. If you wait to taste a dish when it's done, it's often too late to fix anything wrong.

One reason the woman in the supermarket relied on boxed or frozen food was that "it always turned out." Most of the volunteers reported that even careful attention to some recipes yielded bland results. Both stemmed from a fundamental lack of understanding of flavor. Gen had described a recipe for a simple steamed broccoli dish. When I asked if she'd considered adding something extra, say, some lemon or extra black pepper, she shook her head. The recipe didn't say to do it, and she feared "messing it up."

"Slavish followers of recipes, who treat them as gospel instead of guidelines, make the mistake of putting more faith in someone else's instructions than they do in themselves," note Andrew Dornenburg and Karen Page, authors of *The Flavor Bible*. "Many people would do better in the kitchen if they *didn't* blindly follow recipes."

One key is to start with good ingredients, understand their affinity with other flavors, and go from there. Some flavors naturally go together, such as basil and tomato, fig and bleu cheese, or even chocolate and peanut butter. The key here would be to figure out a way to convince the volunteers that spending a bit extra for flavorful quality ingredients was worth it. Most said that when it came to food, cost trumped any consideration of flavor, echoing Sabra's comments that most frozen meals tasted the same to her, so she went for the cheapest options.

This focus on cost versus flavor was not limited to the group or even to this generation. In her 1937 story "Pity the Blind in Palate," M. F. K. Fisher lamented that many Americans shovel in the same fare with dogged regularity, rarely stopping to think about what they are eating. "We eat, collectively, with a glum urge for food to fill us," she wrote. "We are ignorant of flavor. We are as a nation taste-blind." But Fisher acknowledged that if a person sampled a variety of things, stopping to ponder the sensations and subtle differences, then hope existed to awaken the palate.

But how would I get this point across? As I often do when I've got something to think about, I went to the supermarket.

At nearly 10:30 P.M., the place was relatively quiet, with few shoppers. The scent of floor wax drifted over to the canned-goods aisle. I started to spend more time in the center aisles, where I had met the woman with the chicken, hoping to run into her again.

"Mommy, which kind of canned tomatoes do you want?" I turned, hoping it was her daughter. Instead, it was a preteen with braces in a pink fleece sweater over a pink dance outfit and pink sneakers.

Her mother, staring down at her phone, answered without looking up. "Whatever's the cheapest, sweetie. It doesn't matter. They're all the same."

The girl tossed two cans of diced store-brand tomatoes into their cart and the pair rolled away. I stood contemplating the wall of tomatoes featuring nineteen different brands that offered them whole, diced, peeled, fire-roasted, organic, imported, and packed with basil.

Do they taste the same? I thought of M. F. K. Fisher's argument and of the chefs who made us taste everything in order to develop what's often referred to as "taste memory." I thought of the book *The Tasting Club* by Dina Cheney. Essentially, the book suggests comparative tastings of olive oil, cheese, olives, coffees, teas, and the like as a centerpiece for social gatherings. Why not comparatively taste canned tomatoes? I selected nine different varieties of diced and took them in my arms to the checkout. "Someone likes tomatoes," the checker said blithely as he ran them across the scanner.

"Taste is personal. We all taste very differently," Cheney told me later. "We have different sensory thresholds and different taste memories. Ultimately, it's about finding out what we like and trusting our own palates. That's all that matters."

A veteran of more than 150 comparative tastings across the country, Cheney discovered that people are frequently taken aback by how much variety exists within one category of food or drink. In her experience, she found that people remain loyal to one brand or dedicated to the notion of buying the cheapest option, but rarely consider tasting different brands or varieties back to back. "When people do, they're surprised at how many differences there are between, say, various brands of seventy percent dark chocolate bars or canned tuna. They might realize the brand to which they've been so loyal is actually mediocre and they much prefer another one. That's why tastings often change our buying habits."

For the next week, I studied everything that I could find about the issue of taste and flavor. Taste is physical. Our tongues detect only five options: sweet, sour, bitter, salty, and umami, a savory sense of earthiness equated with soy, meat, and mushrooms. Flavor happens in our brains, determined by what we perceive from our senses. Not everyone tastes the same. Some "supertasters" experience certain tastes more intensely than others, particularly salt and bitter.* At the other end of the spectrum fall the "nontasters" with a dulled ability to distinguish individual tastes. Everyone else falls somewhere in between. Most scientists believe genetics is a factor.

So our ability to distinguish taste is nature. But preference is nurture; what flavors we like is something we learn. None of this is new to the wine world, where it's long been accepted that you can "train your palate" to appreciate minute subtleties in wine. That in turn leads to the confidence of someone declaring he's detected flavors such as "black currant," "rotted wood," or "gym socks" after taking a cursory sip from a glass of Cabernet Franc.

Prompted by Cheney's book and my cache of canned tomatoes, I constructed a series of blind tastings with everyday cooking ingredients: olive oil, salt, Parmesan cheese, the tomatoes, and chicken stock. Lisa and I raided our own pantries and then hit a couple of grocery stores. We walked through the aisles and tossed various cans and bottles into the cart.

*"Supertasters" is a term coined by Yale University researcher Linda Bartoshuk, who stumbled on the notion that people's ability to taste varies widely while doing studies on saccharin. Supertasters readily taste a bitter synthetic compound found in saccharin known as 6-n-propylthiouracil. Nontasters can't detect it at all.

We arrived at the teaching kitchen in time to meet up with Lauri Carter, a local chef who had heard about the project and offered to volunteer to teach a lesson on vegetables. Lauri is an energetic petite brunette with deep dimples and a cheerleader-like can-do spirit. I half expect her to break out into a cheer at times, and I mean that in a good way. That summer, Lauri faced her own existential challenge. After four years as the chef and owner of her popular bistro, Moxie, her landlord unexpectedly broke her lease. She found herself covering shifts at a fashionable Spanish wine bar downtown, trying to figure out what to do next. She's smart, a gifted cook, and a good explainer. If anyone could inspire people about vegetables, Lauri could do it. She took the sudden addition of a tasting to her planned vegetable lesson in stride.

As the students wandered in from one of the first sunny Seattle summer days, they looked around, puzzled. Clusters of small plates took up every open countertop. Lisa and I labeled each with a letter or number. As they put on their aprons and grabbed a diaper for their side towels, we handed each person a small yellow legal pad.

"We'll explain what these are for once we cover some vegetable basics," I said. I introduced Lauri and she took my spot at the center of the worktable. She started first with potatoes: russet, red, white Idaho, Yukon Gold, and even purple. The volunteers examined them raw. "The purple ones are so pretty!" Gen said.

To prepare the potatoes, Lauri went on to demystify a commonly misunderstood term—*sauté*. Based on the French word for "jump," *sauté* simply means to cook something quickly in a bit of oil at high heat. "So, where the jump comes in is from the way professional chefs cook. I'll show you." The crew huddled around the big six-burner stove. The skillet looked comically large in her small hand. "First, add some oil to a pan and let it get hot," she explained. "When you sauté food, it should sizzle when it hits the pan." Lauri tossed in a handful of sliced potatoes that hissed when they hit the hot skillet. She shook the pan as soon as they landed. "Shake it right away, enough so that the food moves a bit, and then it won't stick during the rest of cooking." Lauri added a couple of pinches of coarse salt from a small ramekin by the stove.

"So notice the salt in the dish," she said, holding it overhead. "Chefs have dishes with salt rather than shakers. You know why?" The group collectively shook their heads. "If you shake salt from a shaker, you can't see the salt. It's hard to tell how much you're putting in. But with salt in a little dish, you can literally grab a pinch of salt." An "ahhhh" went over the group.

Lauri tugged at the pan's handle and tossed the potatoes in the air, and they fell back into the pan.

"Jump. It makes sense now," Jodi said.

Lauri had each volunteer do at least one shake of the pan. "You want to cook the vegetables until they start to brown. That's known as caramelizing, which just means the heat has drawn out some of the natural sugar in the vegetables. That's when they start to turn tasty."

To practice their knife skills from the week prior, we then dumped about ten pounds of potatoes on the counter. The students huddled around Sabra as she showed off her new knife, purchased from a restaurant supply store.

"Oh, that's a smart idea. I didn't think about shopping at a restaurant supply store," Jodi said. "I thought they might card me at the door or something."

The students dived into the task, peeling and chopping the potatoes. Everyone except Terri held their knives correctly. "Oh, hey, do you want me to show you how to hold a knife again?" I asked her.

"No, I just prefer to hold it this way, but thanks," she said, with a choke hold on the end of the knife. Huh, I thought. I didn't have much experience teaching. Should I force her to do it my way? I decided to let it go.

Soon a rhythmic chopping and light banter filled the room. Lauri demonstrated how to cut a leek, chopping off the hard dark-green ends and then the stubby root. She cut the light green and white portions lengthwise (sticks) and then diced them (cubes). "Leeks sometimes trap dirt between their layers," she advised. "So once they're chopped up, we're going to toss them in a big bowl of water to clean them off."

The potatoes and leeks were destined for a classic *potage parmentier,* potato and leek soup. "Basically, it's always the same," Lauri said. "We're going to sauté the rinsed leeks in some butter and olive oil. Once the leeks soften, we'll toss in potatoes and chicken stock. Once they're soft, we'll puree them and stir in some cream."

"That's it?" Shannon asked.

Lauri nodded. "That's it. You could do a variation of it with almost anything. You could use leeks and asparagus, or onions and broccoli, shallots and cauliflower, onions and carrots. It's just a simple formula. If you've got kids who think they don't like vegetables, I've found they often will eat them when they're made into soup. They'll also eat more vegetables in the form of a soup than they would raw. It's easier for them to eat and digest."

We went through the basics of other common ways to cook vegetables. The volunteers chopped up cauliflower and Brussels sprouts and shoved them into one big collective pan with some olive oil to roast. We set up four portable burners on the worktable and paired the students together to sauté Swiss chard and diced potatoes. The room turned lively. Pans clanked, oil sizzled, people laughed or shrieked, as the smells of the vegetables erupted around the table.

On Gen and Sabra's corner, some potatoes escaped as they shook the pan. "Watch out, we're flying potatoes over here!"

Trish fretted at first. "Am I doing this right?" she asked tentatively as Lauri checked her status sautéing potatoes. "I don't usually cook over high heat."

"Looks perfect to me," Lauri said. Trish seemed pleased with herself.

I brought in my electric steamer. "This sounds cheesy, but it's one of the few things I leave on my counter. Simply add some water, pile in some vegetables, and turn on the timer. It's hands-off; you can forget about them until the timer dings. They never overcook and pretty much any vegetable can be steamed." I threw in baby arti-chokes and small cobs of corn.

Then Lauri explained what Julia Child called "cooking vegetables the French way." The method aims to keep the color and bite of veg-etables such as asparagus, broccoli, green beans, and peas. We brought a pot of water to a boil on one of the portable burners. I set a bowl of ice water next to it.

"Briefly cook the vegetables in the boiling water until they're soft-ened but still a little firm," Lauri said, dropping a handful of green beans into the pot. After a couple minutes, she pulled them out with a slotted spoon. "Then plunge them into the ice water. Actually, cold tap water is fine, too. It slows the cooking process, and it keeps the chlorophyll intact. When you keep boiling them, the chlorophyll evaporates and you get . . ."

"The gray vegetables that my mother used to serve," Trish said.

"Exactly," Lauri replied. She offered a green bean to everyone around the table.

"These are nice, crisp, and so green," Trish said. "So fresh tasting. If my mother would have served me these, I might have thought I liked vegetables growing up."

Done with the vegetables for now, we shifted from cooking to tasting.

I said, "Okay, all this stuff you see laid out around the room? We're going to taste all of them. There is no right or wrong. Just taste each ingredient and write down your impressions. Compare all the olive oils to one another, then the chicken stock, and so on."

At first, people were tentative. A light dip here, a scribble there, but no talking. Then came a chorus of "I don't know if this right" and "I don't know what I'm supposed to taste" and "This just tastes like salt."

After fifteen minutes, they grew bolder. They started to compare notes. The room grew louder, busy with voices. "Did you like num-ber six in the olive oils? No? Me neither." "Didn't that chicken stock taste odd?" "Yeah, I thought so, too."

People dodged from the nine types of olive oil to the eight types of chicken stock to the twelve cans of tomatoes, comparing notes. The salt was the hardest, and in retrospect we overdid it by offering nine varieties: standard table salt, kosher salt, sea salt, Himalayan pink salt, French gray sea salt, *fleur de sel,* black salt, and salt substitute, plus a handcrafted sea salt made from Puget Sound water. The salt tasting led to a lot of water drinking and spitting.

At one point, Shannon sat down. "I'm just seriously overwhelmed," she said. "I don't know if I can taste anymore."

We passed around an "aroma wheel," a multicolored circle designed to help wine drinkers articulate what they experience when tasting wine. Soon the students were consulting it after various tastes. This changed the discussions. "That stock was kind of yeasty, don't you think?" "I found those tomatoes astringent." "I'm definitely getting something metallic in this salt."

Then we unveiled what had been tasted and compared notes.

We started with the salt. The expensive artisan salt made from Puget Sound water won best flavor overall. In second, a gray *sel gris* that a friend had brought back from France. The inexpensive coarse kosher salt was deemed "exactly what I think salt should taste like," Andra said. Collectively, the group disliked two of them. First was the salt labeled "E."

Everyone thought it tasted odd. "It's just got a strange taste," Jodi said. "It's harsh and like a chemical."

"It tastes too salty but also kind of like metal," Sabra said.

The dreaded E turned out to be standard iodized table salt.

"Oh, that stuff is awful," Shannon said, shaking her head. "I am not using that anymore. I had no idea that salts could taste so different."

The other loathed salt was option D, which most of them referred to as harsh and bitter. Lisa developed a chemical burn on her tongue after tasting it. "What I think a car battery would taste like," someone wrote.

"The weird thing is that it doesn't really taste like salt at all," said

Gen, the young woman with roommates. She'd been relatively quiet up to that point. "It's like fake salt." The culprit: salt substitute.

"I would not have believed this if I had not seen it for myself, but let me read this line on the label," Lisa said. "Consult a doctor before using this product."

Next we looked at the winners in the canned-tomato taste test. Both Hunt's and Cento scored high. "Those two actually taste like tomatoes," Cheryl said. "They're kind of sweet, but not so salty."

"I'm so relieved," Lauri whispered into my ear. "I used to use Cento tomatoes in my restaurant. I was worried they wouldn't be any good."

The biggest loser was also the most expensive, a brand of San Marzano tomatoes from Italy. I didn't like them either after a direct comparison to the others. "It's like they had a slightly sour flavor that left a strange aftertaste," Shannon said.

In the olive oil category, the winner was the delicate flavor of an expensive Italian extra virgin olive oil. "Fruity, subtle," Cheryl said, reading her notes.

"Very delicate, not overly oily," Trish said.

"It's like white grapes," Gen said. "Almost a little bit like honey." Lauri and I looked at each other. We tasted it again. Now that she mentioned it, we picked those flavors up, too.

Olive oil is made by pressing olives to extract their natural oil. The first time olives are processed for oil is known as "extra virgin" and accounts for about 10 percent of all the olive oil produced. Each subsequent pressing extracts less flavor, from "extra" to "pure" to just plain olive oil.

"Use extra-virgin olive oil in something uncooked, like a salad dressing," Lauri said. "It's better to buy good oils in small quantities. People think that oil lasts forever, but it has a shelf life of six months. Keep it in a cool, dark place and *not* next to or above your stove! Heat breaks it down."

"You can use a less expensive kind of olive or vegetable oil for everyday cooking. If you use that a lot, then you can get a bigger size."

Unfortunately, the bulk olive oil that I had bought for class was unpopular. "It just tastes oily and bland," Dri said. "Funny, I have this kind at home and I never realized that I don't like it. I have a lot of it, too."

The Parmesan cheese comparison required a brief education. "The real deal is called Parmigiano-Reggiano," explained Lisa, who had done this spiel a million times at her mom's cheese shop. "It's kind of like champagne. You can't call it Parmigiano-Reggiano unless it's from one of five provinces in Italy. To get the name, the cheese makers have to follow very strict guidelines. So that's why everything else is Parmesan."

The difference extends beyond the name. Commercially produced Parmesan is aged a shorter time and due to its production methods can contain up to 70 percent more sodium than the Italian variety. Most of the Parmesan found in supermarkets is mechanically processed to wrest out extra moisture, which extends its shelf life.

The winner in the category was an aromatic wedge of Parmigiano-Reggiano from Lisa's mother's shop. Shavings of it were stacked up against the pale slices of an American brand and three versions of grated cheese, including the familiar canned variety. Results went as expected.

"This tastes like soap," Sabra said of the exact brand of cheese she had used on her White Trash Garlic Bread. "But this stuff, it rocks," she said, picking up another slice of the Italian cheese.

"The thing about something like Parmigiano-Reggiano is that, yeah, it's more expensive to buy a piece of that," Lisa said. "But it has so much more flavor that a little goes a long way. In the end, you'll use less, so it's a better value than you think."

We concluded by tasting the various chicken stocks.

"I always just thought chicken stock was chicken stock," Shannon said, verbalizing what several had murmured during the class. "There's so much difference, it's amazing." Dri described one as a "salt lick." Others were not "chicken-y."

One had a strange flavor. "It's like how orange juice is so orange-y,"

Gen said. "It's almost as if it is chicken stock made from concentrate. It's also weirdly salty." That one turned out to be stock made from a bouillon cube.

Only one person favored my lovingly handcrafted homemade stock. "It's nice and chicken-y, and it has a good body to it, but it's bland," Trish said.

As usual, I hadn't added any salt to it. They were comparing unsalted homemade stock against mostly heavily salted prepared stocks, some of which had more than a third of an adult's daily sodium intake in one cup. Swanson and Pacific got the thumbs-up, and after a dose of salt was added to the homemade stock, the group preferred that one, too.

"I guess the thing is that after tasting them all, I'd only buy ones with lower sodium," said Trish, her taste buds sensitive to salt because she avoided it. "I use one of these brands and, my goodness! I never realized just how *salty* it was until I actually tasted it here tonight."

Everyone nodded. "One thing to remember, you can always add salt, but you can't take it out," I said. "This is also why you should taste things before you cook with them. Taste the olive oil you're using before making a dressing. Sample a bit of the cheese before you add it to pasta. Try a bit of that chicken stock before you put it into a soup."

With that, Lauri and Lisa unveiled the final test of the night. In the middle of the table sat five bowls of leek and potato soup. Three were the newly crafted *potage parmentier* split into different bowls, one with no salt, one mightily oversalted, and the final bowl seasoned to Lauri's taste. The other two bowls also contained leek and potato soup, one from a condensed-soup can while the other was an expensive dehydrated "gourmet" version.

"Select the one you think tastes best," Lauri challenged. Everyone selected the moderately seasoned soup. "What's wrong with soup A?" she asked. Too much salt, everyone agreed. "What's wrong with D?" Not enough salt, the group said. "So now when you see a recipe that says 'Salt to taste,' that's all it means. If it doesn't have enough salt, like D, then add some. Just make it taste good to you."

The group pondered the remaining two bowls.

"Ugh, I can taste the iodized salt in both of these," Jodi said.

"Yeah, how weird, me, too," Shannon replied.

The canned soup generated a range of intriguing descriptions: "strange mouthfeel," "feels fatty on the back of my tongue," "strange aftertaste," "not particularly leek-y or potato-y," and just plain "yuck." The dehydrated version fared better, but was still described as "too salty," "tastes like chemicals," "odd spices," and—my favorite—"kind of like a bowl of liquid blah."

As she took off her apron, Jodi quietly admitted to Shannon that she had a case of the canned soup back at home. "If I had known it was so easy to make, I wouldn't have bought it, you know?"

⤖ Five Marvelous Ways to Cook Vegetables with "Flavor Splashes"

You just need to know the meaning of four words: sauté, steam, roast, *and* grill. *Vegetables are done when they are tender but still crisp. Err on the side of undercooking. You can also toss in a vinaigrette from chapter 8 or a flavor splash (below), or toss with a handful of grated cheese and broil for a minute or two. There's nothing wrong with plain frozen vegetables. Flash-frozen on harvest, they're often as fresh as or fresher than their produce-aisle cousins. Frozen vegetables do best sautéed or steamed.*

Sauté or Stir-fry

⚜ Virtually all vegetables lend themselves to being quickly cooked over high heat in a bit of fat. Cut them into $\frac{1}{2}$-inch pieces, get a skillet hot, and add 1 or 2 glugs of vegetable, olive, peanut, canola, or coconut oil. Add the vegetables and stir a few times. Most take less than 10 minutes. Firm vegetables, such as potatoes and carrots, take the longest, up to about 15 minutes. Cook greens such as Swiss chard and spinach with a bit of chopped garlic until wilted. Finish with salt and pepper. If you mix firm vegetables with softer ones, be sure to add the harder ones first.

Roast

⚜ This is simple yet yields great flavor. Line an oven-safe pan with aluminum foil or parchment paper. Cut the vegetables into uniform 1-inch or smaller pieces. Toss them generously with oil or butter, and add salt, pepper, and maybe a sprig of thyme. Roast at high heat (475°F) and stir a couple of times while cooking. Once diced, sliced, or otherwise broken down into smaller pieces, the following vegetables will cook in less than 15 minutes: asparagus, beets, bell peppers, Brussels sprouts, carrots, cauliflower, eggplant, green beans, leeks, mushrooms, parsnips, white and sweet potatoes, diced squash (hard outer skin discarded), and zucchini.

Steam

⚜ This is a no-fat way to cook utilizing a multitude of setups. Cut up larger vegetables into 1-inch or smaller cubes. Use an electric steamer, or add vegetables to a pan with a tight-fitting lid filled with an inch or two of water, or simply microwave a small batch of vegetables with a bit of water in a bowl covered with a plate. Cook until just tender. Add salt and pepper after steaming. This method is recommended for asparagus, green beans, broccoli, Brussels sprouts, cabbage, carrots, cauliflower, corn, kale, kohlrabi, onions, parsnips, peas, potatoes, spinach, diced squash, Swiss chard, cubed turnips, and zucchini.

Grill

⚜ If you grill often, invest in one of those square grill pans with holes. Cut vegetables into 1-inch pieces, and toss them with generous doses of oil, salt, and pepper. Put in the basket over hot coals, cover, and stir regularly until they are tender.

~~~~~~~~~~~~~~

FLAVOR SPLASHES

Just mix the ingredients together in a small saucepan, heat briefly, pour onto vegetables, and toss to coat. Each recipe coats enough for about four side servings of vegetables. (For more ideas, see the "Cheat Sheet" to Flavor Profiles in the Extra Recipes section at the back of the book.)

Asian Ginger Lime

❧ Warm 2 teaspoons of sesame oil, then add 1 teaspoon of fresh grated ginger or a couple of pinches of dried ginger, a few squeezes of fresh lime juice, and $\frac{1}{2}$ teaspoon of soy sauce. Heat through for about 3 minutes.

Cajun Oil

❧ Warm 2 teaspoons of olive oil, add 3 finely chopped green onions, and cook until tender, then add 1 teaspoon of Cajun spice blend, a few squeezes of fresh lemon juice, and a couple of drops of hot sauce.

Garlic Citrus Butter

❧ Heat 2 tablespoons of butter, add 2 small cloves of minced garlic, a bit of fresh thyme or mixed dried herbs, and 1 teaspoon of lemon or orange juice, and sauté for a couple of minutes, until the garlic softens.

Herb-Lemon Oil

❧ Warm 2 teaspoons of olive oil, then add the zest of $\frac{1}{2}$ lemon and 1 tablespoon of chopped fresh herbs such as rosemary, oregano, tarragon, thyme, or basil. Heat through.

Thai-Style

❧ Heat 2 teaspoons of peanut oil, then add 2 finely chopped green onions, 1 tablespoon of crushed peanuts, a couple of squeezes from a fresh lime, and a bit of hot sauce. Gently heat through.

CHAPTER 6

⊛⊛

Fowl Play

⊛ LESSON HIGHLIGHTS:
The Value of Learning How to Use a Whole Chicken

"If there's one skill that I think people need to learn, it's how to cut up a whole chicken," said Rick Rodgers, the author of thirty-five cookbooks. "Roast chicken is iconic, we all love it and that's a great skill to learn, but being able to do something with all the various parts of chicken is something even more people need to know in terms of how it fits in with their daily life."

Knowing your way around a chicken is a valuable thing to learn. On average, a whole chicken costs about the same as a package of boneless skinless chicken breasts, whether it's a standard supermarket chicken or a more expensive organic variety. Used efficiently, a single chicken can provide the goods for two or three meals.

The breast can be left on the bone and baked, a boneless breast can be quickly sautéed, the thigh meat can be cut up for a stir-fry, the legs oven-fried, and the wings collected and frozen for snacks. If you decide to roast the whole bird, the meat can be used in a seemingly endless parade of dishes: salads, pasta, burritos, casseroles, sandwiches, and so on—virtually any recipe that calls for cooked chicken. As Rodgers notes, you get not only the eight chicken pieces but all the bones, the back, and the giblets,* too. Given that popular

---

*If you've ever wondered what was inside the chicken, the "giblets" include the neck, the liver, and the heart. They're traditionally stored inside the bird's cavity. Poultry producers often sell chickens without these bits because consumers don't know what

brands of stock average about $2.50 per quart and remnant bones from just one chicken can yield up to two quarts, one chicken can provide about $5.00 worth of stock.

In culinary terms, it's hard to beat the importance of chicken. It's the number one search term on recipe sites such as Epicurious.com, Allrecipes.com, and Foodista.com. On Google, worldwide traffic for "chicken recipes" dwarfs requests for beef, fish, or vegetarian recipes. Americans consume an average of 60 pounds of chicken annually, edging out beef as the nation's preferred meat.* American chicken growers process 38 million chickens daily—one for every man, woman, and child in the state of California every single day. That's 43 billion pounds each year, says the American Meat Institute, equivalent to the weight of 860 luxury cruise ships.

The students arrived, donned their aprons, grabbed a diaper, and selected a chef's knife from the box before heading to the worktable. They were getting to know one another and chatted amiably. I overheard snippets of small talk.

"I threw out all of my iodized salt. I had two of them . . ."

"Yeah, me, too."

"I went through my cupboards and found most of my oils were rancid . . ."

"I made kale, and my boyfriend was like, 'This is so good! Where did you get the idea to make *kale*?'"

Helping out that day was my friend Maggie, a thirtyish streetwise Sicilian American beauty from Chicago with jet-black hair and

---

to do with them. Rodgers suggests simmering them with a few veggies in a quart of water for an easy chicken broth.

*Determining accurate numbers for meat consumption is something of a dark art; the USDA puts the figure at sixty pounds per person annually, while the American Meat Institute says it more like one hundred pounds, with others putting figures somewhere in between. No matter the source, chicken beats beef.

dragonfly tattoos cascading down each arm. A kitchen veteran turned culinary consultant, Maggie agreed to assist with some of the more complicated classes. Just as the students were filing in, she arrived, aggravated from a day at her cupcake client. The small-baked-goods industry appears to be a surprisingly ruthless affair. Her client was locked in a battle for cupcake dominance with an arch competitor and the stress had prompted cutthroat internal politics. That day, she had had to snap at someone, "Does this kind of attitude belong around cupcakes!? I don't think so."

Buoyed by the apparent success of the initial tasting evening, I decided to start each class with one. Today we set out small plates featuring five varieties of Dijon mustard. Now they knew the drill. Each person daintily dabbed a bit of mustard onto a small appetizer plate with a tiny espresso spoon. As each jotted down notes on a small yellow pad, they made thoughtful faces. We talked about flavors and words to describe them. The most common: *sour, spicy, bitter, smooth.* No one liked the cheapest store brand. "It's like chalk," Gen said.

Grey Poupon was the easy favorite, even beating out Maille, a pricey classic French import. "You can taste the white wine in both, though," Jodi said. An expensive organic brand was written off as bland. Shannon summed up the group's general thoughts. "The more that I taste, the more it makes me want to pay attention to what I used to just take for granted."

Although it was past seven P.M., the warmth of the late-June day remained trapped in the room, intensified by the heat of the commercial ovens. Cars buzzed by outside the door, which was propped open in a futile attempt to draw in fresh air. Before we moved on to taking apart the chickens, I rounded up the group around the worktable set with a patchwork of colored cutting boards. Maggie passed around glasses of ice water as we talked chicken.

"Okay, I have a few questions. Have you ever cut up a chicken?" Universal shakes of the head.

"Do you know what *braise* means?" One person ventured a guess.

I asked if anyone had ever roasted a whole chicken. Only Trish raised her hand. "I have, but I've mostly bought them that way," she said.

I lined up four chickens, à la Julia Child in a famous episode of her 1960s TV show, *The French Chef*. In that scene, she described the differences between a broiler, fryer, roaster, capon, stewer, and "Old Madam Hen."* Instead of different ages, I presented differently raised chickens, all broilers weighing three to four pounds. Two were supermarket chickens, a commercially raised standard variety and a free-range bird that cost just less than a dollar more per pound. The third was a certified organic free-range chicken from a butcher. The last was a pasture-raised chicken purchased directly from a local farmer.

The supermarket chicken felt wet, and the breast was noticeably heavier than that of the rest of the chickens. The organic chicken from the butcher and the pasture-raised chicken, which didn't come prepackaged, felt dry. When I sat all four up as if they were lounging upright, the supermarket and the free-range chickens fell forward, propelled by the weight of their overbuilt breasts. I sliced a breast off each one. I held up the largest, from the least expensive supermarket chicken.

"How much do you think this weighs?" They all ventured a guess: six ounces, eight.

"How many servings do you think this is?" Everyone agreed that it was one serving.

Cheryl nuzzled Liam in his baby carrier. "A half a serving in my house. Yeah, Daddy could eat two of those, couldn't he, sweet pea?"

"How much do you think a serving should weigh?"

---

*The primary difference is in the age of the chicken, which in turn determines the weight and tenderness of the bird. A broiler/fryer weighs around three and a half pounds and is about ten weeks old. Roasters that tip the scales up to five pounds can be up to eight months old, while stewing fowl are even older. The odd bird out in her lineup was the capon, which historically was created by castrating a rooster to cause it to become a plump, tender bird; later, synthetic sex hormones were used for the same effect. Due to the industrialization of poultry, capons, stewing chickens, and older hens are rarities.

Donna, knower of all things Weight Watchers, piped up. "About four ounces," she trilled brightly. "A chicken breast is three Weight Watchers points."

I put the breast on a scale. It tipped in at more than a pound. "So this one breast ought to provide four servings." More than two-thirds of the weight of this chicken came from the breast alone. The breast from the pasture-raised bird from the butcher weighed the least, about nine ounces.

As Michael Pollan noted in his book *The Omnivore's Dilemma*, commercial poultry growers have researched how to engineer chickens through breeding to grow significantly greater portions of breast meat. From a monetary point of view, it makes perfect fiscal sense. Boneless, skinless chicken breasts fetch as much as six dollars per pound—roughly five times the retail price for whole chickens and at least twice as much as the other portions of the bird. The downside? To maximize profits chickens are often confined to massive barracks where they are provided an endless supply of feed around the clock but given little exercise. As depicted in the documentary *Food Inc.*, some birds grow so big so fast, they ultimately cannot support themselves under the weight of their mighty breasts and fall down. Detractors of the industrial poultry process say that the system ratchets up the stress level for the chickens and breaks down their immune systems, thus requiring mass poultry growers to use a lot of antibiotics.

By comparison, organic farmers aren't supposed to give their chickens any antibiotics or feed containing pesticides.

"So what does it mean when the package says 'all natural,' like this guy here?" Dri asked, pointing to a supermarket chicken.

"In theory, it means that the chicken doesn't have any artificial flavor, but in practice it's a little meaningless," I said. Chickens are natural products, just like beef or pork. They don't make synthetic chickens, at least not yet. "With some companies, free-range is kind of similar, since the USDA requires only that the chicken have access to a door should it want to go outside, but it doesn't necessarily mean that it ranged anywhere, free or not." The only way you can know how chickens are raised is to know the poultry grower, or if your butcher knows the grower. "Some free-range chicken growers really make an effort to treat the chickens humanely. The farm where this guy was raised," I said, patting the pasture-raised chicken, "they make a point to physically transport the chickens to a grassy grazing area. But he's also triple the cost of a standard supermarket chicken."

A small puddle had formed under the first chicken. Dri pointed. "Um, did that one need the ladies' room?"

"That's probably saline." Producers sometimes inject chickens with water or brine. It keeps the meat moist, plus it adds more weight, adding cost, even though it's water, not meat.*

A whisper went through the group. "That's bullshit," Sabra said. "They shot it up with water so I could pay more?" She shifted from one foot to the other and crossed her arms. She looked ready to kick some commercial-chicken-growing butt.

"Listen, I am not going to say that you should never buy a supermarket chicken because that's just not realistic. But look up the poultry grower at the supermarket where you shop. Ask questions of the butcher in your market. If you don't want your chicken injected with water, tell them. If consumers care about something, it changes the kind of products offered. I try to buy from my butcher because I trust that they know their suppliers, but I don't always do that. Remember, if you're buying something cheap, but then you don't use it all, then it's not quite the good deal it seemed when you bought it."

I didn't want this class to just be about *cooking* chickens. One of the things that I had come across in our kitchen visits reinforced what researchers already know. Most people don't associate chicken, especially in the form of boneless, skinless chicken breasts—with a physical animal. In three kitchens, we found packages of chicken

---

*The Center for Science in the Public Interest reports that water or brine can account for as much as 15 percent of the weight in a package of chicken, and estimates that this practice generates $2 billion in added revenue per year for the poultry industry.

meat well past their sell-by dates in the fridge. "Oh, no, I forgot about those," one of the volunteers had said of a family-sized package of chicken breasts. She picked them up to look at the date and shrugged, then tossed it into the trash. "I hate wasting money like that."

Chickens are living creatures, a lesson that I learned early in life growing up on a farm in Michigan that has never left me. I told the volunteers the story about it.

"On the farm where I grew up, we kept chickens," I started. A slightly askew chicken coop graced the far corner of the barnyard, and shortly after buying the house in late winter, my folks went to get some chicks from the local farm-supply store. The weathered old man who owned the place suggested that they purchase 125 chicks to start. "And I'll tell you what"—he rolled a piece of hay around with his dark teeth. "You buy that 125, I'll give you 125 for free."

An hour later, they packed five crates with 250 wildly cheeping chicks into the back of Dad's battered Chevy pickup. My brothers and sisters loved the chicks, but lost interest in them after about a month. About the same time, my parents began to realize that the chicks had been a great deal—for the guy who sold them. He made his real money off chicken feed. My parents stopped by to purchase massive bags every few days to satisfy the voracious chickens. The adorable yellow balls of fluff grew at a startling pace. As adults, they turned into a massive and noisy gaggle of feathers that moved as a single wavering blanket of white.

After a couple of months, panic set in. "We were going broke feeding them," my mom told me later. They traded some chickens for seed to start the garden and gave others away. It didn't put a dent in the flock.

The day after school let out for the summer, Mom rounded up the kids. She set up the chickens into a production line in the barn. A teenage neighbor caught the birds, and then held them down as she whacked off their heads, gutted them. Then she handed the carcasses to my oldest brother, Milton, to plunge into her huge canning pot filled with boiling water to loosen the feathers. He was only eleven years old. The other kids sat around for days plucking, the feathers sticking to their sweaty legs and arms in the Michigan heat. In one day, they killed and gutted twenty chickens. They would take a three-day break, and then fell another twenty more days later. Within two weeks, they killed one hundred and twenty chickens.

When you've got that many birds in the freezer, you make a lot of chicken. Roasted, braised, sautéed, ground up for spaghetti in place of hamburger—Mom did it all. But one thing she always did was avoid waste. "Oh, no, not after all that work. And besides, I could remember when that chicken was still walking around. I would feel too guilty," she said.

"When you're starting with a whole chicken, it helps to remember something important—that this was a live animal. For a lot of people, knowing that makes it harder to throw parts of it away." The group nodded somberly. That was a buzz kill, I thought.

Discussion over, we got to work. Lisa pulled a huge plastic bin heaped with chickens from the walk-in. She set one in front of each student.

"First, we'll break them down," I said, glancing at the clock. "Do this once or twice and it gets easier." I could sense the resistance. "Go ahead, touch it. Don't be afraid."

The volunteers stood in a semicircle around the worktable, apprehensively eyeing the whole chickens resting on their cutting boards. Sweet Donna pulled back and curled her hands against her chest. Dri tentatively poked hers with an index finger. Even Cheryl's eight-month-old, Liam, stared at the chicken suspiciously from the safety of his Björn carrier. "C'mon, you're not going to get salmonella from touching it. If you're going to cut up a chicken, you're going to have to put your hands on it."

Sabra went first, caressing the pale skin of the breast with neon-green fingernails that matched her eye shadow du jour. "It kind of reminds me of Thanksgiving, you know, when you've got the whole turkey," she said. "But instead, it's a chicken. Like a little turkey. Kind of sweet, really. I've never felt a whole, raw chicken before."

It's not surprising that none of them had ever handled a whole chicken. When Julia Child debuted in the early 1960s, shoppers purchased more than half of all retail chickens whole. Now it's around 10 percent, and that's with an uptick in sales in the midst of a recession. As the students stared at their chickens without touching them and the clock ticked down, I worried that perhaps the night's agenda was a little too ambitious.

I started by holding up one of the legs and pulling it away from the body. Then I turned it upside down, and the leg splayed away. Using my knife, I cut around the "oyster," the soft, tender round of meat tucked at the top of the thigh joined at the back. As I cleaved the leg from the body, I explained that the French think the oyster is the best part of the chicken. "They even have a phrase for this, *le sot-l'y-laisse,* which means 'only a fool leaves it behind.'" Then I slid the tip of the knife along the breast bone and carefully sliced against the rib cage until the breast fell free. I felt for the shoulder joint that pins the wing to the bird and located the soft spot to push the knife through.

On the other side, I put my blade atop the sternum and leaned with my weight on top to crack it open, leaving the bone attached to the breast meat. With pressure on my knife, I cut through the rib bones on the side of the bird around the breast until it detached. The wing came off the same way, and thunked solidly onto the cutting board.

Now it was their turn. Brow furrowed, knife in hand, each volunteer gamely attempted to cut up her chicken. Donna held the wings ever so daintily, trying to minimize her contact. To my left, Gen cut the leg right off, perfectly. "I did it! Look!"

Elsewhere around the table there were varying levels of success. Maggie, Lisa, and I circled the table offering advice. Terri, the one most resistant to the ways of a knife, started to saw with vigor into the backbone. Trish tried to hack through the leg bone, missing the joint completely.

"Okay, wait. If you find a bone, stop. Take a deep breath. Pull your knife back. You shouldn't get that much resistance if you're doing it right."

It's hard to teach what's become second nature. How do you articulate the feeling of knowing you've hit the joint at the right angle, so it comes off easily? Then I had a morbid idea.

"Touch your knuckle," I commanded. Everyone touched their first knuckle with their other hand. "Now feel down at the leg joint on your chicken. Can you find a similar knuckle? Feel around for it."

Terri poked around the leg joint until she found it. "Now take your knife and cut through it." She hit the joint and it fell away easily. I observed as Donna followed the curve of the leg and in one quick motion separated it. Without realizing it, she let out a quick squeal of delight and threw her hands overhead in a cheer. "I did it!" Then she looked around and pulled her arms back down, embarrassed.

Legs separated, we shifted to the breast area. The sound of cracking filled the room as the volunteers cut through the bones. Lisa brought over a big bowl for each cut of meat and a plastic container for the mound of remnant bones.

Knives down, Maggie whisked the cutting boards to the dish area and the students rotated through the hand-washing station, merrily belting out various renditions of "Happy Birthday." I eyed the clock; half an hour behind already and we hadn't even started cooking. The goal for the night was to demonstrate roasting, baking, sautéing, grilling, and braising.

"First, we'll roast a whole chicken and a few individual pieces. You'll want some kind of fat, maybe butter, olive oil, or sesame oil, plus some seasonings. A little bit of acid is nice, too, maybe some lemon, lime, vinegar, or white wine."

To demonstrate, I took the organic chicken and set it on my own cutting board. Starting with the breast area, I carefully stretched my fingers between the skin and the meat to loosen the membrane between them. In the cavity created, I rubbed in a mix of chopped garlic, fresh herbs, and olive oil, then topped the skin with salt, freshly ground black pepper, and a bit of cayenne pepper and rubbed it in. To finish, I wedged pieces of lemon into the center cavity along with two cloves of garlic.

"Forget the idea that you need a lot of complicated cooking equipment," I said. "All you need is an ovenproof pan with sides at least one inch high that is not too much bigger than the chicken. You can even use a skillet, as long as it can go in the oven." A roasting rack can make life easier, but it's not necessary. In this case, we used a simple rectangular pan from the catering supplies. I scattered a few hunks of carrots, celery, and onions on the bottom and then perched the chicken on top. "The vegetables should elevate the chicken a bit, allowing fat to drain off. Plus, they keep it from sticking."

Dri raised her hand. "Okay, so it seems like Julia Child was always trussing a chicken. It was all truss, truss, truss."

Everyone laughed. "You know, at Le Cordon Bleu, we learned a complicated way to truss that stitched the whole thing up like a tight little football. But you don't need to do anything, really. I like to at least tie the feet together to help it keep its shape, but it's not mandatory."

There's heated debate among chefs around the "best" roasting technique. I keep it simple. "Put it in at high heat, about 425 degrees. When it occurs to me, I turn it over after forty minutes to brown the other side, but if you're not so keen on getting tongs out to turn over a hot chicken, by all means leave it alone. Lisa doesn't turn hers, do you?" Lisa shook her head. "See? Some cookbooks advise roasting at 350 degrees, others at 400 degrees. This isn't science, it's more of an art. After an hour, check it with an instant-read thermometer to see if it registers close to 175 degrees, or if the juice that runs off when you pick it up looks clear. Pink? Put it back. Clear? Take it out. Let it rest for a few minutes, lightly covered with foil."

Meat will continue to cook for several minutes after leaving the oven. It's called "carryover cooking." Sitting also allows the juices to reabsorb into the meat.

"What if you undercook poultry?" Shannon asked, bringing up

something we had talked about in her kitchen. "I am always worried about it, so I just cook it and cook it and then cook it some more. I think that's why mine always turns out so badly. I mean, you're supposed to cook chicken pretty much to death, right?"

"Suggested cooking temperatures tend to be higher than what's really needed to kill off any latent bacteria," I said. "Cooking it past that point isn't going to do anything. It's kind of like trying to get more pregnant. If you're really worried about undercooking chicken, just spend a few dollars and get a meat thermometer. It will take out the guesswork."

A blast of hot air hit the worktable as I shoved the chicken into the upright oven to roast.

Next, I grabbed a whole chicken breast with the rib bone still attached and set it on my cutting board. "Again, it's what gets put under the skin, just like a whole roast chicken. You need a bit of fat and a bit of flavor." As a demonstration, we used a recipe from Ina Garten of *Barefoot Contesssa* fame that involved smearing a bit of goat cheese under the skin and then sliding in a couple of whole basil leaves. I drizzled the top with olive oil, coarse salt, and pepper. Everyone did the same, and we put all the breasts onto a sheet pan topped with parchment. We put them into the kitchen's other oven at 375°F. "These will stay in for about a half hour."

We moved on. "*Braise* simply means cooking something covered at a low heat with a bit of liquid." Lisa and I started with the big bowl of thighs and legs. We had settled on a classic mustard chicken dish, utilizing some of the Dijon from the tasting.

"Dark meat is great for braises because it can take long, slow cooking," I said. The volunteers gathered around the commercial stove as Lisa added oil to a large pot and waited for it to heat. "First, we're going to brown the meat. Getting a nice, dark color makes a big difference. What you want is a hot pan with hot oil," I said as Lisa set up a large pan to demonstrate. "Then add your food and give the pan a shake, just like Lauri demonstrated last week. That's how you keep food from sticking."

Lisa put a thigh into the hot oil with long tongs. As if in protest, the pan crackled with a loud persistent sizzle. I added a few more pieces.

"Do you hear that?" I asked. This was an important lesson. "Don't cook just with your eyes. Teach yourself to cook with your ears. Listen. It's loud, it's sizzling and sounds sort of angry. That's what you want. Most home cooks are afraid of high heat. Don't be. Smell this chicken right now." Lisa waved them closer. "Seriously, get close and take a whiff. What does it smell like?"

Donna, Shannon, Terri, and Sabra leaned close to the pan and wrinkled their noses. In unison, they said, "Hot oil."

"Exactly. When it starts to smell like chicken, then you're getting somewhere." We shifted back over to the worktable, where Maggie had replaced the cutting boards and set out big bowls of onions, carrots, and celery. Lisa stayed at the stove to tend to the chicken as we moved on to chopping the vegetables. Only two weeks after the knife class, the volunteers grabbed onions, sliced them in half, peeled, and chopped as if they had been working a restaurant line for ages. Only Terri struggled. Maggie tried to help her again with holding a knife. Terri nodded and thanked her. When I checked back after a few minutes, she had reverted again to her former hold. Was this willful resistance or a deep need of remedial instruction? I didn't know. It troubled me.

I asked if anyone was practicing at home. "Oh, yeah! Did I tell you that I got my knife sharpened? It's so great. It goes so much faster now," Shannon said.

"I haven't bought baby carrots since that class," Jodi said proudly, without even glancing up from her cutting board. "My husband likes carrots in stir-fry and my son will eat them now, so I am going through about two or three pounds of carrots a week. So instead of paying two dollars a pound, I'm paying sixty cents or something. It saves a lot."

I walked to the end of the table where Donna was chopping. During Donna's home visit, she had said that her husband often mocked her when she used a knife. In their relationship, food seemed like a feast of control issues. I noticed that she'd brought in her own knife today. I casually asked how it was going at home.

"My husband and I made dinner the other night and guess what? I cut up all the vegetables." She looked up and smiled, dimples flaring. "Now that I've been coming here, I can say, Hey, I know what I'm doing. Leave me alone." She chopped silently for a minute. "I told him that I was going to start shopping."

"How did that go?" I ask.

She kept her high-pitched voice low. "We're still discussing it." Her face flushed crimson. Something in Donna brought out my maternal instincts. I wanted to hug her, but I settled for patting her shoulder instead.

As we finished the last of the vegetables, a powerful smell of chicken hit the worktable. The group looked up, as if they could see the scent hovering overhead. "The chicken . . ." Shannon said, thinking out loud.

We gathered around the stove as Lisa pulled out a piece with the tongs. After ten minutes, it had taken on a dark brown hue, the skin a bit shrunken and crinkly.

Cheryl raised her hand. The baby looked up. "So does that seal in the juices, when you brown it like that?"

"A culinary myth," I explained. "Heat actually releases juices inside the meat, not seals them in. You brown the meat to caramelize the exterior of the meat, drawing out sugars and extra flavor in the process."

"Or, in other words, browning equals delicious goodness," Lisa said, and turned to put the thigh back into the pot.

"Exactly," I said. "Braising is always the same. First, you brown. Add some vegetables and enough liquid to cover the meat halfway, cover the pan, and simmer. That's it. Brown, vegetables, liquid, cover, and simmer. Learn this one technique, five words, and you can cook almost anything."

I removed the chicken to a bowl and tossed the onions, celery, and carrot that we'd just chopped into the pot. While they softened over the heat, we returned to the worktable. Each volunteer brushed a browned chicken piece with some Dijon mustard. We put them back into the pan and added some chicken stock, a few herbs, a bit of white wine. I covered the pot and set it inside the oven to simmer.

"The biggest problem with cooking chicken breasts is that while the poultry industry strives for a bigger breast, it hasn't developed them into a uniform shape or thickness. So they tend to be much thicker in the middle and thin on the ends.

"Here's a trick that I do at home." I laid a boneless breast on my cutting board, then sliced it through the center horizontally, resulting in two thinner fillets. I held them up. "Now the chicken breast is half as thick and more uniform, so it'll cook more evenly. Not to mention, it's a more realistic serving size."

"That's a great tip," Shannon said. "Usually the center isn't cooked all the way through while the edges are overcooked and tough."

To give breasts a bit of flavor, I showed them a lesson that I learned years ago from an aging Italian grandmother during a cooking class outside Florence. "She called it a *'bacio di sapore,'* or a kiss of flavor." I combined a bit of olive oil, a squeeze of lemon juice, salt, pepper, and dried thyme in a bowl. I added my two slices of breast meat and mixed them together. "Let this sit for a few minutes. Then it's onto the heat."

We circled around the stove. I grabbed a small sauté pan and added oil. Once it was hot, I slapped the breasts into the pan with a pair of tongs, was greeted by a hearty sizzle, and gave the pan a shake. I turned them after three minutes. After three more minutes, I added a hearty splash of stock, turned down the heat, and covered the pan for a few more minutes. "At a restaurant where I once worked, the chef added some liquid like stock or wine at the end of cooking and I do that all the time now," I said. "It infuses it with both flavor and moisture."

Maggie handed out forks for everyone to take a bite. "This is great," Shannon said, using the edge of her fork to cut off another bite. "I mean, it tastes good, it's not dry. Mine never turn out like this."

Trish had also commented on tough chicken during our visit. "Neither do mine. I wonder if it's because I usually cook them at lower heat and longer," she mused. "Well, a lot longer."

"Now it's your turn," I said. While I'd been cooking, Maggie and Lisa had assembled a collection of oils, vinegars, garlic, herbs, and spices from around the kitchen. From the walk-in, they had gathered jars of pesto, sun-dried tomatoes, gingerroot, lemons, and limes. The selection now sat as a jumble in the center of the worktable. Each person had a small bowl.

"First, you'll slice a breast in half like I did. One part we'll sauté, the other we'll grill," I said. Maggie walked around the table distributing chicken breasts from the chickens we had broken down earlier. "Then make your own kiss of flavor. Think of what chefs call 'flavor profiles.' These sound all chef-y, but they're easy. For instance, what flavors does Asian food have in common?"

Jodi raised her hand. "Sesame oil, soy sauce, maybe rice wine vinegar?"

"Great," I said. "Put those together. What does Italian food taste like?"

Donna ventured a guess. "Olive oil, Italian herbs, maybe pesto?"

And so it went. Caribbean? Jerk seasoning, hot sauce, limes, a bit of coconut oil. Tex-Mex? Corn oil, chili powder, garlic, and cumin with a bit of lime. The group erupted briefly in unmanageable enthusiasm. "This is actually fun!" Jodi said. "I mean, I can do this!"

One key is to evaluate the flavor of each ingredient. "Smell or taste the oil and the vinegar, try a bit of the spice. As you taste each one, think how it will interact with the others you're using."

The volunteers started to pick up various bottles and jars, sniffing and sometimes tasting with one of the dozens of small spoons set in a plastic shoebox on the counter. A couple looked tentative, watching the others for clues. The three of us wandered around the table offering suggestions until each volunteer came up with a flavor kiss in which to briefly bathe her two chicken breast halves. Maggie put small bits of masking tape with their names on dinner plates. As each person finished sautéing one of her breast halves, it went on her plate. Then they moved to the gas grill adjacent to the stove.

"The thing to remember about grilling chicken breasts is to avoid placing them directly over a flame. The meat's too fragile. An easy trick for grilling chicken is to cover it with a metal bowl. It will surround the chicken with heat, making it cook more quickly and keeping it from drying out. Use tongs to put it in place and lift it up so you don't burn yourself."

The grilled chicken went onto their plates. The baked chicken came out of the oven, and everyone claimed their pieces. The roast chicken emerged deeply brown and highly fragrant.

Back at the worktable, clutching knives and forks and giddy with anticipation, everyone took a bite of their chicken.

"This is so good. And it took what? Less than ten minutes?" Shannon said. "I don't know why I never thought of cutting it like that or just putting a bit of oil and seasoning on it first."

Sabra jumped up and down after tasting her sautéed chicken. "Seriously! This is awesome. Taste mine." She offered her plate to Gen. It gave me an idea.

"Hey, everyone shift to the right," I said. "I want you to taste everyone else's."

Like a continuous Chinese fire drill, the students shifted from plate to plate to plate. The consensus: Donna and Sabra had the best-tasting sautéed chicken of the bunch, while Jodi and Trish won the baked chicken round. Cheryl had not wanted to get near the stove with baby Liam in the carrier but had seasoned all of her food and Lisa had cooked it. Her spicy Tex-Mex combo won rave reviews.

Maggie retrieved the mustard braise at nearly ten P.M., as everyone was preparing to leave. The dish had the classic elements of a good braise, deeply flavored and so tender it fell off the bone. We packed up the leftovers and a full meal's worth of braised chicken in takeout containers that Lisa had picked up at a local restaurant supply store.

Sabra could barely contain herself. "This is the best class ever! I've done stuff tonight that I've never done before!"

As she clutched her takeout box, Trish lingered, reluctant to leave until she was the final volunteer in the kitchen while Maggie, Lisa, and I started to clean up. "What is it?" I asked her.

She wiped her eyes. "Tonight I learned things that I really ought to have known. Why didn't I ever just learn it?"

"Julia Child said she didn't learn to cook until she was thirty-two. Until then, she just ate. So you see, it's never too late." I gave her a hug and then handed her a takeout box. "See you next week."

◎ Your Basic Roasted Chicken

Chefs around the world continually debate the best possible way to roast a whole chicken. Don't overcomplicate it. You don't need a fancy roasting pan. Any kind of ovenproof pan, skillet, or sauté pan with sides one inch or higher in which the chicken fits comfortably will work. A rack is nice, but you can just roughly chop up carrots, onions, and potatoes to spread them across the bottom and balance the chicken on top to allow the juices to drain. Include some kind of fat such as oil or butter, plus salt and pepper, and baste it at least once. I prefer to start the bird breast side up and then, using tongs, turn it over for the last twenty minutes of cooking to brown the other side, but that's optional.

BASIC TECHNIQUE FOR A WHOLE CHICKEN

❧ Preheat the oven to 425°F. Mix up some flavorings. Remove the giblets from inside the chicken cavity.

❧ Gently ease your fingers under the chicken's skin to separate it from the bird, creating a cavity across the top of the breast and around the legs. Shove your flavoring under the skin. Smear a bit over the top and generously season the skin with coarse salt and ground pepper.

❧ If you want to, tie the legs together with some string; this will help the bird keep its shape and cook evenly.

❧ The larger the bird, the longer it will take to roast. Depending on your oven and your bird, a standard 3-pound chicken will take about an hour; allow about 10 minutes for each additional half pound. After half an hour, baste it by using a spoon, pastry brush, or bulb-style baster to collect the juices from the pan to moisten the skin.

❧ If desired, turn the chicken over for the last 20 minutes of cooking. Baste again.

❧ See if it's done. The best method is to insert an instant-read thermometer into the thigh meat and again into the breast, avoiding the bones. It should read close to 180°F, but double-check by pulling the thigh away. If the juices that ooze out are clear, it's done. If they are pink, baste the chicken again and put it back in the oven for another 10 minutes. Repeat as needed.

❧ Let your chicken rest for about a few minutes before serving.

~~~~~~

TEN WAYS TO FLAVOR ROAST CHICKEN

❧ Add coarse salt and pepper to each combination, and be generous with the oil, butter, or other type of fat; the excess will run off and it will help to keep the meat moist. Mix each into a paste before applying it to the bird. You can't go wrong shoving some fresh herbs, some lemon, a wedge of onion, or a couple of cloves of garlic inside the bird's cavity, along with some salt and pepper.

Lemon-Herb Butter
$\frac{1}{4}$ cup fresh lemon juice; put the leftover lemon inside the cavity
3 tablespoons butter, softened
Handful of chopped fresh tarragon, thyme, or rosemary

Italian Herb Oil
3 tablespoons olive oil
2 teaspoons grated Parmesan cheese
2 garlic cloves, chopped
2 tablespoons finely chopped fresh herbs, such as thyme, oregano, parsley, or basil (or about 2 to 3 teaspoons dried herbs)

French Dijon
3 tablespoons butter, softened, or olive oil
1 tablespoon red wine vinegar
3 tablespoons Dijon mustard
$\frac{1}{2}$ teaspoon red chili flakes
1 teaspoon dried thyme

Soy Ginger Oil
2 tablespoons peanut or vegetable oil
1 tablespoon sesame oil
2 teaspoons soy sauce
1 tablespoon rice wine vinegar
1 teaspoon freshly grated ginger

Pesto-rama
$\frac{1}{4}$ cup any kind of pesto (basil, sun-dried tomato, etc.)

Goat Cheese with Prosciutto and Herbs
1 ounce finely minced prosciutto or pancetta or crumbled cooked bacon
2 tablespoons goat cheese
3 tablespoons olive oil
Handful of chopped basil or 1 teaspoon dried oregano

Thai-Style

2 tablespoons coconut oil

1 teaspoon sesame oil

1 tablespoon finely crushed peanuts

3 tablespoons fresh lime juice

$2\frac{1}{2}$ teaspoons Thai curry paste

2 tablespoons finely chopped fresh basil or cilantro

Greekesque

$\frac{1}{4}$ cup plain yogurt

4 garlic cloves, minced

1 tablespoon chopped dill

2 teaspoons fresh lemon juice

China Spice

3 tablespoons sesame oil

1 tablespoon orange juice

1 tablespoon Chinese 5-spice powder

4 green onions, minced

3 garlic cloves, minced

1 teaspoon soy sauce

Tex-Mex

3 tablespoons vegetable oil or butter

$\frac{1}{4}$ cup lime juice

1 teaspoon chili powder

2 garlic cloves, minced

1 teaspoon dried oregano

$\frac{1}{2}$ teaspoon ground cumin

Pinch or 2 of cayenne or a few drops of hot sauce

FOR INDIVIDUAL CHICKEN PIECES

❧ You can add any of these flavorings to individual pieces to roast separately. Again, press the flavorings under the skin. Put the pieces on a baking sheet atop aluminum foil or parchment or in an oven-proof baking dish in an oven preheated to 375°F. Thighs and legs will take about 45 minutes, bone-in breasts about 30 minutes, and boneless breasts about 15 minutes, depending on the thickness and your oven. Aim for a final internal temperature of around 165°F. If roasting mixed pieces, remove them as they're done and keep them warm by covering them with foil.

ᑩᑫᑫ

Cruise Control

We Interrupt This Project for a
Cruise to the Mediterranean

ᑫ The morning after the chicken class, I received a frantic call. "Can you be in Rome next Tuesday?" a woman's voice said. "A chef canceled. Ten-day cruise on the Mediterranean. It would *really* help me out."

Such things never happened in my corporate life. Months earlier, Holland America had invited me to work for a week on one of its ships as a "guest chef." When Mike and I joined the cruise on the *MV Amsterdam* for its final leg from Honolulu to San Diego, we met Erika, the manager of "culinary entertainment" for the cruise line. Mike and I liked her instantly and bonded with her over the short trip. Back on land in Seattle, we kept in touch. Now she was in need of a replacement guest chef for one of the line's culinary-themed cruises—stat. "I'm racking my brain thinking about who could go on such short notice," she said. "We'll pay your airfare." She called not realizing the trip would fall during our fifth wedding anniversary and Mike's forty-fifth birthday. We'd have to reschedule two weeks of classes, and I worried about losing momentum with the project, but then I looked at the itinerary: Rome, Monte Carlo, Barcelona, Palma de Mallorca, Tunis, Palermo, and Naples, with three days at sea during which I was expected to entertain cruisers with cooking demonstrations and hands-on classes.

I immediately called Mike. "I know you've been planning something for our anniversary, and this is so crazy last-minute. But what do you think?"

"I don't think I can top that," he said. "Let's do it."

Within four hours he'd sorted flights and scored a last-minute deal on a hotel room in Rome. Just three days later, swarms of buzzing Vespas escorted our death-defying taxi ride from the airport into the city center. We abruptly turned off a main road to creep along a narrow, ancient street to the Hotel de Ville nestled at the top of the Spanish Steps.

It felt decadent jetting into a foreign city with no itinerary on short notice. On our first night, we walked arm in arm to dinner at the restaurant Tulio. Mike ordered us each a glass of champagne to start. We eavesdropped on conversations around us and flirted across the table. I ordered the day's special, handmade fettuccine pasta dosed heavily with eggs. Mike splurged on a bottle of earthy Italian wine. As the immaculate waiter shaved slices of black truffle onto my plate of hand-cut noodles, I jumped up and down in my seat, giddy with anticipation.

Mike took my hand across the table and twisted his fingers in mine. "I love that you can get this worked up over pasta," he said, and tenderly kissed the back of my hand. The scene was impossibly perfect: a romantic candlelit restaurant in Italy, Mike in a smart jacket, my complete disregard for carbohydrates.

"You want to hear something?" I whispered. He leaned in across the table. "I would marry you all over again just for this one moment with you."

The waiter cleared his throat. We had failed to notice his return. He stood over us with the bottle of red. We politely waited for him to pour while my heart pounded. I picked up my fork to start on my pasta. I stole a quick look up, assuming Mike would be tending to his plate of osso bucco. Instead, he was looking at me. Without a word, he picked up his glass of wine in a toast.

"To five more years," I offered.

"No, wait." He stopped me as I held my glass up in midtoast. "I believe we agreed to forever." We clinked glasses.

The next morning, he lazily threw an arm around me as we started the slow ascent of waking from our jet lag. He nuzzled his chin against my hair. "You still smell like truffles," he murmured softly.

Being a guest chef on a cruise ship is not quite work, but it's not exactly a vacation. To earn my passage, I had to perform two live cooking demonstrations before an audience, and then conduct two hands-on classes for a small group of guests. The demonstrations took place in the ship's Culinary Arts Center, a no-expense-spared TV studio–style demonstration kitchen set atop a stage in front of about three hundred plush upholstered audience seats. Huge plasma screens showed the action live to the audience, while the audio-visual crew pumped the "show" into every single stateroom on the boat. So it was more like planning two forty-five-minute live cooking shows with an unfamiliar kitchen crew plus cooking a tasting for hundreds of audience members. Piece of cake.

On the *MV Noordam,* guest chef activities were coordinated by party planner Linda. Fun spirited and high energy, she spoke in a throaty northern England accent and was a dead ringer for Patsy from *Absolutely Fabulous,* although the similarity ended there since she's not a shallow drunk. Guest chef status provides access to parts of the ship most cruisers never see. Behind the gilded mirrors and velvet wallpaper exists a maze of kitchens and prep areas that span five decks. Linda led me to Chef Don, the executive chef in charge of the kitchens. He noticed my bare head and fished a paper chef's toque out of a drawer. I'd never worn a tall toque before. It didn't quite fit and kept falling off as I walked through the sea of Indonesian and Central American kitchen workers, all 337 of them male. Women kitchen workers, much less chefs, are a rarity. The sea of workers parted as they saw me. They smiled sweetly and nodded furiously. "Oh, *hello,* Lady Chef."

Chef Don and I zigzagged through the vast kitchens stacked on multiple floors. The scale of the operation overwhelmed. The *MV Noordam* served eleven thousand meals a day from five separate restaurants, plus busy stateroom room service and special events. One area equipped with a floor mixer the size of an impressive Jet Ski turned out nothing but the morning pastries and evening desserts. Rows of tables stood at the ready in one prep room awaiting the hundreds of plates the crew assembled each day. Don took me through two baking kitchens and an entire floor dedicated to *garde manger* that managed cold foods such as salads and refrigerated desserts. A full-time butcher worked in a walk-in cooler the size of my first apartment tucked deep belowdecks. During meals, the kitchen buzzed at a frantic yet practiced pace. At ten A.M., it might be quiet in the fine dining kitchens, but the crew of the Lido Deck buffet—the hub of breakfast onboard—was just clocking out. "At every hour of the day, there's someone working somewhere," Chef Don said. "We never really close, we just slow down production."

On our tour, Chef Don asked, "You want to see something?" We took an elevator down to the cargo hold in the belly of the ship. In front of us, pallets the size of double-wide trailers held tons of produce. "We have a crew who spend their days getting the food off the pallets and moving it to the right parts of the kitchens," he said. "It goes faster than you can imagine."

Chef Don explained that the complexities of the supply and thin profit margins of the operation required a delicate balancing act. "Managing our food supply is one of the most critical things that we do. We can't go through it too quickly or we will run out before our next port. But we can't afford to let it go bad or waste too much food either," he explained. "We try hard to figure out how to maximize everything yet never run out." My thoughts went to the volunteers and to my own kitchen, and to the larger issue of wasted food. Just how many wilted vegetables in our crisper awaited my return?

In the elevator heading back up to the kitchen, Chef Don glanced again at my demonstration list. "Paella? I can't wait. You have much experience with it?"

As it happens, for a girl from Michigan, paella has odd prominence in my life. It was the subject of the first food story I ever published back in the early 1990s. Days after we got engaged in Spain, Mike and I happened upon a paella-making competition in the heart of Valencia, home of the classic rice and seafood dish. Knowing that, our chef friend Ted built a custom-made box and shipped his three-foot-wide paella pan across the country from Seattle to Florida for our rehearsal dinner on Anna Maria Island. If that's not friendship, I don't know what qualifies. The pan was so massive that Ted rented a portable commercial four-burner stove to ensure adequate heat. Our seventy-five guests hovered, clutching cocktails in the sweltering Florida night, as he browned chicken, cooked sausage, sautéed onions, and added the rice and stock, stirring with a spoon the size of an oar. To finish, he tossed in a plethora of Gulf-fresh seafood from Cortez, a historic fishing village nearby. As a tradition, we've made paella every year to commemorate our wedding; it's as much a ritual in our lives as turkey at Thanksgiving. By fate or sheer coincidence, my last demonstration was scheduled for the Fourth of July, our fifth anniversary— right after we'd visit two ports in Spain. We both agreed that I had no choice but to make paella, and to pick up a pan along the way.

However, we arrived in Barcelona on Sunday and most of the stores were closed. Instead, we hung out at La Sagrada Familia, the famous unfinished church designed by artist Antoni Gaudi. Before that trip, I'd seen the church only from a distance; the spires always remind me of tapered candles left out too long in the sun. It's impressive on many levels. But what I admire most is that Gaudi started a church that he knew he would never live to see finished, perhaps the ultimate definition of faith.

The next day, the ship docked at the Spanish island of Palma de Mallorca. We stepped up our hunt for a pan. Mike confirmed that standard paella pans are crafted from carbon steel and thus would not work on the induction* burners in the ship's Culinary Arts Center. The best way to tell if a pan will work on an induction burner is to see whether a magnet will stick to it. Mike sent me on my way and headed into town on his hunt armed with a tourist magnet from the Sagrada Familia. I'd booked a day-long excursion to watch a Spanish chef make paella over a blazing fire in the countryside. A bus delivered me and two dozen cruisers to a restaurant set up in a stone farmhouse.

Under a small wooden pavilion, the chef's crew commenced with threading three whole baby pigs onto monstrous wrought-iron poles. The poles hooked into a medieval-style spit device over a row of white-hot fires. The distraught look on some of the cruisers' faces signaled that many had likely never seen a whole pig, much less witnessed an iron rod jammed up one's backside. Only a cruise passenger skewered and put onto the spit could have yielded more horrified stares.

As the crew tended to the pigs, the chef worked the paella. He started with hacked-up pork bones on a flat, shallow pan nestled above another bracing fire in the 102-degree heat. Chef tossed out points in Spanish to his young Catalan assistant, who caught and translated them for the group. "Chef says that he likes to start with bones because the marrow will caramelize and add richness to the dish," she said. The pork crackled and snapped as the pool of fat slowly widened and the remaining meat on the bones darkened with its own sugar.

Chef stooped over the heat to place two dozen white chicken thighs into the pan. Each sputtered as it hit the oil. Then he tossed in bowls of chopped onions, tomatoes, peppers, and rice, one by one. Finally, he poured in a bucket of dark chicken and fish stock. The watching crowd sat mesmerized, most slightly drunk from drinking

---

*Induction works through magnetic transference; one molecule excites another through direct physical contact. When I was asked this question the first time during a demonstration, I thrust the microphone at Mike. He was forced to define it on the spot. It sounded quite sensual.

sparkling wine in high heat at midday. Chef handed a long paddle to a clean-shaven midwestern guy in a golf shirt. He eagerly took it. Everyone took a turn stirring, including an eighty-four-year-old man in Sansabelt trousers who teetered over his walker as he pushed the oar around in the rice.

"Dad, are you okay?" his concerned daughter asked, approaching. "It's pretty hot over these coals. Maybe you should sit down."

He waved the paddle at her, nearly falling off his walker. "Back off! I'm having a good time," he said gruffly. "That chef isn't much younger than me, you know. This is the first time I've cooked any-thing in years and I'm liking it." She slunk away.

The area took on a meaty smell that mingled with the aroma of charred onions and peppers, joined later by the sweet scent of mas-sive, lobsterlike langoustines, the final addition by the chef near the end of cooking. When finished, the pan was substantial enough with the rice and other ingredients that it required four strapping Span-iards to haul it away. Armed with fireman-style gloves, they squatted in unison and with a collective grunt hauled the pan up and walked it inside the dining room like pallbearers.

As the food arrived, I noticed that even women who had been aghast at the sight of the skewered pigs now happily gnawed on the pieces of roughly cut pork. The room went silent as everyone con-centrated on lunch. The chef's assistant emerged from the kitchen with one last tip. "Try a bite of paella and then a bite of the raw green pepper slices you'll find on the table. It enhances the flavor." He was right. It drew out the earthy, soft, and sweet flavor of the saffron rice and the light sea-scented stock.

The bus dropped us back in Palma, a town filled with beautiful Spanish architecture and populated by women dressed in beach attire even in the middle of downtown. Mike alerted me to meet him in the kitchen section of the department store El Cortes Inglés. He'd located two paella pans that he thought would work on the ship's burners. After some debate, we purchased both. We then boarded a bus whose destination was "Airport/Harbor."

Mike asked, "Are you going to the harbor?"

"Yes," the driver replied.

After a few stops, we realized that we were heading out of town to the airport. We nervously looked at our watches.

At the airport, Mike talked to the driver again. "Are you going to the port next?"

"Yes," the driver said.

"With the ships?"

"Yes."

"Do you go to the moon?"

"Yes," the driver answered, nodding.

Mike waved me off the bus. "Let's take a taxi back to the ship."

The night before, we'd barely made it onto the ship in Barcelona before the crew pulled up the gangway. Once again, we ran through the port, this time each of us clutching a paella pan.

The next day, I told the story of our chef friend Ted and our wedding. "Oh, it's not fair that you have to work on your anniversary," a woman from Asheville, North Carolina, said.

"Are you kidding? If I was at home, this is exactly what I'd be doing, making paella."

When we recounted the trip back home, we both measured the days in meals and countries: lunch in Monte Carlo overlooking a white sand beach populated with beautiful topless French women (crisp salad Niçoise thick with anchovies, roasted whole fish with fennel and tomatoes); in Barcelona, a late bite just off Las Ramblas (spit-roasted rabbit, broiled mussels with garlic and parsley sauce); the hike to a hillside cliff for hot, sweet tea above Tunis (sugary date-heavy Tunisian pastries); a bite in an ancient square in Palermo, Italy, after being overcharged by a crafty seventeen-year-old Sicilian cart-and-buggy driver (handcrafted pizza with fresh tomatoes, grilled squid with sweet fennel sausage); and, finally, the best *pasta vongole* (pasta with clams) of my life high above the harbor on the island of Capri.

◈ Paella Valenciana

Paella sounds complicated, but it's just a casserole that originated as a poor fisherman's supper designed to use up scraps left in the nets. Make it once, and then adapt the technique to make a one-pot dish that's simple or extravagant based on what you've got on hand. Just keep intact the base aromatics known as the sofrito: *onions, garlic, and tomatoes. I've made paella with and without meat, with green beans, asparagus, fresh corn, rabbit, garbanzo beans, scallops, andouille sausage, littleneck clams, and even Dungeness crab.*

Paella takes its name from the traditional pan, a wide, flat-bottomed carbon-steel double-handled skillet with flared sides. This recipe is designed for paella pans from twelve to fifteen inches wide. If you don't have one, a twelve-inch or larger shallow skillet or similar-sized pan will work. In Spain, paella is often cooked over an open fire, but it can be cooked on a stovetop and finished in a 450°F oven or over a large, round barbecue. Lovely with a rioja, either red or white.

SERVES 6 TO 8

Shrimp-Flavored Stock

1 pound medium shrimp, deveined, shells reserved
1 quart chicken stock

Seasoned Chicken

6 chicken thighs and/or legs
Coarse salt and freshly ground black pepper
1 teaspoon dried thyme
Couple of pinches of cayenne

Basics

2 tablespoons olive oil
8 ounces chorizo, cut into bite-sized pieces

4 garlic cloves, minced
1 large yellow onion, diced
1 green pepper, diced
2 large tomatoes, seeded and chopped
2 bay leaves
1½ cups uncooked Bomba, Arborio, or other short-grain rice
Pinch of saffron threads (about ¼ teaspoon crushed)

To Finish

One 14-ounce can artichokes
1 cup frozen peas, thawed
2 ounces diced pimento
About 1 pound mussels, bearded and scrubbed
2 or 3 lemons, cut into wedges
Strips of green pepper

❧ Combine the shrimp shells and chicken stock in a pan, and simmer until needed.

❧ Season the chicken pieces with generous doses of coarse salt and pepper, the thyme, and the cayenne.

❧ Heat the pan over medium-high heat or a hot grill. Add the oil and sauté the chorizo until it is partially cooked, about 5 minutes. Add the chicken to the pan and brown it well, turning occasionally, for about 15 minutes. Remove the chorizo and chicken and set aside. Add the garlic, onion, and green pepper to the pan and cook until the vegetables are softened and starting to brown. Add the tomatoes and bay leaves and cook another 3 minutes. Meanwhile, strain the shrimp shells from the stock.

❧ Add the rice to the vegetables and cook, stirring, for a couple of minutes, until gently toasted. Add the strained stock, saffron, several cranks of black pepper, and 3 pinches of salt. Stir as the mixture comes back to a boil.

❧ Return the chicken and chorizo to the pan. Cover loosely with aluminum foil and keep at a bubbling simmer for about 25 minutes, until the rice is tender. If excess liquid remains, remove the foil and cook until it is absorbed. Scatter the artichokes, peas, and pimentos on top of the rice, then press the shrimp and mussels into the hot rice. Cover again until the seafood cooks through, about 8 to 10 minutes. Remove the pan from the heat and let it stand, covered, for a few minutes before serving. Discard any mussels that are not open after cooking. Remove the bay leaves before serving. Serve with the lemon wedges and strips of raw green pepper.

PART II

❦❧

A Bit About Meats, Bread, Pasta, Salads, and Vinaigrettes

"The smell of good bread baking, like the sound of lightly flowing water, is indescribable in its evocation of innocence and delight."

—M. F. K. Fisher

"How can a nation be great if its bread tastes like Kleenex?"

—Julia Child

Trish makes bread

CHAPTER 7

❧❧

The Bread Also Rises

❧ LESSON HIGHLIGHTS:
   No-Knead Artisan Bread, Simple Pasta Sauces

On the farm, my parents made bread twice a week. In one of my
earliest memories I perched atop a wooden chair in the hot farmhouse kitchen on a snowy winter's day. I drew hearts on the steamy
window, my small fingers cold against the pane of glass as my father
shaped and patted loaves of dough into four pans.

Dad moved a chair over to the table. "Time for sugar!" he said. I
leaped up on the chair and pressed my tiny right hand on top of each
petal-soft loaf and he drew an outline of my hand with a butter knife.
My tiny handprint, Dad said, replaced any need for sweeteners. I
helped him fold laundry warm from the dryer while the yeasty sour
fragrance grew fierce as the bread finished baking. Dad turned the
pans upside down and shook the still-warm loaves from them with
a thump. He smeared half a stick of butter across the top of each one,
the butter creeping into my handprint, distorted by the heat, like a
melting clock from a Salvador Dalí painting.

By lunchtime at school, such pleasant memories faded fast. Taking sandwiches with thick slabs of homemade bread to school made
kids of my era look both poor *and* distinctly uncool. By first grade,
I longed so desperately for soft white store-bought bread that I saved
up for a month to buy a loaf with my allowance, assuming it would
taste like candy. Compared to our bread, it had the flavor of what Julia
Child once described as Kleenex. The bread did offer remarkable

127

sculpting qualities when softened with water, so it wasn't a total loss. I molded tiny statues rather than eat it.

When I was in first grade we moved from the farm into the town of Davison, a suburb of Flint, Michigan. An early sign of our improved social standing: store-bought bread. When Mom discovered a series of barely touched PB and J's in my Scooby-Doo lunchbox, she assumed I'd developed a sudden dislike of the entire concept of sandwiches. It wasn't that; I missed my parents' homemade bread. But they seemed too busy to make it anymore, and I didn't want to hurt her feelings. She abruptly started to shove quarters in my hand every morning for hot lunches. I would sit with my hard plastic tray eating soggy Tater Tots and stare at the kids in the bagged-lunch ghetto unwrapping their thickly sliced sandwiches. As they sometimes had to risk dislocating their jaws to open their mouths wide enough to take a bite, I turned away, distressed by the depth of my envy.

Despite my inherent love for homemade bread, I never mastered it. Single life in a series of tiny kitchens, with a deficit in counter space, and dodgy ovens did not inspire many forays into bread making. The curriculum at Le Cordon Bleu merely glanced at the subject. In France, *boulangerie* equates to both a high art and a culinary science that warrants its own focused study, like butchery or patisserie. My personal reference to homemade bread made the whole thing feel so intimidating—until I came across no-knead artisan bread.

Most people became aware of the no-knead bread phenomenon thanks to Jim Lahey of the Sullivan St Bakery in New York when food writer Mark Bittman documented his method in a 2006 story for *The New York Times*. As Bittman noted, breakthroughs are rare in something as fundamental as bread making, so developing a strategy to transform freshly made bread into almost a convenience food counted as a groundbreaking achievement. I tried Lahey's version, and later versions from various books on the subject. The result: a crusty, artisan-style loaf for about sixty cents. Mike loved the stuff, and he adopted the role of primary baker for our small household.

For the next class, we'd focus on pasta (since I'd just been in Italy) and no-knead bread. "You sure? It's going to be crazy hot in there with burners and that oven going full blast," Lisa said over the phone. I could hear her starting to sweat at the thought. "Also, something's up with Maggie. I don't know if she's going to be able to help out for a while."

During my absence abroad, the ongoing cupcake battle consumed Maggie's schedule. "You won't even believe what I'm going through," she said on the phone, pained. The company was on the brink of opening its third store in two weeks and had scheduled three events back to back that involved handing out thousands of samples. I had heard that a major film being shot in Seattle might feature cupcakes. Maggie said nothing, but if this was true, I imagined pursuit of cupcake placement in a film held the possibility of bloody intrigues worthy of film noir. "I've got to go back to the samples now," she said with a weary voice. I felt bad for Maggie. The idea of a business consultant having to help frost thousands of mini-cupcakes struck me as one of Dante's circles of Hell.

I hung up and wandered downstairs to find Jeff. In an odd confluence of events, my former upstairs neighbor in London arrived in Seattle ready to relocate, but in the brutal job market of 2008 had yet to find work. Mike and I live in a 1902 Dutch Colonial that had been rebuilt into a duplex thirty years ago by an architect and his son. We live upstairs and rent out the larger main level. Mike was in the middle of an extensive remodel of the kitchen in the downstairs unit. Jeff arrived as our renters moved out, so Mike set him up in the place for free but warned him that he would be without a kitchen for at least a couple months. That didn't bother Jeff.

"Sure, I'll help out with your project. You know, you should teach risotto. I made it in a hotpot in the bathroom last night," he told me as he ironed his trousers. "It came out pretty well." He seemed genuinely pleased with his ingenuity. "I think you should write a whole book about cooking in the bathroom with a hotpot. I bet *that's* never been done before. Oh, hey, I've got pinot gris chilling in a bucket in the bathtub. Want some?"

By lunchtime on the day of the bread-making class, the air refused to budge outside. It was even hotter inside the kitchen; the catering crew had the ovens and commercial stove at full blast for most of the day. When we arrived, the kitchen's thermometer registered 101°F. After we set up most of the gear, we needed a break. Mike and I headed for the walk-in cooler. Jeff followed with a cold bottle of sauvignon blanc and three glasses. We perched on produce boxes and sipped wine to cool down. "This is really nice," Jeff said, sitting with his legs crossed atop a crate of cabbage. "Maybe we can do the whole class in here."

The door flew open. "What, there's a party in the walk-in, and nobody told me?" exclaimed Lisa, who looked wilted from a hot, horrible commute. We got her a glass before the four of us returned to the hot vat of a kitchen.

Shannon and Cheryl were the first to arrive, the latter without baby Liam. "I'm liberated!" she said. "I'm ready to get near the big stove, and of course it's too hot outside to want cook anything."

Without a word, the early arrivals put on their aprons, grabbed a diaper, and headed to the hand-washing area. Then they found a spot at the table to start chopping. As each person arrived she joined in, like a bystander jumping into a moving parade. "Hey, are there any more vegetables?" Terri asked. After her initial struggles, she seemed to finally get the hang of it and made quick work of a few zucchini. "We've run out of things to chop."

I scoured the table. "Nope, that's it. Today we're going to make pasta and sauces as promised, and we're also going to make bread." Half fanned themselves limply with copies of the recipes we'd handed out at the start of class. As I said the word *bread*, most instinctively looked at the commercial ovens. I could almost hear what they were thinking. *Bread? In this heat? You've got to be kidding.*

Traditional bread has just four ingredients: flour, salt, yeast, water. I started the class by revealing a plastic sleeve from a loaf of supermarket bread. I read the ingredients out loud:

Refined white flour, water, high fructose corn syrup,* contains 2% or less of: wheat gluten, soybean oil, salt, molasses, yeast, mono- and diglycerides, exthoxylated mono- and diglycerides, dough conditioners (sodium stearoyl lactylate, calcium iodate, calcium dioxide), datem, calcium sulfate, vinegar, yeast nutrient (ammonium sulfate), extracts of malted barley and corn, dicalcium phosphate, diammonium phosphate,† calcium propionate (to retain freshness)

I stumbled through the polysyllabic words. I was familiar with high-fructose corn syrup (HFCS), the heavily processed sweetener made from starch-rich corn. HFCS is common in baked goods, as it helps stave off spoilage and keep breads soft. Recent studies have linked high intake of HFCS to childhood obesity and diabetes. But in research that I conducted for the class, I was surprised to learn that soybean oil is so ubiquitous, a leading researcher has stated that some nutritionists believe it makes up as much as 20 percent of all calories consumed in the United States. Diglycerides are simply fancy names for fatty, often hydrogenated oils or trans fats.

By the end of it, the sweaty crew stood with their mouths agape. "Some bread is healthier than this one. Read labels. Consumers have a voice in a free market. If people buy bread without a lot of additives, you'll see more bread without them. Or you can make your own. You can control what's in it, and it's way cheaper."

Jeff settled a big plastic container with flour on the worktable. "Okay, first we're going to talk about the right way to measure flour. Don't dig a measuring cup into it. Instead, use one measuring cup to fill another." I spooned flour into a stainless steel cup measure. "When full, use a knife to scrape it level across the top."

---

*Presumably due to bad press, in 2010 the HFCS lobby asked the Food and Drug Administration for permission to shift its name to corn sugar.

†Diammonium phosphate, also known as DAP, used as a yeast nutrient here, is also used as a fertilizer, to enhance the flavor of nicotine in cigarettes, and is widely added to fire-fighting agents.

Trish raised her hand. "So I've always heard that, but why do you do it?"

Jeff fetched a kitchen scale from a side table. I set a metal bowl on top and zeroed out the scale. I measured a cup of flour as I'd just demonstrated and plopped it into the bowl. "Okay, 150 grams." I poured it back into the flour bin, set the bowl atop the scale, and zeroed the scale again. This time, I dug the scoop directly into the flour and scraped the top. "This is 190 grams. If you add 40 grams on each cup, you'll completely ruin a baking recipe. In baking, weight is more precise than volume. That's why most professional recipes are outlined in weight, not cups."

Dri slapped the table. "I think this explains most of my baking failures."

Yeast went in next. "Any yeast will do. You can buy fresh yeast in the supermarket, like this," I said, holding up a cube of fresh yeast. "Or you can use instant yeast in the packets or jars. If you think you'll make a lot of bread, buy a block of yeast at a warehouse store. Then invite a couple of your friends over, show them how to make this bread, and divvy up the yeast with them."

"Yeast is a living thing, be nice to it," I continued. I reached for a pitcher of warm tap water on the table and measured out a cup and then stuck an instant-read thermometer into the water. It registered 100°F. I handed it to Cheryl. "Feel this and pass it around. It should feel lukewarm. If it's too cold or too hot, you'll kill the yeast. Go for around body temperature." The little metal cup went around the table as each person dutifully stuck a finger into the water. As it got to Donna, she shook her head.

"And *this* explains a few of *my* baking failures. I think sometimes my water is too hot," she said, passing the cup back to Jeff, who drained it into the sink.

I measured the water, yeast, and salt and added them to a large bowl, dumped in the flour, and stirred. The dough became a stiff, lumpy, sticky, and moist mass. "That's it. Here, pass it around. Smell, touch it, so you can remember what it's like." Everyone peered into the bowl, sniffed, and tentatively poked a finger into it. As it made the rounds, I pulled out a five-quart clear plastic bin.

Earlier, I'd made a double batch of the same dough recipe. We'd left it in the back of our car while we shopped for ingredients for class, a point that reminded me of the state health exam and the question about not leaving meat to defrost in the trunk of one's car. It had shifted from a dense, gloopy mass to a bubbling, airy beige blob three times the size. I took back the original bowl and compared them side by side. "So this is 'The Blob.' It's what it looks like after it has risen." The volunteers looked suitably impressed. "Now we're going to shape some loaves."

Everyone grabbed a hunk of the risen dough with floured hands and slathered it in a cloak of flour. Mike, our resident baker, stopped videotaping the class for a moment. "The point is to cover it lightly all over," he advised. "I think of it like creating the shape of the top of a mushroom by smoothing and stretching the dough out and tucking it under the loaf." He and I went around the table helping everyone mold their little grapefruit-sized balls of dough into round *boules*. The volunteers smiled and patted their blobs tentatively at first, and then with a bit more gusto, rather like kids making mud pies. Jeff carefully set up trays lined with parchment paper and cast a generous handful of cornmeal on each to keep the loaves from sticking. I watched as Dri set her loaf on the sheet and wrote her name next to it on the parchment paper. She gazed at it wistfully. If no one had been watching, I wondered if she might have kissed it. I knew the feeling. Baking can do that to you. The loaves needed at least a half hour to rise, so we moved on to pasta.

Pasta earned its place as a household staple in the space of a generation. Italian immigrants started commercially producing the tender, pleasantly neutral-tasting white pasta known to most diners in the early twentieth century, back when it was considered an ethnic food. In the United States and Canada, pasta consumption doubled between 1975 and 1995. Even with the rise of low-carb diets and an increased appetite for gluten-free foods, dried pasta is still a nearly

$2-billion-a-year business. Ever since the major food companies took notice, they've found big profits trotting out various forms of flavored, prepackaged pasta dishes. We may have a vision of a group of Italian grandmothers in some countryside locale turning out noodles, but the retail arena is controlled by a handful of multinationals. In the 1990s, Hershey's was the largest pasta manufacturer until it divested itself of a couple of brands to focus more on its main business, chocolate and confectionaries.

One of my longest conversations with the woman in the supermarket was around her presumed inability to make a simple sauce. Pasta was a staple in the diets of all the volunteers, more ubiquitous than even chicken. But not all pastas are made the same. For that day's tasting, I had compiled a wide selection, including traditional white spaghetti and a couple of gluten-free alternatives, but mostly focusing on whole wheat options, mixing expensive and inexpensive brands. Shifting from white semolina pasta to 100 percent whole wheat pasta can double the fiber and nearly triple the protein of any dish.

While we were all playing with dough, Lisa tended six pots of boiling water, preparing to cook the twelve different types of pasta to the same exact level of al dente and keep track of them all. On its face, this seems a simple task. Some had to cook for six minutes, others fourteen. As the rest of us worked on the bread, I could hear her clanging around in pots to dig out pasta to settle into colanders and slapping down a dozen small plates on the stainless side table.

By the time we were ready to taste, Lisa looked ready to melt. The walls behind the stove dripped condensation. "Okay!" she said, blowing out a huge sigh. "Ready?" As everyone circled the plates, she disappeared into the walk-in cooler and shut the door behind her. I'm fairly sure that Jeff was already in there, possibly with the wine.

Everyone nibbled. The results intrigued. Favorites included the store-brand whole wheat pasta from a warehouse store. "It's got a nice nutty flavor to it," Terri noted. The least favorite was a national whole wheat brand that I had bought months earlier but left untouched after Mike insisted on referring to it as "dirt pasta." I used to give him a hard time for not liking it, but then I discovered no one else did either.

"No, it really does taste like dirt," Shannon said earnestly. "I mean, it's got a strange grit thing going on. My kids would never eat that." She set down her small plate and pushed it away.

Mike leaned out from behind the video camera. "See?" he said, vindicated.

Trish pointed at some brightly colored rotini on her plate. "What are these colored pastas? They're kind of odd tasting." They were pasta spirals flavored with vegetables, another pasta reject from my household. "Oh, yeah, I bought these for our friend's kids who come over to visit a lot. Neither of the girls were crazy about it, though."

Tasting one of the two white pastas, Donna said that she detected something fishy. "It's like tuna. I mean, that's probably not right. That's just me." Then we looked at the package. It contained omega-3. That would explain the fish flavor. No one else had picked it up, but on tasting it again, it was obvious.

Shannon seemed enthused. "This is a great tasting to do," she said. "I'm going to start buying a couple of different pastas and trying them out with my kids. In some ways, I think this was my favorite tasting so far since it's something that I cook all the time."

When it comes to cooking pasta, a few tips make or break the whole experience. First, be sure that you use plenty of water. Second, the pasta will take on the flavor of the water that it's boiled in. One classic way to add flavor to pasta is by salting the water. "The water for pasta should taste salty, kind of like the sea," said Lisa, who was back and looking refreshed from a turn in the walk-in. Finally, don't overcook it, especially whole wheat pasta.

"Don't rinse the noodles," I added. "Sauce will stick better to drier pasta."

"Why do they say to rinse it, then?" Terri asked.

"As long as it's hot, it will keep cooking," I replied. "In fact, if you're going to put pasta into a sauce, which you will be doing in a couple of dishes, undercook it a bit. It will cook a little bit as it cools down and a bit more when it sits in hot sauce."

"Did any of you know that?" Dri asked the group. They shook their heads and kept listening intently. "Okay, good, I thought maybe it was just me."

"Pasta can be a fridge-clearing powerhouse," I explained. "Clean out your crisper drawer, chop up the contents, sauté, steam, or boil them, and add them to a bowl of pasta. Add a little olive oil and some Parmigiano-Reggiano cheese or a classic tomato or Alfredo sauce, and voilà, dinner."

We began with a basic cream sauce. Having worked in a restaurant that served a popular Alfredo dish, Lisa grabbed a whisk and a pan and took over. "Okay, I know it's hot, but everyone over to the stove," she commanded. "You know that fifteen dollars you pay at the Olive Garden for Alfredo pasta? Here's what they start with," she said, and she poured two cups of cream into a pan atop the six-burner stove. "It's just cream reduced with a little bit of pasta water. It's such a simple recipe that you'll wonder why you ever bought it in a box with a flavor packet."

The stove still radiated massive heat from the earlier pasta cooking. She pointed at the cream gurgling in the pan. "See how it's starting to bubble? When this happens, add in half a teaspoon of salt." She kept stirring. Large glassy bubbles popped then died on the surface slowly and then quickly until it resembled slow and lazy foam. The smell changed from bland milk to a strong, intoxicating, almost cheeselike scent. "Smell that? Now let it keep doing that until it thickens." After a minute, she took a spatula and pulled it across the bottom of the pan, painting a wide swath in the stainless steel. She grabbed a spoon from a holder near the stove and stuck it into the sauce, then held it up. The cream cleaved thickly to the back of the spoon, melting in a glacial slide of goo.

"When the sauce thickens enough to cover the back of a spoon or leaves a clean line in the bottom of the pan, it's time to add some pasta water." She dug a ladle into one of the still-hot pots of pasta water and splashed it into the pan with the cream. She simmered it over medium-high heat until bubbles erupted again. "Now add a little bit more cream, heat it through, and then add some shredded cheese, maybe some garlic, and a few cranks of pepper. Jeff, can you hand me some of that cooked pasta?" Jeff brought over a colander of cooked linguine. She took hearty grabs with tongs and swirled the strands into the sauce.

"And that's it. Cream, pasta water, some cheese, maybe some garlic. Easy, right?" She poured it into a pasta plate. "That's just a start. Add in some leftover chicken, some ham, peas, sautéed mushrooms, steamed asparagus, cooked shrimp, and chopped basil, whatever. Just think of dishes you've seen on restaurant menus when you're looking in your fridge thinking, Huh, what could go into pasta? You want to make macaroni and cheese? After the cream reduces, just add shredded Cheddar cheese and macaroni."

She brought the warm pasta with the Alfredo sauce to the work-table. Jeff ladled out a serving to each person on a small plate. For comparison, I had asked Jeff to prepare a boxed version of fettuccine Alfredo. The fresh Alfredo was white with a velvety texture and had a faint scent of garlic in the warm cream. The boxed version had a thin sauce and an unnatural sheen; it smelled strongly of cheese.

"Don't make us eat that," Jodi said sternly, screwing up her face. I knew from the inventory that I had made of her overstuffed pantry that she had at least half a dozen boxes of this exact same stuff.

"Oh, come on," I said. "You need to taste the difference."

She sniffed it. "I can actually smell the iodized salt in it." She took a bit and put it on her plate, then lifted it to choke down a bite.

The rest of the group tentatively picked up a single ribbon of the boxed pasta. "This doesn't taste anything like that," Donna said, motioning to the freshly made sauce. "It's not terrible, but it's not good, especially compared directly to the real version we just had. I never thought to do that."

I tried both, too. The cream sauce had a luxurious, fat mouthfeel with the slightest spikes of pepper and garlic. By comparison, the boxed version had an almost overpronounced sweet cheesy flavor at first bite that vanished into a salty aftertaste. It was an obvious knockoff, like an inexpensive purse attempting to stand in for an authentic Italian leather bag.

"Oh, wow, look at the bread!" Dri said as we set the first of the baking trays onto the worktable. In the half hour that had passed, the raw loaves that they had left to rest had plumped and softened. Mike grabbed a chef's knife and slashed three diagonal slits lightly across the top of the loaves as I explained: "Scoring the bread allows a bit of steam to escape during baking, resulting in a better crumb and a prettier loaf. You can do a pattern if you want."

Armed with their knives, the women found their loaves and exchanged murmurs. "It's so soft!" and "Look, it's starting to look like bread." Most carefully sliced slashes in theirs; Sabra branded hers with a star. Jeff waved everyone away from the oven and pulled open the doors. The heat blast felt almost like a physical punch. I slid the two sheets of bread into the oven. Earlier, I had set a small pan in the bottom. I poured water into the hot pan. As it hissed and steamed violently, I slammed the door shut. The steam helps the dough "spring" in the oven with a sudden burst of heat.

As it baked, we moved on to a basic tomato sauce. Many jars and cans of spaghetti sauce include significant amounts of added sodium and sugar. Also, given that a sauce is little more than some aromatics, seasonings, and tomatoes, it's often less expensive to make at home. During the Alfredo lesson, Jeff had set up five portable electric and propane burners from the kitchen's inventory around the table; it was simply too hot to keep cooking over the big stove.

"Who wants to demonstrate?" Gen raised her hand. She skipped around the table and grabbed the spoon. "Okay, Gen, warm some olive oil in a pan. Add some garlic, onions, and herbs until the onions are soft." While she stirred I opened a can of diced tomatoes, and when the vegetables were ready, Gen plopped them into the saucepan along with a couple of pinches of red pepper flakes and salt, some water, and a bay leaf. She brought it to a boil and then reduced the heat to a simmer. "And let's have a big hand for Gen and her sauce!" I said. Everyone clapped. Gen took a bow.

As the sauce bubbled lightly, we shifted to another burner for a quick *pomodoro,* or fresh tomato sauce. I took off my watch and asked Cheryl to time the process. The sauce started with heating olive oil, then adding chopped garlic, sliced cherry tomatoes, and a splash of the pasta water. We let it simmer briefly and then added two handfuls of cooked linguine to the sauce along with a toss of chopped basil. Start to finish, the sauce clocked in at less than five minutes. By the time it was done, so was the spaghetti sauce.

"Now it's your turn." I waved my hand over the center of the worktable, where bowls sat holding the vegetables chopped at the start of class, along with some cream, various cheeses, cherry tomatoes, fresh basil, cilantro, parsley, and lemon. Lisa brought over bowls of cooked spaghetti, penne, and macaroni. Everyone shifted into action, grabbed a pan, found an empty burner on the table or stove, and settled in to work.

I observed their selections. Each person made something completely different. Terri faithfully replicated the *pomodoro* sauce. Sabra made creamy macaroni and cheese. Jodi sautéed all the vegetables quickly, then added the penne, chopped basil, and olive oil and lovingly grated Parmigiano-Reggiano cheese over the top. With a graceful, seemingly practiced move, she dropped it into a pasta bowl, then she stood back to admire her work. "Wow, look at this," she said to herself. Then she turned to Shannon. "Can you believe that I made this? It's so pretty."

Ding! We retrieved the dark blond loaves from the oven. Although it's best to let bread rest and cool, the smell insisted that we try one loaf almost immediately. Steam escaped as Mike held a hot loaf in a diaper and broke open the crust. "I like to rip bread," he said. "It's not the same if you slice it." The kitchen went quiet as everyone lingered, dipping the still-hot bread into small bowls of olive oil laced with herbs and garlic. The crusts of the other loaves crackled as they cooled on a nearby counter. "I could do this, I could really do this," mused Jodi. "I bet my son would eat this, too." Jeff brought out a bottle of white wine and poured short glasses. Everyone sampled one another's pasta sauce, plus the *pomodoro* and spaghetti sauces. The room erupted into a series of "mmmm's" and "yumm's."

"It's all good, I mean really good," Dri said. "It's kind of surprising, really, all the different dishes you can do with a few ingredients."

The group collected their pasta and still-warm loaves to take home. Sweating under my own apron, I wished everyone a good night. Mike took my hand and led me across the street. We sat on the curb cloaked in shadow in the cooling night air. Late on a Monday, the normally busy thoroughfare was quiet. A waning moon lit the sky. "It's amazing," Mike said. "Last week we were on the other side of the world looking up at the moon, remember?" I leaned my head on his shoulder.

Then we heard a voice, a familiar one. "I made bread. Yes, me. Yes, really." Donna emerged, balancing her cell phone on her shoulder, holding a box of pasta and a loaf of bread in her arms. "I have pasta, too." Pause. "No, *I* made it. Yes, *me*. Don't sound so surprised!" She got into her car and drove off into the night.

No-Knead Artisan Bread for Busy People

This recipe is adapted from the master recipe in the excellent book Artisan Bread in Five Minutes a Day *by Jeff Hertzberg and Zoë François. It's simple to prepare and the dough keeps in the fridge for up to two weeks. I often add a tablespoon of dried thyme, rosemary, or herbes de Provence to the water to infuse the bread with extra flavor. The recipe was designed to work on a baking stone, but I get similar results with a shallow cast iron skillet. A cookie sheet will work, but your loaf may not get quite as brown and crusty. You can find the original recipe plus helpful photos and variations at www.artisanbreadinfive.com.*

YIELDS ABOUT FOUR ONE-POUND LOAVES

3 cups lukewarm water (about 100°F)
1½ tablespoons yeast
1 tablespoon kosher salt
6½ cups (32 ounces/900 grams) unsifted unbleached all-purpose
 white flour
Additional flour to create loaves
Cornmeal

❧ Combine the water, yeast, and salt in a 5-quart bowl or plastic food container with a lid. Stir to mix. Add all of the flour at once and mix with a wooden spoon until the dough is wet and sticky with no dry patches. Cover with a lid or plastic wrap, but do not seal airtight. Let it rise for about 2 hours at room temperature. If you are not using it immediately, refrigerate the dough, covered, for up to 2 weeks.

❧ To make a loaf, lightly sprinkle some flour onto the dough's surface. Scoop up a handful the size of a grapefruit, and cut or tear it away from the remainder. Rub the dough with a layer of flour while gently stretching the top around to tuck the sides into the bottom to form a round, smooth loaf. Put the loaf on a pizza peel or cutting board dusted with cornmeal to prevent sticking. Let it rise, uncovered, for at least a half hour or as long as 90 minutes. The loaf will plump but not change radically in size.

❧ About 20 minutes before baking, preheat the oven to 450°F. Place a broiler tray or other metal pan on the bottom rack of the oven. Put the baking stone or cast iron skillet on the middle rack.

❧ Dust the loaf liberally with flour. Slash the top with a cross or three lines with a sharp knife and slide it onto the preheated baking surface. Carefully pour about 1 cup of hot water into the broiler tray or metal pan and close the oven door to trap the steam. Bake for about 30 minutes, until the crust is browned and the loaf feels light and hollow. Cool to room temperature.

Note

For a "lazy sourdough," mix the next batch in the same container without cleaning it first. You can substitute 2 cups of whole wheat flour for the white flour if desired.

~~~~~~

ᏋᎽ Basic Alfredo Sauce

This is a great way to use up leftovers such as shredded chicken, cooked shrimp, grilled vegetables, and so on. Just toss them in near the end of cooking. Use cream, not milk. Start cooking the pasta before you begin the sauce. As an easy shortcut, toss chopped vegetables such as broccoli, asparagus, peas, artichokes, and the like into the pasta water to cook them briefly; frozen vegetables work well. Add cooked chicken, vegetables, diced ham, cooked shrimp, and whatever you have on hand with the pasta and heat through.

MAKES 3 TO 4 SERVINGS

8 ounces cooked pasta
2 cups heavy cream (2 tablespoons reserved)
$\frac{1}{2}$ teaspoon salt
$\frac{1}{2}$ cup grated Parmesan or Parmigiano-Reggiano cheese
1 garlic clove, minced (optional)
Freshly ground black pepper

❧ Prepare the pasta according to package directions. Carefully reserve one cup of the pasta water to use in the sauce. Over medium-high heat, add all but 2 tablespoons of the cream to a sauté pan or skillet. When it bubbles, add the salt. Small bubbles will erupt into larger bubbles. Stir. When the sauce thickens enough to cover the back of a spoon or leaves a clean line in the bottom of the pan when you pull a spatula across it, add the pasta water. Cook over medium-high heat for about 3 minutes, until it bubbles again and the sauce thickens. Add the reserved 2 tablespoons of cream, heat through, and then add the cheese, garlic (if using), and a few cranks of pepper. Taste, and add more salt if needed. Add the cooked pasta and any additional ingredients and stir well to coat.

CHAPTER 8

Tossed Salad & Scrambled Eggs

৩৯ LESSON HIGHLIGHTS:
**Salads and Omelets as Vehicles for Leftovers,
and the Miracle of Vinaigrette**

The autumn before I started the project, I donated the first of several cooking-class dinners to charity. A sweet couple forked over seven hundred dollars to a worthy cause for my services, blissfully unaware that, at the time, I had never taught a cooking class.

As Lisa and I arrived at the door clad in chef's jackets and armed with cooking gear, an elegant woman with a bob of highlighted blond hair holding a white wine spritzer opened the door. "Hi, we're all so excited!" she greeted us enthusiastically. "Yep, it's the chef. She's here!" she yelled over her shoulder to her guests. She kept one hand on the doorknob and waved us inside with the other clasped firmly on a flute of champagne. She smelled vaguely of Chanel No. 5.

Her guests gathered around the granite-topped kitchen island littered with wineglasses. The house was a well-decorated atomic-era ranch style with an expansive backyard blanketed with lush green grass and ringed by evergreens. The friends stood around in casual summer attire, the women in capris and the men in Dockers and button-down short-sleeved shirts. Two of the men put down their drinks and left to help Lisa lug in the rest of our cooking gear from her truck. As I exchanged pleasantries with the hosts, a dark-haired fellow holding a gin and tonic cheerfully asked, "So, Chef, where's your restaurant?"

Ugh, that question. "I don't have one. I'm a food writer," I replied. "Oh, so you're not a real chef," he said, a little confused.

The hostess interjected, "Don't put her on the spot. Of course she's a real chef! She went to culinary school. In Paris, no less!"

Booze comes in handy for dodging questions. "Oh, hey, I almost forgot! We brought champagne to make kir royales."

After I made a round of cocktails, I opened the fridge door to put the remnant champagne inside. Three dozen bottles of vinaigrette clanked like wind chimes caught in a Category 1 hurricane. "That's quite a lot of dressing you've got in there," I said to the hostess. "Why don't you make your own?"

"Oh, I'd have no idea how," she said, fingering her pearl earrings.

"Do you have a jar?" I asked.

We ransacked the cupboards, pulling a motley collection of barely touched bottles of oil and vinegars of seemingly every shape, size, and flavor and set them on the kitchen island. "Okay, everyone, gather around," I said. As I explained the impromptu tasting session of oils and vinegars, the guests exchanged dubious glances.

"But are those even edible alone?" a woman asked.

"Of course," I said. "You need to know what each tastes like so that you'll have an idea when you put them together."

We started with the oils, a variety of olive, canola, safflower, and sesame and a small aging bottle of walnut. We set aside a bottle of olive oil that had turned rancid. "Oils don't have the shelf life most people think," I said. "It's, like, six months, and less if you store them over the stove like you're doing here because the heat breaks down the oil." Lisa and I had everyone taste the good oils and then the bad oil. "Rancid oil isn't bad for you, but the unpleasant flavor and acrid taste will ruin whatever you decide to do with it." We moved on to the vinegars, which ranged from cider to white wine to red wine to balsamic.

Then Lisa explained that vinaigrette dressing is just a simple ratio. "It's generally three to one," she said. "Three parts oil, such as olive oil or sesame oil, to one part acid, such as vinegar or citrus juice."

The hostess and I measured three tablespoons of olive oil and one tablespoon of balsamic vinegar into her empty jar. We added some salt and pepper. I gave it to the hostess to shake fiercely.

"Now what do we do?" she asked excitedly.

"Congratulations. You just made vinaigrette," I said. She looked proud and held it above her head as if she'd won a trophy at Wimbledon. Everyone cheered. A month later, she sent an e-mail thanking me for the class, adding, "I haven't bought a bottle of salad dressing since that night. This sounds crazy, but it changed my life. It made me start to wonder what else I have been buying that I could just be making myself."

I printed out that e-mail and brought it to the next class. I told the volunteers the story, and then read the e-mail aloud to them as they gathered around the worktable. Only one short week after the numbing heat of the pasta and bread class, the kitchen temperature was nearly twenty-five degrees cooler.

"That woman had everything she needed to make vinaigrette," I said. "She was missing only one ingredient: the know-how to make it."

Vinaigrette is one of the more expensive products to buy by weight at a grocery store. A sixteen-ounce bottle of dressing can run anywhere from $3.60 to more than seven dollars. At an average of thirty-two cents an ounce, that's nearly forty-one dollars per gallon. Yet it's one of the easiest and cheapest things to make at home.

After the story, we circulated copies of a basic vinaigrette recipe. At the top of each page: "oil + acid = yummy."

Lisa and I led the volunteers on a raid around the kitchen to collect oils, vinegars, soy sauce, jams, chutney, fig paste, cheeses, garlic, dried coconut, gingerroot, spices, red wine, lemons, limes, olives, and some of the Dijon mustard from the chicken lesson. We broke the class into two-person teams. "If you can think of something you had eating out, consider the flavor profiles, the way we did in the chicken class. What flavors make something taste Italian? Name them." We went around the table: Parmesan cheese, oregano, red wine, tomatoes, basil.

"Thai?" Basil, coconut, curry, lime, hot chilies.

"I usually buy a strawberry balsamic. How would I make that?" Shannon asked.

"In summer, you can add mashed-up fresh strawberries. The rest of the time, you can just use a bit of strawberry jam," I said, an answer that generated a collective "ah" of enlightenment.

The group went to work tasting and talking, a cacophony of whisks in motion, stopping and tasting again. Jodi and Dri made an Asian version with sesame oil, grated gingerroot, soy, and lime. Another team crafted a balsamic with fig paste and bleu cheese. Sabra and Gen made classic mustard and white wine vinaigrette with fresh thyme thrown in.

Then we stopped everyone. "Okay, whisks down!" Lisa commanded. She and I had bought a couple of packages of mixed greens. We set them on the table. "Pick out different salad leaves and dip them into your vinaigrette. You want to see how the flavor pairs with your lettuce, since all lettuces taste different," she explained. "Remember, there is no right or wrong answer. Whatever tastes good to you is all that matters."

Everyone stopped and delicately selected a few leaves—radicchio, butter lettuce, romaine, arugula, frisée among them. The group chatted and murmured. "This one's bitter." "This one doesn't go with the ginger." "Huh, it's great with the arugula but terrible with that red leaf."

Then each pair rotated around the table, tasting the other teams' creations with all manner of lettuce. They were all good, but the fig and bleu cheese balsamic knocked it out of the park. I made a mental note to try it myself.

Everyone had such a great time with the salad and vinaigrette lesson that it was tough to pull them away from it. But it was time to move on to the eggs.

"Omelets don't get the respect they deserve," says Jamie Oliver. He's so right. An omelet is inexpensive, easy, satisfying, and a good way to use up leftovers. Plus, who says that eggs are only for breakfast? A famous food writer, Elizabeth David, wrote a whole story about the beauty of an omelet and a glass of wine for dinner.

One of my chefs at Le Cordon Bleu used to say, *"Apprendre à faire une omelette et vous n'aurez jamais faim."* If you learn to make an omelet, you'll never go hungry. He told my Intermediate Cuisine class a legendary story about Napoleon Bonaparte. His army was traveling in southern France and spent a night in a small town, Bessières. The owner of the inn where Napoleon stayed made him an omelet. He had never had one before and found it so wonderful that the next day he requested the townspeople to gather up all the eggs in the village to prepare an enormous omelet for his army. They won the battle, of course. If they hadn't, no one would make omelets.

"Omelets are great for leftovers because, well, you can put almost anything into them and serve them for breakfast, lunch, or dinner," I said. "I've made omelets filled with every possible leftover including steak and bleu cheese. Otherwise, the method is always the same."

I put a seven-inch nonstick skillet over one of the portable burners and dropped in a dollop of butter. As it warmed, I cracked two eggs into a bowl, added salt, pepper, and a bit of thyme, and whisked. The eggs made a "shhhh" sound as they hit the surface of the warmed pan. I turned the heat to low, then tilted the pan around to assure that the egg coalesced evenly. Once it had cooked through, I added a bit of cheese, folded it over with the edge of a spatula, and slid it from the pan. Voilà.

Each volunteer made an omelet. There may be nothing more gratifying than watching someone make an omelet for the first time. Some came out better than others, but student after student had the wide smile of accomplishment as she watched hers fold onto her plate. Andra openly chuckled. "This is so easy! I don't know why it never worked when I tried them. I'd start out with an omelet but end up with scrambled eggs."

"Funny you mention that—making scrambled eggs is the last lesson of the day."

The trick to great scrambled eggs is to start with a cold pan. Add a couple pats of butter and the eggs, and then turn the heat up to medium-low and stir regularly. It's a longer process but yields a softer result than the classic high-heat version in which the eggs take on an elastic flavor and a rubbery consistency. Lisa whipped up some cream and added a bit of cayenne to it, then spooned it over the scrambled eggs, a variation on a recipe by famed chef Jean-Georges Vongerichten. "This is so good; I could eat a mountain of these eggs," Andra said.

I had been worried that everything we taught was too simple. Yet that day I was reminded that in an unsure world, few things are invariably as good and true as a humble omelet, a simply dressed salad, and a glass of wine. Later, Gen told me that shortly after the class, she found herself without a plan for dinner one night. "But I realized that I had eggs, so I made an omelet. I chopped up some leftover asparagus and threw it in. My roommate was so impressed. She was like, 'Wow, I can't believe that you just made an omelet, just like that.' So I taught her how to make one, too."

~~~~~~

Ꮐ DIY Vinaigrette

Vinaigrette is among the simplest things to make yourself, yet one of the most additive-riddled items in the supermarket. Extra vinaigrette will keep for a few days in an airtight container in the fridge. Experiment. Use leftovers for inspiration. If you hate it, you've wasted thirty cents in ingredients. Some lettuces reduce an acid tang while others amplify it, so taste your concoction with a leaf or two to taste before serving.

Here's the basic formula:

1 part acid + 3 parts oil = fabulous stuff

Acids	Oils
Vinegar (red, balsamic, white wine, rice wine)	Any vegetable oil
	Nut oil (hazelnut, walnut, peanut, almond, macadamia, etc.)
Citrus juice (lemon, lime, grape-fruit, etc.)	Fruit oil (olive, avocado, coconut, etc.)

❧ In a bowl, combine the one part acid, a pinch of coarse salt, and a few grinds of fresh pepper, then whisk in the three parts oil, or add them all to a jar and shake vigorously. Taste. Congratulations, you've made vinaigrette. If it's too acidic, add oil. If it's too sour, add a little sweetener. If it's too oily, add more acid. Just add very small amounts until it tastes balanced and good to you. If you have time, let it rest for at least 15 minutes, then taste again.

❧ Acid and oil don't like to stay mixed, so you can add an emulsifier, like an egg yolk or a dab of mayonnaise or mustard or honey, before adding the oil. Additional seasonings to consider include some minced shallots or garlic, herbs, or spices.

❧ Want fancy designer gourmet vinaigrette? Raspberry balsamic, for example? Add a handful of berries, fresh or thawed from frozen, or a teaspoon of berry-based jam. Asian vinaigrette? Try some combination of lime juice, ginger, garlic, miso, sesame oil, peanut oil, soy sauce. French? Dijon mustard, shallots, tarragon, white wine vinegar. For more help developing vinaigrette flavors, check out the "Cheat Sheet" to Flavor Profiles in the Extra Recipes section at the back of the book.

~~~~~~

❧ Your Basic Omelet

Omelets cook quickly, so assemble any fillings that you want to add before you start. For a two-egg omelet, you can use a seven-inch nonstick skillet; bump it up a size for three eggs. Otherwise, all you need is a small bowl, a fork, and a spatula. I like to use a dab of olive oil and butter to give the omelet a little bit of flavor. If you want to use vegetables such as onions, peppers, or mushrooms, you may want to precook them briefly.

2 or 3 eggs
Salt and freshly ground black pepper to taste
A pinch of dried thyme or mixed herbs (optional)
A splash of milk or water (optional)
About 1 teaspoon oil (such as canola or olive), cooking spray, and/
   or a pat of butter
Ingredients to fill your omelet, such as cheese, ham, vegetables,
   etc.

❧ Combine the eggs in a small bowl. Add a pinch of salt, a couple of grinds of pepper, and the dried herbs, if using. Add a bit of milk if you want a fluffier omelet. Whip using a fork or a whisk. The longer you whip, the fluffier the omelet.

❧ Heat a nonstick pan over medium heat. Add the oil, cooking spray, or butter. Add the egg mixture. Tilt the pan around so that the egg runs to the open areas of the pan to form a consistent layer. Let the egg cook through briefly and then carefully use a spatula to pull up one side and let the remaining uncooked egg go under the omelet to the pan's surface. Once the egg layer thickens, lower the heat and add the other ingredients, such as cheese, vegetables, and cooked meat or seafood. Heat the omelet just until the egg is cooked through, but not too browned on the bottom. Using the spatula, carefully tuck around the edges to ensure that the omelet will slide freely from the pan.

❧ Fold your omelet in one of two ways. Carefully fold it in the pan using your spatula, and then slide the finished omelet onto the plate. Or put a serving plate on the counter and carefully tilt the omelet toward it. Once the edge of the omelet hits the plate, use the spatula to guide the other edge over in a fold.

Udder Confusion

ᏩᏪ LESSON HIGHLIGHTS:
**When It Comes to Meat, It's Worth Knowing
Your Butt from Your Round**

Not long after I moved to London in the autumn of 1999, I scanned
newspaper headlines while waiting for a bus at Oxford Circus on a
dreary winter's morning. TWO MORE DEATHS LINKED TO MAD COW,
screamed one headline. TODDLER ORPHANED! blared another.

Like a lot of people living in the United Kingdom in the wake of
the BSE epidemic, I stopped eating red meat. The problem wasn't
limited to British beef,* although the issue had the greatest impact
in the United Kingdom. I swore off poultry and pork, too. What
tripped me up were the crispy, fragrant ducks hanging in the windows of the city's small Chinatown area that I passed by on my way
home from work. I tried changing my route, but the ducks, shiny as
if varnished with a chestnut-colored lacquer, called to me like an
artful siren luring the unsuspecting to treacherous rocks.

I relented the way I imagine alcoholics fall off the wagon. I went
into Lee Ho Fook's alone late one night. I'll just get a few steamed

---

*By the end of 2008, more than 184,500 cases of BSE had been confirmed in the
United Kingdom, according to the Centers for Disease Control. In humans, the disease manifests primarily as Creutzfeldt-Jakob disease (vCJd), and as of October 2010,
a total of 217 cases of vCJd had been reported in eleven countries. In the United
Kingdom, the epidemic peaked in 1999. In North America, twenty-one cases of BSE
had been reported by mid-2010, three in the United States and eighteen in Canada.

pork dumplings, I told myself. I can stop anytime I want. Everyone knows that dumplings are a gateway food. Before I knew it, I'd inhaled half a duck. I sorted through the remnants, prying tiny bits of dark meat from the bones with the enthusiasm of someone who has just returned from a space mission and subsisted on nothing other than gel packs and Tang for months. I walked home through the busy environs of Chinatown with my head down. I swore that it would never happen again. The next night, I went back. Settled in a discreet booth and wearing dark glasses, I broke the land speed record for consuming a full order of moo shu pork. After that, the floodgates opened. I bought my first whole chicken in more than three years and I never looked back.

All this transpired not long before I started studying at Le Cordon Bleu in Paris. I felt particularly unprepared for the routine dismemberment of lambs, ducks, chickens, and beef that was de rigueur in the course of culinary school.

Even more than chicken, beef comes with baggage. So many people buy chicken in nonoffensive white breast meat hunks that it's ubiquitous enough that the "meat thing" doesn't even factor into the discussion. It's kind of like that scene in *My Big Fat Greek Wedding* when an aunt, on hearing that the main character's fiancé is a vegetarian, cannot fathom that it's an issue. The aunt replies, stunned, "He don't eat no meat?! What do you mean, he don't eat no meat? Oh, that's okay, I make lamb."

During the kitchen visits, many of the volunteers expressed that the meat department in their local supermarket was often a place of confusion. How to tell what cuts work for different types of cooking? "I look at packages of meat and it's just baffling," Shannon said. "I know that a T-bone is a good steak, but I am not sure what should be roasted and what should be grilled. And what the heck is chuck?"

Cheryl shopped at a local food co-op. The labels confused her. Choice? Prime? Natural? Pasture-raised? Grass-finished? She didn't know what they meant.

They're all good questions. I didn't know the answers to many of them either, especially around meat classification. So I did some research.

Unsurprisingly, beef is big business. The United States produced nearly 27 billion pounds of it in 2008, the result of processing about 33 million head of cattle. On average, Americans consume about 54 pounds of beef per capita each year. That's nearly one Quarter Pounder from McDonald's for every man, woman, and child in the United States every day of the year.* More than 40 percent of all cattle raised meet their destiny as hamburger.

I wanted to break the lessons out of the grind, so to speak, so I felt it was time for another guest teacher. I'd recently met Robin Leventhal, the former chef/owner of Crave, a minuscule wedge of a restaurant in my neighborhood that specialized in beautiful comfort food. For the past few years, Robin had been winning a battle against two forms of lymphoma, yet lost the lease on her popular restaurant after a protracted negotiation with her landlord.

"It was both devastating and liberating," she said on reflection. "For once, I wasn't a slave to my phone twenty-four hours a day." Released from the pressures of a restaurant, on a whim she auditioned for *Top Chef* and earned a place as a cheftestant in the sixth season of the series from a field of thousands of candidates. Over a couple of celebratory cocktails, we ended up chatting more about her background. She started life in the art world, earning a master's degree in ceramics. "I didn't want to be a starving artist," she said. Instead, she went to work feeding people. In food, she found a creative outlet that paid the bills and that was as emotionally satisfying as art. "For me, feeding people is primal and maternal. It's arguably the most satisfying experience in the world."

A week later, thinking about her comment, I called to ask if she would be willing to teach a class. Among the best dishes that I'd had in years were her simple braised specials at Crave. She agreed. For her class, we'd focus on cuts of meat, how to prep them and get the

*Denmark has the highest consumption of ground beef internationally.

most from inexpensive cuts. But I hoped some of the ethos that Robin felt about cooking and her passion to nourish people would come through in the lesson as much as anything she could tell the volunteers about shoulder roasts.

When I told Lisa and Maggie that Robin was coming in to teach, they had identical reactions. "No freakin' way," Maggie said. No cupcakes would keep her from that class. "Seriously, whenever I would go to Crave, the waiter would start to rattle off specials, and once he said 'braised whatever,' I'd just say, 'I'll take that.' The server would say, 'Don't you want to know what it comes with it?' I'd say, 'Uh-unh. Don't know, don't need to know. Just bring it.'"

The day of the class, Lisa and I raided a local supermarket to collect twenty-two packages of beef, lamb, and pork, essentially clearing out the "manager's special" discounted area. We had ribs, round steak, tri-tips, oxtails, London broil, T-bones, beef shanks, lamb shanks, lamb steaks, pork shoulders, and something called chuck Denver steak. We dragged nearly forty pounds of meat into the teaching kitchen. To witness that much meat in one place is both impressive and disturbing. The students filed in, and as each one approached the table she stopped dead in her tracks. "Oh, wow, that's a lot of meat," Cheryl said, summing up the group's reaction.

Robin has stores of quiet energy, yet a big personality. She's also physically impressive, a square-jawed, solid woman with dark, olive skin and black eyes. Her black short-sleeved shirt accentuated hard biceps. Whenever I saw her, I made a mental note to check out Pilates and never to cross her because, frankly, she could take my pale carcass in a fight without breaking a sweat. She stood demurely behind me as I introduced her. "In two days, she'll be on the first episode of this season's *Top Chef,* but tonight she's going to be teaching something very important—meat."

Everyone seemed suitably impressed. She was going to be on TV! We handed out diagrams of cows and pigs with dotted lines to demarcate various cuts. Even at the paper version Trish recoiled a bit. As Robin talked, Trish pulled me aside between two towering metal racks of dried goods and tableware as everyone took turns washing their hands. "So, this is kind of awkward," she said, literally wringing her hands, the way she had when I visited her kitchen. She cast a glance back at the dense collection of red meat on the work-table. "We don't eat much meat now, so I may not be able to stay for the full class." Her anxiety was palpable. I assured her that I understood and told her of my fling with vegetarianism.

We started with a basic lesson on recognizing cuts. The July heat crept into the kitchen. Two minutes into the explanation, half the class started fanning themselves with the meat diagrams. Their collective eyes started to glaze over as Robin and I began to discuss chuck and sirloin. I looked at Maggie and Lisa. We all sensed we were losing the audience already. Lisa bent over abruptly.

"So, everybody, look at me, I'm a cow," she said loudly. Possible comebacks rattled around my brain. The students exchanged glances and snickered. Lisa waved a finger good-naturedly at the group. "No wisecracks!" she warned. "Okay, see my shoulder? It gets a lot of work. Feel your shoulders and arms. There's a lot of muscle there. It's tough. This is where chuck comes from," Lisa said. The group snapped out of its stupor. Each person started to feel her own shoulders.

Then Lisa slapped her thighs. "This is where shank and brisket come from, and you'll want to braise them the way we did with the legs and thighs in the chicken class. We'll do another one tonight." The class kept their eyes on her, feeling their upper legs. "The meat near the ribs is tender. It isn't used as much. This is where you get your prime rib and rib-eye steaks." She put her hands on her lower back. "Behind the ribs are the short loins and then sirloin. That's where the most expensive cuts come from. Think tenderloin, filet mignon, that kind of thing."

As they prodded their own backs and ribs, it struck me that while effective, there was something curiously macabre about demonstrating meat cuts using the human anatomy.

Lisa took one last fling as a cow and put her hands on her buttocks. "Feel your butt. Round, right? That's where round comes from. It works a little harder than the back, so it's tougher." Then she bolted upright. "Okay, I can't believe that I just did that," she said, laughing. Everyone clapped, and she took an embarrassed, quick bow.

Then we quizzed them. "Where is your short loin?" The group tentatively reached to their lower backs.

"Round?" Looking at one another and stifling giggles, they grabbed their buttocks.

"Your chuck?" They pointed to their shoulders.

We then looked over the vast assortment of meat on the table. Maggie videotaped the class as Lisa, Robin, and I started to pick up various packages and explain how to prepare them. We grouped them by cuts. Robin took over. "Most people know steaks or ribs, so we're just going to focus on the lesser-known cuts. Anything that says chuck is tough, so these are great for stews, pot roast, or braising.

"The other one is round," Robin continued. "If it says round, just think of that as a cue to marinate it before you cook it. For instance, London broil is a cut from round, and normally you marinate that and then grill it."

Every so often, though, you may run into a cut you've never heard of. "For instance, let's discuss this Denver chuck steak," Robin said as I picked up a vacuum-packed oblong cut of beef. It turned out to be one of the "new" cuts developed by the National Cattlemen's Beef Association. The good folks at the Cattlemen's Association dedicated $1.5 million and five years to finding new ways to market lesser cuts of meat. Cuts that might have normally found their way to hamburger had been salvaged as whole pieces, including the Denver, an inexpensive, well-marbled piece of chuck that could be cooked like a steak.

"This piece used to be ground into hamburger. You'd pay three or four dollars a pound or whatever for it. Now that they call it a steak, they can charge seven to twelve dollars a pound. I'm not saying that it's a bad cut of meat, it's just that meat producers are always coming up with new things, so don't get discouraged if you don't recognize it."

Robin picked up two T-bones. "But this is a good example of why you should learn a little about meat cuts, or get to know your butcher," she said. "This should have meat on both sides of the bone. One side is a strip steak, and the smaller part is the tenderloin. But the butcher cut off the tenderloin and left just the strip steak. The difference?" She selected another package of meat. "Here's a New York strip. It's $8.99 a pound. This T-bone is $12.99 a pound. But you didn't get half the T-bone, or the most expensive part of the steak. It's hard to know if this was a mistake or if it was on purpose. But if you bought this, you'd have been robbed."

Everyone had questions. Among them, what the difference is between organic and "natural," two common distinctions, and the controversy over grain-fed beef.

To start, it's worth knowing what's in commercially produced meat. About 70 percent of all the antibiotics produced in the United States are fed to healthy livestock, including pigs, chickens, and cows.* Most commercial beef breeders in the United States and Canada inject their cattle with hormones designed to promote rapid growth. The beef industry maintains that the hormones have been vigilantly tested for safety. Critics argue that hormones cause everything from early onset of puberty to increased predisposition for certain types of cancer.†

Most commercially produced cattle start on an individual farm but are "finished" in a feedlot by being fed copious amounts of corn

---

*This figure is based on studies by the Union of Concerned Scientists, which argues that heavy antibiotic use in animals may be a contributing factor in the rise of antibiotic resistance in humans who eat commercially raised meat.

†The European Union is not so keen on North American beef. A blanket import ban has been the subject of intense political and legal wrangling. The World Trade Organization probably wishes the whole thing would just go away.

and grain, foods that cows are not physically designed to eat.* But much of that stems from consumer demand; many people prefer corn-fed beef and its more heavily marbled texture to the leaner flavor and mouthfeel of grass-fed beef.

By contrast, organic beef farmers are prohibited from giving their charges antibiotics, growth hormones, or anything other than organic feed. The "natural" description for beef† allows more flexibility, but generally the beef must be free from growth hormones and antibiotics and minimally processed, although in some cases it simply means that it wasn't ground into hamburger.

"A lot of smaller farms that produce grass-fed beef don't meet organic requirements, and some organic beef comes from cattle raised in feedlots that are just fed organic corn," I said. "I sound like such an old saw on this, but the only way you know the difference is to know the company that developed your beef. Look up the companies that supply your supermarket or butcher. Ask them questions."

Robin chimed in. "Meat isn't cheap. Look at your grocery bill for a month. How much are you spending on meat? It's probably a bigger investment than you think. So it's worth thinking about."

Beyond cooking, I wanted to instill the idea of considering the provenance of meat, not just its cost. So I told them the story of Betsy, the one and only cow we ever had on the farm growing up in Michigan. Betsy was a gentle bovine with a lazy disposition and impossibly long eyelashes. When we named her, my mother was not pleased.

"Don't name the cow," Mom said.

My brother, a gifted artist, drew a loving portrait of her. "Don't draw any more pictures of the cow," Mom said.

The kids spent hours taking turns walking her through our ample

*Corn is so complex that entire books and films are devoted to the subject. Two I recommend are the documentary *King Corn* and the book *The Story of Corn* by Betty Fussell (University of Mexico Press, 2004).

†The reason why the term "natural" is less meaningful for chickens is because growth hormones are prohibited in poultry in general; the USDA allows minimal antibiotic use in "natural" chickens but doesn't specify the amount.

meadows blanketed with clovers and petting her rough brown coat. "Don't pet the cow," Mom said.

One day in autumn, a man in faded gray overalls showed up at the farm with a trailer. Dad said that he was going to take Betsy to a nice farm for the winter. Betsy docilely filed past the kids, who stared, stunned, and then, as if on cue, started bawling in unison. My sister couldn't take it. She tore herself away from my dad's leg and ran over to her, dramatically throwing her small arms up toward the cow's neck. Sobbing, she kissed her good-bye. "We'll miss you, Betsy! I will dream about you every night until you come back next spring." My father gently pried her away.

About two weeks later, my sister discovered new paper-wrapped parcels in the chest freezer in the barn. The first night we had spaghetti made with beef, she looked up at my brother's charcoal sketch of Betsy and then stared back down at her plate. She ate it anyway.

Half the class looked mortified. "You ate your cow," Donna said flatly.

"Yes, and all this"—I waved my hand over the remainder of the meat we'd moved to the side table, still covered in plastic wrap—"was once a Betsy," I said. "But we knew what *she* ate; she didn't get any antibiotics or hormones. She also didn't eat any corn. She just ate grass, which is what cows are supposed to eat. So the closer you can get to meat from a cow like Betsy, the better."

Although we could have talked about beef all night, the clock was ticking. We set out bowls of onions, carrots, and celery. Everyone plowed through their mirepoix as if they'd been doing it for years. What would have taken a half hour in the first class took less than ten minutes. "Wow, you guys are good," Robin observed as Lisa and I collected it all in bowls. I felt like a proud stage mother.

Then we shifted to pork to practice on a cut no one in the class had ever purchased: pork shoulder.* Robin, Lisa, and I handed a

---

*Pork shoulder is also known as pork butt or Boston butt, a historical reference to the butchering style used by Boston-area butchers that left more meat and less bone

hunk of pork shoulder to each student. Robin guided them through breaking down the larger pieces, feeling for bones and removing unwanted pieces such as gristle, tough sinew, and hard tracts of white fat.

Trish, the gentle sixty-one-year-old part-time vegetarian, gave it her best. I watched her from across the room. She looked anguished as she held her chef's knife poised above her pinkish meat. But then she calmly set it down, stood back from the table, and purposefully took off her apron. Trish walked over to where I stood near the door. "I'm sorry, but this is just too much meat for me," she said apologetically. She picked up her purse and left.

The rest of the class, however, seemed transfixed. While they had seemed so squeamish around the chicken, they had no such inhibitions with beef or pork. Most had never tackled a chunk of meat, and who could blame them? Given this era of prepackaging, you can go your whole life never having to cut anything beyond the bite-sized portions required for mastication. No reason exists to explore the sinew, to feel the complexities of muscular development, or to feel the stiff line of a bone giving way to softer flesh unless you plan to break it down as we were doing that day. Dri, who had been so reluctant to touch her whole chicken, now maneuvered her knife with the laser focus of a passionate scientist. Jodi explored the flesh with her fingers, massaging it and trying to understand the contours.

Robin wandered around the table inspecting, offering advice and quiet support. "Exactly, let your blade follow the line of the meat," she told Shannon. Cheryl had seemed a bit intimidated to start. Robin literally held her hand. "Just like that. You're doing really well. See? You can do it." Cheryl asked if she'd learned about meat in culinary school. "Oh, no, I didn't go to school," Robin said. "I kind of fell into cooking. A chef took me under her wing and I never looked back."

Standing next to Cheryl, Shannon overheard the conversation.

---

on the shoulder cuts. The pieces were typically shipped in casks or barrels, colloquially known as "butts," hence the term.

"Was your mother a big cook?" she asked without looking up as she tenderly cut her meat into cubes. I thought of Shannon's response on her initial questionnaire, that her own mother had invariably shooed her out of the kitchen.

Robin let out a robust hoarse laugh. "Ha, no! My mother is a terrible cook. Her ideal house would contain no kitchen. I think part of the reason I started to cook was to rebel against her."

We shifted to start the evening's braise. This time, we handed out a two-quart sauté pan to each person and gave her the option of a single gas or electric burner at stations around the kitchen. "We can also have at least two people at the big six-burner stove," I said. Like a shot, Dri moved into position before anyone could take it away from her. During the classes, some of the students had seemed intimidated by the high heat emitted from the commercial stove. Not Dri. She seemed almost ready to trade her urban planning job for a spot on a restaurant hot line.

As we had for the chicken, we started by searing the pork in hot oil to brown, nearly crispy. Then each volunteer added the mirepoix, some stock, wine, and some herbs. The air took on a heady, meaty fragrance. One by one, the volunteers covered their pans and shifted them into the oven, holding the hot handles with their diapers. "Remember where you put it in the oven, so you can remember which one was yours," I advised as we slammed the oven doors shut.

"Great!" Robin said. Aware of the time, she moved swiftly onward. She heated a large skillet on one of the electric burners and waved everyone to join her around the worktable.

"One simple way to add a lot of flavor to any cut of meat is to coat it in a spice rub," Robin began. Spices have a shelf life of about a year, less if exposed to light or heat. Spices left intact in their original form, such as allspice berries, cinnamon sticks, or whole nutmeg, last significantly longer. "I'm as guilty as the next person. I've got ground oregano that I've had for twenty years in my cupboard. I'm sure it tastes like nothing. But one thing you can do, either with whole spices or those that you've kept around a little too long, is to bring out the flavor by toasting them."

She demonstrated by adding cardamom to the pan. A common ingredient in Indian curry, cardamom pods resemble sunflower seeds shrouded with a light green or dark brown papery exterior. "Notice I'm not using any oil," she said. "We're just dry-toasting them." She swirled them around in the pan. After a minute, everyone started to sniff at the air as the pods released their strong licorice-like scent.

"I can smell that, totally," Sabra said. Everyone nodded.

Robin smiled. "Mmmm, doesn't it smell great? After a last swirl, she dumped the pods onto a plate. "Next, I'm going to do the same with cumin. A lot of people know it from making chili and usually buy it ground." She tossed the oblong, ridged, beige-hulled seeds into the pan. Again she swirled them over the heat. "Just heat until you can smell them and dry them a bit further." Cumin has a distinct scent, at once reminiscent of a pot of chili and falafel. It's a common ingredient in both Tex-Mex and Middle Eastern cuisine, arguably one of the few things those two regions have in common.

When the toasting was over, Robin grabbed the large gray marble mortar and pestle from the kitchen's spice rack. She combined a few pinches of both the toasted cardamom and the toasted cumin in the heavy bowl along with some coarse salt and whole peppercorns. "Who owns a mortar and pestle?" she asked. "These are a great investment," she said as she put her weight into the pestle, crunching and crushing the whole seeds into the bottom until they crumbled into dust. "You know, you can get one for about ten bucks. You can buy whole spices and then grind them up. They'll store longer and taste fresher. Plus it's therapeutic, a great way to take out the frustration of a bad day."

Robin put a spoonful of the powder on a plate. She instructed them to smell or taste it and passed it around the table. "It's really powerful, almost pungent," Shannon said. "That's just something that I would never have thought to do."

"Now we want you to make your own," Robin said. "Just think of flavors you like. Your taste is something to listen to. Trust your instincts," she said. In many ways, it was a reprise of the vinaigrette lesson, but this time without oil or vinegar. "Be bold," Robin advised. "Experiment. Strong flavors make good rubs."

As she talked, Lisa and I had gathered up all the various dried herbs and spices in the kitchen and put them into a jumble on the worktable. At Robin's invitation, the women exploded with activity, grabbing for jars and canisters, inhaling deeply, rejecting or selecting one here and there to spoon onto their plates. A few took turns at the mortar and pestle. Everyone seemed happy and talkative yet mindful of their own creative mission, rather like kindergartners at art time. "Taste it," Robin said. "If it's strong or spicy, just put a tiny bit on the end of your tongue."

Dri and Jodi looked at each other as they daintily tasted a dab and started laughing at the sight of their outstretched tongues. "Tongues are *so* not attractive," Jodi said, once she regained her composure. "But this cumin tastes yummy."

Each person coated a small piece of steak or a pork chop with her spice rub. One by one they rotated through the grill. "The key to grilling something like this is to start it hot," Robin said, swirling her tongs around the preheated portion of the commercial grill. "You want to sear it on one side until it's slightly caramelized with a good brown color, but then move it off the fire to a cooler spot and cover it. Do the same for the other side."

Gen shrugged. "That explains why I always end up with charred meat. I must be leaving it on the actual fire for too long," she said, which led to a lot of discussion around grilling mishaps.

Once again, Maggie put a piece of tape with each person's name onto a plate. As the meat came off the grill, each of the volunteers took a bite of her own and then passed it on. The rubs varied from a fiery combination of cumin, cayenne, and oregano to a sweet one seasoned with cardamom, brown sugar, and cinnamon. "The great thing about rubs is that you can use them on anything, even vegetables. They're good for last-minute seasoning and they can be simple or complex. Just trust yourself," Robin said.

One by one, Lisa and I pulled the hot pans with the braised pork from the oven. The heat from the center of the table felt as if we'd set a fire. Each person claimed hers and tasted.

"This is great," Jodi said of the pork. "It tastes . . . I don't know, like *home*. Does that make any sense?" Everyone went quiet, eating. She noticed. "Wow, this must be good. No one is saying anything."

"This is better than food that I've had at a restaurant, and I made it. I mean, really made it, from scratch. Cutting up the meat, everything," Dri said. "It makes me feel like I'm cooking *Top Chef* food or something." It was an offhand reference, but particularly amusing given that we had a cheftestant teaching the class.

Everyone thanked Robin profusely. As she packed up her knives and we cleaned, we tried to pry some gossip about the season from her. Robin wouldn't share anything other than that she was the only contestant who didn't have a culinary degree. In past seasons, that had always been an obstacle. No one without a culinary degree had ever won. Robin had never worked in fine dining, nor did her résumé include a stint under a famous chef.

"All I can say is that my food is heartfelt and not pretentious because that's who I am, so that's the way that I cook. That's what you'll see."

That season I watched Robin struggle on *Top Chef*. Her lack of culinary training did put her at a disadvantage at times when challenges called for complex dishes with tactics such as deconstruction or refined haute cuisine techniques. She was criticized more harshly by her fellow contenders than she was by any of the celebrity judges. At one point, I cringed when a chef in his twenties referred to her as "Grandma"; Robin and I are around the same age. Another complained that she wasn't even "a real chef."

What defines a chef, anyway? What defines any of us? I had a culinary degree, but Robin had spent a dozen years cooking in the culinary industry and owned a successful restaurant for five of those.

If lack of a culinary degree disqualifies, what about all the Michelin-ranked chefs who worked their way up the food chain as apprentices?

It takes guts to go on a national reality show, especially one essentially devoted to fetishizing the entire concept of cooking. It was that foodie bubble all over again. In my kitchen, she was generous with her knowledge, patient, and encouraging. It struck me that in a curious way Robin could be a stand-in for home cooks looked down on by culinary elitists.

I thought back to the original questionnaires. Shannon's mother had snipped that she burned everything, but in the space of six weeks, I'd seen no evidence of anything other than someone with terrific curiosity and an unrealized natural talent in the kitchen. Another person had admitted that she ate Tuna Helper while watching Gordon Ramsay. When I pressed her for a reason why, she responded that cooking felt beyond her reach and not worth attempting. She was so discouraged by her cooking skills that she declined to be a part of the project—and it was *free*.

"I think that one of the things that has ruined home cooking are the TV cooking shows," said veteran cookbook author Rick Rodgers. In his life, he's taught more than five hundred cooking classes and met his share of struggling cooks. "First, the majority of the shows teach lots of stuff but cooking is not one of them." When he sees twentysomethings obsessing about foam or rushing around the kitchen in a competitive cooking challenge, "it's kind of like watching pornography. I think I'd love to do that, but I'm afraid I'll throw out my back."

I suppose that's what made Julia Child so endearing. Not long after the meat class, I looked up the episode of *The French Chef* in which she attempts to flip a pan-sized disk of potatoes. "When you flip anything, you just have to have the courage of your convictions," she stated, even though she looked less than convinced that the whole thing was going to work. She gave the pan a shake and a hearty flip, but rather than landing neatly back in the pan, half of its contents fell and splattered on the stovetop. As she investigated the fallen pieces, she explained what went wrong. "When I flipped it, I didn't have the courage to do it the way I should have. You can always pick it up."

Then came the moment that sealed her fans for a lifetime: "Besides, if you're alone in the kitchen, who is going to see?"

"Julia's little kitchen catastrophe was a liberation and a lesson," wrote Michael Pollan in a story on the decline of home cooking in *The New York Times* in 2009. She offered a simple but obvious observation. "The only way you learn to flip things is to just flip them! It was a kind of courage—not only to cook but to cook the world's most glamorous and intimidating cuisine—that Julia Child gave my mother and so many other women like her."

Perhaps that was her greatest contribution. She didn't limit herself to offering instructions on how to execute a particular dish, but instead imparted a more generalized sense of courage for cooks willing to navigate unfamiliar culinary terrain.

How often are we rewarded for going off the map anymore? Or given the freedom to trust ourselves and the permission to make mistakes, cooking or otherwise? My mother has many phrases, two worth noting here. "Who says you can't?" with emphasis on the "who" was her invariable refrain whenever any of her kids alleged that something simply couldn't be done. The other: "In a hundred years, no one will know the difference."

So *who* says you can't cook? Not every meal has to be from scratch, nor does everything you consume have to be organic, locally sourced, and pasture raised. Try to find a comfortable place somewhere between Tuna Helper and *Top Chef*. If you burn, scorch, drop, overcook, undercook, underseason, or otherwise put a meal together that's less than a success, in the end it doesn't matter. It's just one meal. You'll make another one tomorrow. In a hundred years, no one will know the difference.

~~~~~~

ᕗ Your Basic Braise

The term "braise" promotes much confusion, yet it simply means to cover and simmer something with a bit of liquid so that it cooks slowly with moist heat. Braising can yield comfort foods on many levels; a traditional pot roast is a simple braise; so is beef bourguignon.

There are plenty of reasons to add braising to your bag of culinary tricks. Long, slow cooking provides great meals from the most inexpensive cuts of meat by gently breaking down the connective tissue, yielding a tender, flavorful result. Second, once you put it in the oven, it's pretty much on autopilot, leaving time to devote to other tasks or pleasures. Braises provide a star turn for entertaining, as most can be made a day ahead and reheated. Leftover braised meats can be used in a variety of ways, from inclusion in tacos or burritos to folding into omelets or scrambling with eggs, or they can be added to soups, beans dishes, salads, pasta, or sandwiches. Braising infuses great flavor into vegetables for side dishes, too, notably carrots, asparagus, green beans, onions, leeks, and Brussels sprouts. In a skillet, lightly brown vegetables in butter or oil, add a bit of water, stock, or wine, cover, and simmer for about 20 minutes or until tender.

The Basic Technique

❧ Season the main ingredient with coarse salt and ground pepper.

❧ Brown the meat thoroughly in oil over medium-high heat.

❧ Sauté a mix of aromatics, such as onions, garlic, shallots, leeks, carrot, or celery, or even fruit, such as apples or pears, in some oil.

❧ Add some liquid, such as water, stock, or wine. Stir to scrape up any browned bits on the bottom of the pan; this is known as "deglazing."

❧ Return the meat to the pan and cook until thoroughly tender, from 2 to 5 hours.

❧ If desired, take out the meat, vegetables, or fruit from the pan and remove any extraneous fat. Thicken the sauce by boiling it until some evaporates; this is known as "reducing."

A Few Tips

❧ Use a heavy pan with a tight-fitting lid (see note on Dutch ovens on page 171).

❧ Don't use bouillon cubes in place of stock; the result will be too salty. If you don't have stock, use water instead.

❧ Tougher cuts of meat, such as shoulder roasts, short ribs, brisket, and shanks, work best for braising. Whole chickens or dark poultry braise beautifully; boneless chicken or turkey breasts tend to overcook and stiffen.

❧ You can simply focus on braising meat, or extend it with vegetables, such as potatoes, cabbage, carrots, leeks, parsnips, or squash. Vegetables cook faster than the meat, so add them during the last hour of the cooking process. Here's an example:

ᕬ Braised Pork with Potatoes and Cabbage

Not enough people braise pork, yet it's an inexpensive dish resulting in deeply useful leftovers. You can replace the pork with beef, chicken thighs, or even a couple of meaty lamb shanks. If the meat is on the bone, leave it. If you start with a larger piece, just try to cut the meat into chunks roughly the same size so that they cook evenly, and trim off excess fat. This can be served alone or pairs nicely with wide pasta noodles or mashed potatoes.

SERVES ABOUT 6 WITH GENEROUS LEFTOVERS

3 tablespoons vegetable oil
About a 3-pound piece of pork shoulder or picnic ham, cut into
    1- to 2-inch cubes
Coarse salt and freshly ground black pepper
1 large onion, chopped (about 1½ cups)
2 carrots, chopped (about 1 cup)
2 stems of celery, chopped (about 1 cup)
4 garlic cloves, peeled
1 bay leaf
Several sprigs fresh thyme, or 1 teaspoon dried thyme
About 1½ cups chicken stock or water

Vegetables

½ head cabbage, shredded or sliced thin (about 8 ounces)
2 to 3 large tomatoes, diced, or one 14-ounce can diced tomatoes
1 large potato, peeled and cubed (about 1½ cups)

❧ Preheat the oven to 325°F. Heat 2 tablespoons of oil in a 5-quart Dutch oven over medium-high heat. Season the meat with coarse salt and freshly ground black pepper. When the oil is hot, add the cubes of pork, working in batches if needed to avoid crowding, which will steam the meat rather than brown it. Brown well, about 3 to 6 minutes per side. Remove all the meat from the pan and set aside. Add or remove oil so that there are about 2 tablespoons in the pan. Reduce the heat to medium.

❧ Add the onion, carrots, celery, garlic, bay leaf, and thyme. Sauté until the vegetables are soft. Add the browned pork and enough stock or water to come to the top of the meat. Stir and scrape up any browned bits on the bottom of the pan. Cover and put the pot into the oven to simmer for about 2 to 2½ hours, or until the meat is tender enough to cut with a fork.

❧ Add the shredded or sliced cabbage, tomatoes, and potatoes to the pot, then return it to the oven for about 35 to 45 minutes, until the cabbage is tender. Remove the bay leaf before serving. Taste to see if it needs salt and pepper before serving.

A Note on Dutch Ovens

A Dutch oven is a squat, thick-walled cooking pot with a tight-fitting lid. You can buy an enamel-coated steel number for as little as fifteen dollars, but for the quality and longevity, I recommend cast iron. A standard black preseasoned five-quart version can be had for thirty dollars, while enamel-coated cast iron varieties start at sixty dollars. Both varieties will last a lifetime with proper care.

The Red Velvet Dinners

To Pay for the Classes, I Invite You to a Series of Unusual Communal Dinners

☙ By the end of July, the bills for the class project started to mount. The rent for the Post-it notes kitchen, the barely above minimum wages for Lisa and Maggie, and the costs for food, business insurance, and even linens such as cloth diapers added up to a couple of thousand dollars. Meanwhile, I'd donated more cooking-class dinners to charity; one fetched thirty-four hundred dollars. The dinners promised to combine elements of the project, including a brief cooking or tasting lesson and dinner. Of course, since they were donations, all those same costs would apply—out of our pocket—to the tune of a few hundred dollars per dinner. Mike and I had a discussion about the mounting costs.

"It's a nonprofit research endeavor," I said, making the case for the project. "And those dinners are for good causes."

"*We're* not a charity," Mike said. "How are we going to cover all this?"

My culinary-school friend who had led me to the teaching kitchen, Anne-Catherine, had offered communal dinners in the space and had made a small profit. Another friend had done the same on Vashon Island. A communal dinner simply means that everyone shares one big table. No tables for two or four, but rather tables for twelve or twenty or thirty-two, with one menu shared family style. I decided to try a few dinners to raise money for our little charity project. We'd ask people to bring their own wine and suggest a donation. The first was nothing short of a haphazard affair.

Mike arranged the tables and chairs the catering company used for events. Jeff ironed white linen tablecloths to an immaculate finish and artfully crafted bits of the lavender growing outside into small glasses and littered the table with tea lights. The result resembled a *Martha Stewart Living* magazine spread.

By coincidence (or fate?), we held the dinner on what would have been Julia Child's ninety-seventh birthday. I expected fourteen guests, yet twenty-two showed up. I forgot to add salt to the dough, so even though Mike led a great lesson on fashioning lovely loaves, the final bread had little flavor. My chef friend Ted and I hustled to cook the food, but the scene took on a strange Keystone Kops aura. We bought six dozen oysters but forgot to pack an oyster knife. The pilot light went out on the stove and we struggled to figure out how to relight it. Once Ted and Mike got started, my side towel caught fire. I dropped a huge vat of cooked green beans on the floor. The sole meunière fell into pieces as we started to cook it. We served the final dishes around eleven P.M.

Due to the steady stream of wine, few seemed to mind the lateness of the dinner as most everyone was hammered by the time the food hit the table. Due to clumsy execution, we collected less than we needed to cover the cost of the food, much less earn anything toward the project.

Julia Child consoled chefs by reminding them that they were alone in the kitchen, but this was not true in ours. The small dining room was open to the entire kitchen, so there was no escape. Before the next dinner, Mike engineered ceiling-to-floor-length inexpensive red velvet curtains from IKEA along the length of the kitchen to separate the cooking area from the tables. As he stood back to evaluate whether he needed to improve the torque to keep the heavy curtains level, Jeff stood next to him. Mike asked him whether perhaps he needed a turnbuckle, a piece of hardware, to keep the line straight. Jeff responded that the drapes needed more pleats.

"Pleats?" Mike's voice scaled up.

"Oh, yeah, I think they're tight enough, they just need more pleats. I can take care of it," he said. "My sisters and I used to put on musicals when we were kids. My job was always fixing the sheets so they looked a bit fuller when we used them as curtains. If the pleats aren't even, they look cheap." He borrowed our car to hit a store for small clamps and then spent the next ninety minutes moving a stool along the length of the curtain, painstakingly adding perfect pleats. I have to admit, the result looked fabulous. With that, the Red Velvet Dinners were born.

After the dubious start, I strategized the next dinners as if executing a battle plan. In earlier years, I'd been known for over-the-top dinner parties, and even then I planned the menus weeks in advance. Invariably, though, the party buzzed in the kitchen, drinks took prominence, and dinner arrived on the table late, often very late.

When someone pays for a meal, it's different. An entrée served hours late isn't charming; it simply shows you failed to plan. The French chefs would not be pleased. Learning as we went along, we became more proficient at performance. Maggie and Jeff, both experienced kitchen hands, agreed to help prep food and manage the tables. I made time lines, schedules, and multiple versions of the menu. I even started to litter the kitchen with my own Post-it notes. "Do NOT touch dough. For RVD only!" The menu for the first series included the following:

Salt tasting
Calvados and peach sorbet (palate cleanser)
Fresh sweet corn soup with chili oil and seared scallops
Pear and lemon verbena sorbet
Artisanal beef tasting
Seasonal green salad with local goat cheese and cherry vinaigrette
A cheese tasting with savory tart and fresh fruit

The red curtain invited something . . . sexy. We decided to add an "entertainment" to the dinners. "What about burlesque to go with the steaks? Kind of fits, doesn't it?" asked my friend Deirdre. She'd recently directed a documentary on the neoburlesque movement, and she knew all the best performers in town. She helped me arrange for The Shanghai Pearl, a nationally known burlesque artist, to perform during a break in the dinner.

For the beef tasting, a friend organized a variety of grass-fed beef options. Ted set his own Weber grill on the sidewalk in front of the storefront, tasked with cooking twelve steaks from four different purveyors to exactly the same degree; it was so complicated, it would likely have been easier to dribble three basketballs at once.

The lovely Shanghai was no diva. The first night, she arrived at the back door in jeans and a simple T-shirt, an odd combination with her intense stage makeup, which included bright blue drag-queen-like eye shadow and glitter lipstick, and a complicated updo. "I'm so sorry, I've lost my voice," she whispered hoarsely. She held up a bulky garment bag. "Where can I change?" I directed her to the bathroom. "Oh, here's my music." She went to change. I turned to give the CD to Mike, who was managing the audio. Instead, I bumped into Ted, lurking in the rear of the kitchen with a postgrilling glass of Syrah in hand.

He looked awestruck. "Uh, wow, she's, um . . . ravishing."

Moments later, Shanghai emerged in a scarlet-sequined hip-slit burlesque costume strutting in five-inch heels with two large red plume fans balanced in one hand. A massive blood-red flowery ostrich plume sprouted from the side of her head. Ted tried to look casual as she readied herself behind the red velvet curtain. She turned to him. "Do you think you could hold these fans and hand them to me on cue?" she whispered hoarsely. "When I've stripped, can I hand you my dress? Do you mind?"

Ted stared at her and nodded without blinking. "Yes, I think I can handle that."

He took the job seriously, watching transfixed as the dancer bumped, grinded, and charmed the tiny audience around the long table while she strutted through her set. As she discarded gloves, garters, and portions of her dress, Ted dutifully caught them and carefully smoothed them over his arms. She concluded by removing a tiny red silk bra to reveal bright silver pasties and bowed in time to finish with her music. The dinner guests exploded in cheers. Nothing completes a dinner like a beautiful naked woman. As she returned behind the curtains, Ted handed her back her dress and accoutrements. "I can do this anytime you want," he assured her earnestly.

Maggie, Jeff, and I watched from the sidelines, clutching tumblers of wine. As her act concluded, Maggie leaned in to me. "I'm fairly sure that after The Shanghai Pearl, no one is going to remember any of the food," she said. "I mean that in a really nice way."

Empowered by that success, we developed more dinners. Demand overwhelmed the seats available. At first, the dinners were open to friends only, then friends of friends. Then we invited people to get on "the list." Within a week, we had 370 names.

Six of those with reservations could opt to come early to help prepare dinner via a cooking lesson. After they chopped vegetables, plated the cheese course, or made pasta, they then sat with the rest of the patrons for the five- or seven-course dinner. All of them followed a variation of the first dinner: a main course that featured a comparative tasting, such as oysters, salmon, or differently raised types of poultry. Each featured an entertainment—usually live music, but once we brought in a tarot card reader.

For Halloween, we took the Red Velvet Dinners on the road to the upper floor of the Richard Hugo House, a literary center set in a rambling 1902 Victorian that once served as the city morgue. The house has been featured in news outlets from ABC's *Nightline* to National Public Radio for one simple attraction—it's haunted.

I did not know this minor fact when I rented a writing cubicle situated in the former morgue. I heard whispers past midnight. Doors slammed when no one was around. At two o'clock one morning, I caught the sound of what sounded like silverware rattling atop something metallic. It's such a cliché, but the hair on my neck did, in fact, stand straight up. Later, I understood the sound when I heard the clang of medical instruments atop a tray at my dentist's office. The next day, I put my name in to transfer to a different writing office.

For the masquerade dinner, we shifted the drab six-foot classroom tables into one comically long dining tabletop set with three-foot-high candelabras, immaculate linens, and the ramshackle mismatched thrift-store plates, forks, and glassware from the center's own kitchen. All twenty-eight guests arrived in costume and character for a mystery dinner, masks intact. Hugo House doesn't have much of a kitchen, so we stuck to an elegant yet simple menu:

Trays of figs, duck liver pâté, olives, assorted soft cheeses
Cassoulet with duck confit, garlic sausage, and braised lamb
Autumn green salad with Riesling-soaked pears
Apple tarte Tatin with brandy sauce

That night's cassoulet dinner by candlelight had an air of sensuality. Champagne flowed. People flirted behind their masks. As everyone dug into three steaming vats of the traditional French white bean casserole and started to eat, the room went eerily quiet. A door slammed somewhere unexpectedly. Everyone suddenly looked around, startled. "I think I left a window open in the other room," I said. Everyone returned to their dinner.

I never left a window open. But how do you tell people that it might be the sign of a ghost signaling his displeasure at failing to get an invite?

The last of the series featured an Italian theme. The evening included an olive oil and olive tasting, plus handmade pasta in a fragrant saffron broth with shrimp and tomatoes, a reprise of something I'd taught during the hands-on classes on the cruise earlier that summer. The scheduled entertainment was an opera singer performing excerpts from the works of Italian-born composer Giacomo Puccini.

It was a last supper, so I invited all the guests into the kitchen early to cook, and more than a dozen of them took me up on it. I'd developed the recipe as a lesson on tackling that issue so often mentioned by the volunteers: How do you keep a recipe from tasting bland?

After everyone helped to make the pasta and left it to dry on trays stacked on the counter, I discussed some classic seasoning points from Italian cooking. "Buy a basil plant and keep it in your kitchen window all year long," I started. "You can just pull off a few leaves at a time and it will add freshness to the end of a dish, and it won't die in the bottom of your crisper. While you're at it, consider getting a thyme plant, too." Next tip, keep lemons or limes on hand; the acid brightens flavor. Garlic adds bite and hot chili adds punch.

I made one very bland plate of pasta and let everyone taste it. Then we divvied the pasta into three bowls and let them experiment with shifting the flavor by adding lemon, fresh herbs, and hot chili. In another batch, this time dosed with garlic. "Wow, this is pretty boring without garlic," one guy said.

"*Life* is boring without garlic," replied another.

Afterward, as the "cooks" took off their aprons to take their seats at the tables with the other guests, a woman approached me. "I can't get over how the lemon and the garlic changed everything," she said. "I can't tell you how often I make a recipe and it's kind of blah. It will need *something,* but I can't figure out what, and, well, I've always been kind of afraid to add anything because I'm afraid I'll screw it up."

As a little girl, I used to play restaurant, and in some ways, this was simply the big-girl version. With each dinner, I gained more confidence in the kitchen. I managed a regular crew, and we bonded in our kitchen camaraderie, quietly plating entrées behind the curtains. The dinners required developing menus, managing food costs and budget, and the full responsibility of what went right or wrong.

For the first time, I felt like I was starting to earn the title of chef, whatever that meant. The odd thing was that just as I thought that I might warrant it, I decided it wasn't all that important anymore.

Spicy Shrimp in Saffron Tomato Sauce

To appear short, many recipes for "quick" meals often leave off steps that would upgrade the flavor. This recipe utilizes four important concepts to awaken otherwise bland dishes: fresh herbs, acid, garlic, and spice. Frozen shrimp is a great freezer staple, but try to opt for wild-caught North American shrimp over Asian farmed varieties. If you can find only peeled shrimp, c'est la vie. This recipe cooks quickly, so be sure to prep and measure all the ingredients in advance. This is equally charming served over fettuccine pasta, basmati rice, or saffron rice. No shrimp? You can substitute bay scallops (take care not to overcook them), a solid white fish (such as cod), extra-firm tofu, or boneless chicken breasts cut into half-inch cubes. You can substitute turmeric for saffron and dill or cilantro in place of the basil.

SERVES 4

1 pound uncooked large shrimp
½ cup chicken stock or water
2 teaspoons plus 1½ tablespoons olive oil
Coarse salt and freshly ground black pepper
½ teaspoon red pepper flakes
Half a lemon
½ cup dry white wine or vermouth
Pinch of saffron threads
2 or 3 large garlic cloves, minced
1 tablespoon tomato paste
One 14½-ounce can diced peeled tomatoes in juice
1½ teaspoons dried oregano or mixed Italian herbs
Handful of minced basil or flat-leaf parsley

❧ Peel the shrimp. Add the shrimp shells to the chicken stock or water and simmer until needed. Toss the shrimp with 2 teaspoons of the olive oil, a couple of pinches of coarse salt, a few grinds of black pepper, the red pepper flakes, and a squeeze of juice from the lemon half. Combine the wine and saffron.

❧ Heat $1\frac{1}{2}$ tablespoons of olive oil in a large sauté pan over medium-high heat. Cook the shrimp until they are opaque, about 2 to 3 minutes, then transfer them to a bowl with a slotted spoon or tongs. Add a bit more oil to the pan if necessary. Cook the garlic for about 1 minute, then add the tomato paste and the wine and saffron, and cook for about 3 minutes, until some of it evaporates.

❧ Remove the shells from the stock with a slotted spoon and add the liquid to the sauce. Next add the tomatoes and dried herbs. Continue to cook over medium-high heat, stirring frequently, about 8 minutes, until it is reduced to a saucelike consistency. Taste to see if it needs more salt or pepper.

❧ Add the cooked shrimp and simmer until they're heated through, about a minute or two. Remove from the heat, then stir in the minced basil or parsley and add a few squeezes of lemon over the top. Serve over hot pasta or rice.

Easy Habits for Good Flavor

These "tricks" are the kinds of things chefs do to elevate what could be a bland dish into something much more satisfying:

❧ Preseason protein with a few simple seasonings before cooking, such as a bit of olive oil, coarse salt, pepper, simple herbs or seasonings, a squeeze of citrus, or a splash of vinegar.

❧ Use fresh garlic. It adds punch the way jarred garlic doesn't. Some markets offer cloves of peeled garlic as a time saver; they are commonly used in professional kitchens.

❧ Spice it up. Many cuisines add spicy ingredients as an inexpensive way to add a sassy, satisfying note to otherwise simple dishes.

❧ Finish dishes with a "bright" flavor at the end. Normally this is a bit of acid and/or an herb, in this case lemon and fresh herbs. Small amounts of vinegar, especially flavored ones, can add a lot of flavor in a finished dish.

PART III

Seafood, Soup, and the Importance of Leftovers

"So long, and thanks for all the fish."
—Douglas Adams

Donna and Dri with their fish

CHAPTER 10

ʕʔ

The Pleasures of the Fish

ʕ LESSON HIGHLIGHTS:
How to Buy Fish, Plus Plenty of Ways to Cook It

One of the first things I discovered about Mike was that he didn't like fish. Sure, he was a fan of fish and chips, but most people would probably eat a brick if it was deep-fried. In Paris, when I brought home a complicated dish from culinary school featuring monkfish stuffed with delicate crab meat and wrapped in prosciutto coupled with a beurre blanc sauce, he simply said, "It's not bad. It tastes like chicken."

In the years since, he's warmed up to fish. But the reasons for his initial resistance were often expressed by many of the volunteers. They felt uncomfortable selecting seafood, and I suspected this led to the inadvertent purchase of lower-quality fish. They told tales of fish stinking up kitchens and relentlessly overcooked fillets that turned out too tough, too oily, or too bland.

North Americans eat relatively little seafood, about sixteen pounds total per capita per year, a paltry showing compared to the sixty-plus pounds of chicken we consume each year. Just 7 percent of our diet includes fish and shellfish. By comparison, it makes up more than 25 percent of that in Asian countries. Most health-care experts suggest increasing fish consumption to ensure adequate levels of omega-3 fatty acids. A growing body of research suggests that omega-3 can help deflect everything from heart disease to stroke, Alzheimer's disease, cancer, and even clinical depression.

I was gung ho on teaching a class about fish—until I went to see a screening of the utterly depressing documentary *The End of the Line*. If you're unfamiliar with this, it focuses on the havoc wreaked on various fish species due to commercial overfishing and is often referred to as *An Inconvenient Truth* for the oceans. Overfishing happens based on consumer whims. Take the blackened redfish craze that gripped the nation in the 1980s. To feed the extraordinary and sudden demand from restaurants and retailers, commercial netters caught redfish by the millions, devastating the species within the space of a few years. When Chilean sea bass* ended up on every menu years later, the same thing happened. More than twenty species are included on various overfished lists.

So my initial enthusiasm shifted into a dilemma: Should I even do a class on fish? Most of the students commented that they might eat more if they knew how to make it.

"Are you kidding? You have to do a class on fish," Lisa said. "This is Seattle. The airport has bronze salmon embedded in the floor. Why don't you bring in Ted as a guest teacher? He's a total Jedi master when it comes to fish."

I mention my chef friend Ted often but fail to point out that he trained at the Culinary Institute of America and spent a dozen years in the industry. His early career during the 1980s involved catering for the PBS channel in Boston. As a result, two of the regular visitors to his kitchen were Paul and Julia Child. "She'd come in and ask, 'What are you making, Chef?' But then she'd have to go out and mingle," he told me. "You could tell she'd rather have been in the kitchen." Although he's now a financial consultant to the tech industry, Ted never lost his appetite for the kitchen.

Several of the volunteers arrived early. I took it as a chance to catch up with them as Ted, Jeff, and Maggie set everything up.

"So we've started to buy vegetables regularly from this farm stand

*On page 200 of my first book, *The Sharper Your Knife, the Less You Cry,* I call for Chilean sea bass in a recipe. I suggest you try another responsibly caught whitefish instead. Thanks.

near our house," Gen said. "We told them we were going to a Mexican-themed party that night. Seriously, you should have seen the reaction from the owner!" She seemed anxious to tell the story. "He and his wife went back and forth, insisting that we had to make this amazing sangria from a recipe his grandmother brought from Peru."

The farm-stand owners gave Gen the recipe and helped the pair organize all the stuff to make the sangria. Just when they wondered if perhaps it was a grand marketing ploy to persuade them to purchase extra produce, the owner asked if they wanted any tamales. "They were making tamales for this big party. We said sure, we'd try some. They gave us this huge bag of tamales for free."

Gen and her boyfriend rushed home. "We were using this big wine jug for the sangria, trying to shove the fruit through the itty-bitty hole at the top," she said, pantomiming the scene and laughing. "It was kind of chaos. We had to cook all these tamales and make the sangria and rush to the party." But they were the hit of the night. People were impressed.

"It's funny, but that made me realize that there's a whole world beyond the supermarket," Gen said. "That kind of interaction would not happen at a grocery store. I feel like I've made friends with them. We're part of this little community. It's really kind of cool, and I don't know, this sounds sort of dorky but it makes me feel like, wow, cooking can be fun in a way I never imagined."

Jodi had arrived in time to hear the end of Gen's story. She joined the discussion.

"That's so crazy you just used the word *fun*," Jodi said. The past weekend, her friend had come over to cook to see what she was learning from the project. "After an hour of cooking together, my friend turned to me and said, 'Hey. What's up with you? I can just feel the tension! You are like a madwoman. Cooking is supposed to be fun!'"

Jodi said that she looked at her friend, sipping wine and relaxing. "It just kind of hit me. I realized that cooking is not supposed to be so stressful. Why do I put myself through all this anxiety? There was always a part of me that worried about screwing something up. But at that moment, I don't know, I just had this moment of clarity." She paused a minute. "God, I sound so confessional!"

Just then, Maggie clapped her hands. "Ladies? We have some salmon for you to taste."

Ted had sautéed five pieces and placed them in a line from least to most expensive: farm-raised Atlantic,* keta,† sockeye, coho, and king. Side by side, they looked remarkably different. The keta and Atlantic versions appeared pale, while the sockeye was a vivid orange-red, its denser meat marked by thick waves. The coho was almost magenta. Meanwhile, the king had the deep color of a ripe peach with a softer texture.

The group was torn on their favorite. Some preferred the "classic" salmon taste of the sockeye. Others thought the coho was more complex. "The king tastes buttery, if you can say that about a fish," Dri said. The keta and the farm-raised Atlantic were judged "meh" by the group.

As a group, we contemplated the uncooked salmon, halibut, and black cod fillets set out on the table atop a bed of ice. "The most important thing to remember is that fresh fish doesn't smell fishy," Ted said. "Take a whiff. What do you smell?" All the women leaned in. Among the responses: cucumbers, cantaloupe, sea air, the brine of an oyster. "See? No one said 'fishy.' Those are all nice, clean fragrances. That's how fresh fish should smell," he said.

Whether you buy fish at a grocery store or a dedicated market, you should ask to smell the fish first. If it's still whole, you should be able to touch it.

"If the guy at the counter doesn't grant letting you smell it without

---

*Farm-raised salmon is controversial. It takes three pounds of wild fish to grow one pound of farmed salmon, according to the Monterey Bay Aquarium. Most are farmed in open pens and cages in coastal waters, and it's easy for waste, parasites, antibiotics, and diseases from the penned fish to seep into open water. (Imported farmed shrimp has similar issues.) If you buy farmed salmon, try to stick to those that are referred to as "tank-raised" or "tank-farmed."

†Keta is the salmon formerly known as "chum." In terms of quality, it's generally considered at the bottom of the salmon totem pole.

question, find another place to buy your fish," Ted said. "Since smelling it is so important, try not to buy it wrapped in plastic. Ideally, you want to eat fish the day you buy it." If you must store whole fish, put it belly down in crushed ice, and remove the water as it melts to keep the fish relatively dry. "If you don't live somewhere where you can get good fresh seafood, fish that's been flash-frozen on the boat is a great option. That's true of shrimp, too."

As consumers, we can be part of the problem or part of the solution based on what we opt to buy. I handed out copies of the pocket guide to buying fish from Seafood Watch.* The card offers suggestions ranked as "Best Choices," "Good Alternatives," and "Avoid." Everyone perused the cards. We reviewed the fish on the table in front of us. Good choices included the wild-caught Alaskan salmon and halibut and the trout. Bad choice? The farm-raised Atlantic salmon.

I told the group that former *Gourmet* editor Ruth Reichl made a comment at a conference I attended that stuck with me. "You only get to vote for a president once every four years," Reichl said. "But you get to vote three times a day, every day, with your dollar."

Ted picked up on that. "Exactly. Ask questions. Ask them, 'Is this fresh? Is it frozen? Where is it from? How is it caught?' I personally try to avoid eating shrimp from Asia if I can help it. If that's the only kind of shrimp available, I change my meal plans."

Someone else asked about the constant refrain that eating too much fish leads to mercury poisoning. Longer-living large fish such as tuna tend to be more susceptible to mercury contamination. "I recently heard that one good rule is to avoid eating any fish that's longer than your arm," I said. "Smaller fish are good both for you and for the environment. Anchovies and sardines are wicked good for you." As with the beef discussion, we could have gone on all night. But it was time to cook. First, the crew dutifully spent a few

*Regional guides are available for download at http://seafoodwatch.org.

minutes chopping up all the necessary vegetables for the class. As they did, they chatted.

"Oh, you'll find this funny," Jodi said, clearly fine with her confessional mode now. "We were cleaning out the garage and we found one of those appliances to make roast chicken. I had forgotten about it. But now it seems strange to think that we once bought a *machine* to make roast chicken knowing what I know now."

Sabra said that she and a friend had started to cook together once a week. "Yeah, it's pretty cool. My friend comes over and we cook. This week we made beef stew and it was pretty awesome." Then she looked around. "Oh, is that it? No more vegetables?"

We started with a dish that I learned from an Italian friend I met in London. In a roasting pan, I added handfuls of freshly sliced red pepper, onion, asparagus stalks, garlic, and chopped black olives and covered them generously with olive oil, salt, and pepper.

"Basically, you just roast a whole bunch of vegetables, and then you nestle some fish into it," I said. "I've done it with chicken breasts, too." I put them in a hot oven to roast. "Okay, Ted, you're up."

He slapped his hands together. "Now let's fire up some fish!" He grabbed a sauté pan and heated it over one of the portable burners on the worktable. As with chicken, it's key to start it on high heat and cook it quickly to get the center hot. Ted turned up the heat on the burner and added a small pool of oil to the skillet. He coated a small halibut fillet in some flour. "This will help release it from the pan." He slapped the fillet into the skillet and it popped and hissed loudly as it hit the oil. Ted talked loudly over the sizzle. It sounded like incessant static. "Always cook the presentation side first. If there's skin, then you put the side *without* skin down first. It will get the most even heat and so it will be nicely browned."

He gave the pan a quick shake. "I'm sure you've heard this before, but if you shake right after you put it in, then it's not going to stick." He watched it closely. After about five minutes, the bottom and edges of the translucent white fish shifted to opaque. He flipped the fillet over, covered it, and turned off the heat. "For a fillet that's less than an inch thick, the heat of the pan will cook it through. Let it continue for about the same amount of time you did the other side."

"Now you need just one tool to see if the fish is done," he said, and held up his right index finger. Theatrically and with great purpose, he slowly brought it down to the top of the fish.

"It should feel firm in the center and hot to the touch." He took a fork and pulled off a section "When it comes away in layers like this, that's called 'flaking.' That's what you want." He slid the fish onto a plate.

"Now we'll make a quick sauce in the same pan." He turned the heat back on. "See, there's flour stuck to the bottom of the pan." He held it up for everyone to see. "This is what we call '*fond.*' It means foundation in French. This stuff has a lot of flavor."

He poured in a bit of white wine and it steamed immediately. "When you put cold liquid into a hot pan to release the fond, it's called 'deglazing.' I'll tell you a trick, too. It's also a way to clean out a pan that's got a lot of gunk stuck to it." He added some sliced onions, zucchini, and red bell pepper, then seasoned them with salt and pepper. After a couple of minutes, he poured it over the fish. "And bang! It's done." He clanged the pan down onto the counter. He topped the fish with some chopped basil.

"This is simple and fast. Learn to do this and you can cook a sauce from stuff in your fridge in fifteen minutes. If you don't drink wine or don't have it, a little stock, extra lemon juice, or lime juice will work, too."

Everyone tasted his dish. "Delicious!" Trish said. "I normally find halibut so boring. This is nice. And moist; the sauce really adds to it."

Dri asked if the flavor kisses we learned for chicken could work, too.

"Sure, it's the same concept," I said. "You can try it out right now. Everyone, get a partner."

Watching people cook week after week, I observed something interesting. On their own, the volunteers seemed tentative. When asked to pair in teams, the lesson went quickly and they experimented more freely. Perhaps it was the collaborative nature of cooking with someone else, or maybe it just felt like a safety net for any gaps in knowledge or confidence, or possibly both. It made me wonder if perhaps people ought to cook together more often, to spend some time socializing as they tackle a recipe. Sabra had mentioned that she had started to cook with a friend once a week. Perhaps we should all be meeting for a "cooking break" rather than coffee? Maybe mothers could cook together while their children have playdates.

My attention went back to the activity of the kitchen as each team grabbed a skillet. They carefully selected fillets as if they were either precious jewels or plastic explosives. Dri again took up residence at the big stove, with Donna working by her side. Dri felt confident with the high heat. When she saw Donna shrink back, Dri encouraged her to take over cooking the fish. They finished, each testing it with their index finger. Then they made a quick sauce with garlic, green onions, and sticks of red pepper and zucchini. As they poured it atop their fillet, they could not contain their enthusiasm.

"Check this out! We made this. It could be in a magazine." They were so proud, I got my camera and took their photo.

Sabra and Gen finished their fish so quickly that I never even saw them cook it at all. "We're just pros, that's why," Sabra explained as they nibbled at their fish. Jodi and Andra took the endeavor seriously, carefully navigating each of the steps. Ted teamed up with Trish.

"But how will I know when it's done? I don't know what it's supposed to feel like," Trish asked him. He advised that touching it regularly as it cooked to feel how the fish firmed helps to "train" the ever-sensitive index finger. Like anything, the way to cook fish well is to just do it.

As everyone finished their sauté, I pulled the roasted vegetables from the oven. They'd been in for about ten minutes. "So here's the deal. The vegetables are partially cooked. Now all you have to do is place a piece of fish on top and cover it with some hot vegetables." I laid a long piece of halibut in the center and scooped some of the vegetables over it. "We'll let it roast for another fifteen or twenty minutes and then see how it's doing."

Next, we moved onto cooking *en papillote,* or cooking in paper, a technique wildly overlooked in American households as a simple and fast cooking method, not to mention that it requires no pans, and leaves no dishes to clean. The process is simple. Put a little oil on a large piece of parchment or foil, then add some salt and pepper. Lather a thin fillet of fish with oil or butter and salt and pepper, and then add finely sliced or diced vegetables, some herbs, a bit of wine, perhaps some citrus or vinegar. Fold the parchment or foil in two and crimp the edges tightly. Put it in the oven for fifteen minutes at 400°F. This also works for thin slices of chicken.

"You want to keep the vegetables small so they cook quickly and keep the fish or chicken sliced thin," Ted explained. Then he demonstrated how to close the sides by thoroughly pinching and squeezing the edges together with his fingers. "Be sure to get a nice, tight seal so that the moisture stays trapped inside. It bakes and steams at the same time."

Each team went to work. I wandered around the table to see what they assembled with their choice of thin fillets of black cod, salmon, or snapper. Jodi and Andra added lime, ginger, shallots, rice wine vinegar, a touch of fish sauce, and chopped basil. Jen and Sabra flavored theirs with diced cherry tomatoes, finely chopped zucchini, minced garlic, chopped dill, and lemon. Dri and Donna debated. "Hmmm, would balsamic work or would it be too strong a flavor?" Dri mused. Donna thought about it.

"Let's think about what we like. The olives look good. What would go with them?"

"Tomatoes," Dri offered. From there, they each took some of the sliced vegetables to chop them even more finely. Their fish looked beautiful topped with diced olives, red peppers, onions, shallots, and basil and christened with wine and a touch of white balsamic vinegar.

Each team wrote their names on their paper packets and slid them onto a baking sheet. I pulled out the vegetables with fish and set them on the side table. "Wow, that looks amazing," Andra said. "Smells good, too." I slid the trays with the parchment into the oven.

Everyone chatted, tasting one another's food and the vegetable-roasted fish. "It's all so good, and so easy," Gen said as she sampled her own sautéed piece. "I think that I am truly going to start tackling fish more often."

About fifteen minutes later, Maggie pulled the paper-cooked fish from the oven. Each team carefully retrieved their hot portion and settled it onto a plate. On my signal, they opened their packets in unison by slashing them with a knife. Steam escaped from each and the collective smells burst around the room. Donna clapped her hands in delight.

"It's like opening a tasty present!" she exclaimed. Then the room went quiet as everyone ate. "I'm definitely doing this again!"

"No kidding, I'm doing it, too," Cheryl said. "My husband will be knocked out by this."

That evening made me think of that old saying "Give a man a fish, he eats for a day. Teach him to fish and he'll eat for a lifetime." That always struck me as such a cliché, but as I cleaned up that night I realized that these days, catching the fish isn't the issue, so teaching someone to simply cook it might accomplish the same thing.

ல Fish en Papillote, or Baked in Paper

Simple enough for weeknights and elegant enough for guests, the smell that escapes when opening the package is reason enough to try this. To ensure thorough cooking, use thin fish fillets or chicken breast slices; this works well for salmon and mild-flavored white fish such as snapper and cod. It works best in parchment paper, but you can also use aluminum foil. Use sheets at least eight by twelve inches for each individual packet. Change up the ingredients. For instance, use sesame oil in place of olive oil and add lime, cilantro, and ginger to the package for an Asian flavor. Consult the "Cheat Sheet" to Flavor Profiles in the Extra Recipes section at the back of the book for more ideas.

SERVES 2 WITH INDIVIDUAL PACKETS

$1\frac{1}{2}$ tablespoons olive oil
Salt and freshly ground black pepper
Two 4- to 6-ounce pieces of fish or thinly sliced chicken breast
Few sprigs of a fresh herb (dill, basil, thyme, rosemary, or cilantro)
Few thin lemon or lime slices or a dash of vinegar
$\frac{1}{4}$ cup white wine, water, or stock

Vegetables

About $\frac{1}{2}$ cup finely chopped or sliced vegetables (such as shallots,
   onion, garlic, zucchini, carrots, broccoli, fennel, mushrooms)
   for flavor and garnish

❧ Preheat the oven to 400°F. Start with two pieces of parchment
paper (or aluminum foil), about 10 by 12 inches each. Fold the pieces
in half. On one side of the middle crease of each piece, drizzle the
olive oil and add a pinch of salt and a couple grinds of pepper. Add
the fish or chicken and turn over to coat. Place the herbs, lemon,
wine, and vegetables on top of the fish. Fold the parchment or foil
over like a book and crimp the edges securely to avoid allowing any
liquid or steam to escape from the package during cooking. Place
the package on a baking sheet and bake for 15 minutes. Allow to sit
at least 2 minutes. Open carefully by unraveling the edges to ensure
the fish or chicken is cooked through, then serve.

CHAPTER 11

❧❧

What's in the Box?

❧ LESSON HIGHLIGHTS:
   Why It's Worth Cooking Outside the Box

A fancy KitchenAid stand mixer dominates the kitchens of most food writers I know. In an online tour of her kitchen, famous food author Amanda Hesser introduces her handsome gray model by saying, "I sometimes think of this as my third child. I use it for everything."

By contrast, we have a simple yet heavy chrome 1960s-era Hamilton Beach stand mixer. No pasta hook, no paddle, and certainly no pasta-maker attachment. Ours is limited to a set of standard beaters; its capabilities peak at "heavy mixing." The mixer is one of Mike's most cherished possessions and one of the few items inherited from his late mother. He fondly recalls scraping batter from the bowl forty years ago as the two of them made chocolate chip cookies or—his favorite—yellow cake with chocolate frosting. He cracked the eggs into the bowl. She gave him the spoon to lick. (Yes, with raw eggs. As a nation, we used to be less fastidious about such things.) It was their special time together and remains a sweet memory. Sure, the cake came from a box and the frosting came from a can, but the cake itself wasn't the point: His mother set aside time for him. His emotional connection outweighs any of the functionality that we might gain from fancy attachments. As a mixer, it works great. Although Hamilton Beach gave up on the model two decades ago, Mike lovingly maintains it, sourcing replacement parts from an obscure outpost in Ohio. So we won't be replacing the mixer, and that's absolutely fine by me.

One night after Mike got a little too worked up watching his alma mater's football team take a sound drumming, he snapped off the TV. He abruptly arose from the couch where I sat sifting through a stack of food magazines and announced, "I'm going to make a cake."

This did not surprise me. Whenever he's upset, Mike needs something constructive to do with his hands. He might disappear to rebuild a carburetor, replace a light switch, or, as in this case, bake a cake. He started to ransack the cupboards. "Hey, don't we have any cake mix?"

"We have all the stuff for cake," I replied without looking up. "Just look up a recipe."

"Really?" Mike asked. "You mean you can make a cake without a mix?"

A few minutes later, after looking up a recipe, Mike called out, "So what's in the box?"

"What are you talking about?"

He brought a printout of a recipe for yellow cake into the living room. "You've got to see this. So get this, it's just flour, eggs, baking soda, milk, sugar, and butter. But with a box you already add eggs, milk, and oil, so what's in the freakin' box?" He was agitated. "Just flour, sugar, and baking soda?"

A fundamental truth had hit him: You don't need a box to make a cake.

For the first time in his life, Mike made a cake from scratch with his mother's forty-five-year-old mixer. "So that's it? This doesn't take any longer than doing it from a mix."

As the cake baked in the oven, he had another revelation. "That's ALL that's in frosting? Seriously?" Another first for Mike with the mixer: chocolate frosting from scratch, made with confectioners' sugar, butter, vanilla, cocoa, and milk.

I'm among the minority of women who aren't keen on chocolate and cake isn't my thing, but I had to try the results. The flavor and texture of the cake were more interesting and varied than the one-note sugar sensation from a mix. "It's good, don't you think?" Mike asked as we stood at the counter contemplating the flavor. His voice had a spark of pride, and for good reason. His cake *was* good.

But that led to a great question: What *is* in the box? I went back to the supermarket.

> Sugar, enriched bleached wheat flour (flour, niacin, reduced iron, thiamine mononitrate, riboflavin, folic acid), vegetable oil shortening (partially hydrogenated soybean oil, propylene glycol mono- and diesters of fats, mono- and diglycerides), leavening (sodium bicarbonate, dicalcium phosphate, sodium aluminum phosphate, monocalcium phosphate). Contains 2% or less of: wheat starch, salt, dextrose, polyglycerol esters of fatty acids, partially hydrogenated soybean oil, cellulose gum, artificial flavors, xanthan gum, maltodextrin, modified cornstarch, colored with yellow 5 lake, red 40 lake.

Curiously, in the boxed version, sugar is the ingredient in the largest quantity. Compare that list to the ingredients from the recipe Mike used for his cake:

> Unbleached flour, sugar, milk, eggs, unsalted butter, vanilla, baking powder.

The label for the frosting was equally unsettling:

> Sugar, water, vegetable oil shortening (partially hydrogenated soybean and cottonseed oils, mono- and diglycerides, polysorbate 60), cocoa powder processed with alkali, corn syrup. Contains 2% or less of: cornstarch, salt, invert sugar, natural and artificial flavors, caramelized sugar (sugar, water), caramel color, acetic acid, preservatives (potassium sorbate), sodium acid pyrophosphate, citric acid, sodium citrate.

Mike's frosting contained only five ingredients:

Confectioners' sugar, cocoa powder, butter, evaporated milk, vanilla extract.

Again, there's no oil and no corn syrup in the recipe. The cost for the raw ingredients is roughly the same. Cake mixes aren't even big time savers. Multiple studies conducted from the 1950s onward comparing the time it takes to make a cake from scratch versus a boxed version have found that the average time savings ranges from one to six minutes. So why make cake from a box at all? As it happens, cake illustrates an interesting story about what we think about food and cooking. After World War II, food manufacturers had to figure out other ways to market all the food-science technology developed during the war for army rations. The end of the war meant the loss of a massive market. So instead they focused their sights on our mothers and grandmothers, starting a not-so-subtle decades-long campaign to convince people that at least some elements of cooking were not worth the effort, says Laura Shapiro, author of *Something from the Oven: Reinventing Dinner in 1950s America*.

"The food industry created a basic assumption about cooking generations ago, and it's now fully settled into place as reality. Cake mixes exist, therefore they are easier than real baking, therefore real baking is hard," Shapiro said. "Another factor might be that we have frozen and boxed versions of things that really *are* hard—frozen croissants, for instance—so perhaps the very fact of packaging something gives it that aura of being out of reach."

The difference between a real cake and a cake-mix cake was apparent to most women baking for their families in the fifties. "But as generation followed generation, the number of home cooks recognizing that difference dwindled," Shapiro added. Bluntly put, consumers not only get used to but prefer the flavor of the artificial version, not the real thing.

Many people believe that women started to use convenience foods in droves in the 1950s. But as Shapiro documents, women then as well as now were responsible for the vast majority of meals in homes, and they initially avoided many prepared foods for fear that they'd appear to be shirking their duty as housewives. Boxed cake mixes were a prime example. When they first hit the scene in the 1950s, a homemaker needed to add only water. Women dreaded the guilt of serving such a cake, not to mention the depressing faux egg flavor. So despite initial interest, sales remained stagnant. Researchers found that cooks wanted more involvement with their cakes in order to have the necessary pride of ownership that goes with baking. Food scientists never cared for the outcome of cakes using dried egg whites anyway, so they changed the formula so that home cooks could participate by adding eggs. How delightful! Women could have their boxed cake and contribute, too. With that subtle change, the sales of cake mixes skyrocketed.

Even now, many boxed foods require the addition of eggs, milk, butter, oil, or margarine, even though it's unnecessary given the state of food science. But by requiring those ingredients, they give the perception of "cooking" without too much fuss.

However, the "shortcut" of boxed cake mixes typically includes twenty-two to thirty-three ingredients, many of them polysyllabic chemicals. A friend of mine majored in chemistry in college and later went to work for a major food company. To this day, he refuses to eat ultraprocessed foods. One reason is that the method to approve food additives requires that individual ingredients be tested and weighed in isolation, and as a result no one has any idea how they all interact together.

"When it comes to food additives, we're the mice," he said.*

---

*Issues with food chemicals can crop up years after approval, yet the FDA lacks much power to investigate or pull approved chemicals off the shelves. Since it was introduced in 1993, consumers have filed more than four thousand complaints to the FDA about aspartame, more commonly known as NutraSweet. This chemical accounts for 70 percent of all complaints received by the agency for a variety of health

That isn't all bad. Scientists love mice. Well, they make great subjects, anyway. In *The End of Overeating,* author Dr. David A. Kessler documents the decades-long pursuit of scientists working for food manufacturers to fine-tune heavily processed and fast-food fare. Their goal: to hit a "sweet spot" of the holy trinity of fat, salt, and sugar, trying to turn just the right keys to unlock a dopamine response in your brain. Dopamine triggers neurotransmitters to provide an artificially enhanced pleasure response. Finding that combination for them is like the scene in old movies where a guy uses a stethoscope to listen for clicks in a huge bank vault. Suddenly, he hears the last click and, voilà! The safe opens.

The goal of food science isn't flavor but consumption. "When scientists say a food is palatable, they are referring primarily to its capacity to stimulate the appetite and prompt us to eat more," Kessler noted.

For example, eat a handful of blueberries and you're easily satiated by the natural sugar. Not so with an ultraprocessed frozen blueberry waffle. Even the scent that escapes the toaster has been carefully orchestrated to heighten your anticipation. Perhaps you don't even think it tastes great, yet you still want another one . . . and perhaps another one. This odd response triggered in the brain led researchers to find that rats fed a steady diet of junk food quickly become addicted to it. Waiting for their dopamine fix from high-sugar, fatty, and salty treats, they rejected their normal "rat chow." Some of them starved to death. Notably, serious habit-forming drugs such as cocaine or heroin trigger the same response in the rats.

Targeting this reaction is the reason why more than three-quarters of the sodium that Americans consume comes from ultraprocessed convenience and fast foods. Does a cup of soup really need 38 percent of an adult's recommended daily salt intake to taste good? No. Does a piece of frozen lasagna need three teaspoons of sugar, the equivalent

---

claims. It remains a controversy, with each side claiming the other doesn't have enough proof.

of the amount in a glazed doughnut? No. But both do if the manu-facturers want you to buy more soup and more lasagna.

This explains cravings for potato chips or fast food. It's also why some children reject nonprocessed food. It takes very little time for tiny haywired brains, hungry for dopamine, to reject anything other than what might match the high-fat, high-salt, and high-sugar makeup of chicken nuggets, a frozen pizza, or a box of macaroni and cheese. Jodi's son came to mind. "It's so hard," Jodi told me about trying to feed her son something other than his preferred kid's diet. "I do my freakin' best to be patient, but then we have these scenes. So I admit it, a lot of the time I just give in and give him what he wants."

Many nutritionists believe toddlers should consume no more than 1,000 milligrams of sodium a day; the USDA cites 1,500 milligrams. Yet one can of Campbell's condensed alphabet vegetable soup con-tains 2,100 milligrams. That cup of soup has a teaspoon and a half of sugar, the same amount that's in a slice of apple pie.

Most packaged foods are engineered to mimic a pharmacopoeia of flavors, even if you're expected to consciously taste only one. The more complex the flavor, the more you'll eat. This explains compli-cated variations of fried chicken or dipping sauces for chicken nug-gets. But research suggests that when one or two flavors dominate, people eat less.

"There's the obvious fact that the single most important thing about food is taste," says Dr. David Katz, author of *The Flavor Point Diet*. "If we know that limiting food to simple flavors causes people to fill up faster, it really makes sense that having a wide variety of flavors engineered into foods would make people fill up slower and need to eat more. If you are choosing simpler foods . . . you will fill up faster on fewer calories."

All of these are great reasons to learn to pay attention to labels and focus on cooking simple foods. So for the next class, I brought in Beve Kindblade. She had been a nutritionist for nineteen-plus years and I liked her pragmatic approach. The crew wouldn't be cooking, so I lured them in with dinner. But what to serve for dinner when a nutritionist comes calling? We made lentil soup and organic greens topped with a quick strawberry vinaigrette and baked up some fresh whole wheat baguette that Mike was experimenting with at home.

Beve started by casually asking the group some questions. "So just what brings you to a class like this?"

Gen went first. "So it's kind of funny, but my mother was insulted when she found out that I was taking a cooking class," she said. Growing up, her mother had asked her to make dinners on Monday nights. "She said, 'I taught you how to cook! Why do you need a class? What did I do wrong?' So I had to say, 'Oh, yes, Mom, you're right, you taught me. I just wasn't listening.'"

"Did she teach you anything?" Beve ask.

Gen thought about it. "The only thing that I really remember was tuna curry. It's a can of tuna mixed with curry powder and sour cream. But I still don't know how to make that either."

"That sounds kind of disgusting," Terri said.

"It kind of was," Gen said. "That's probably why I didn't learn to cook from her."

"I enjoy going out a lot more than I like cooking," Terri told Beve. "I feel like the hassle of cooking for just me isn't worth it. But now that I've got high blood pressure, my doctor wants me to cut sodium, and that's hard to do if you eat a lot of fast food, which I do."

"I know what you mean," Dri said. "I don't eat a lot of fast food, but I have to say that when I cook, I tend to make a lot. Maybe it's from growing up in a big family. Then I eat too much of it or I have leftovers forever."

Beve listened to all their stories with genuine interest. Then she spoke about herself, her voice full of Southern twang. Her decision to go into the field came from her own "What's in the box?" moment. Growing up in North Carolina farming country, Crisco was a pantry staple used for everything. "Heck, I even won the Crisco is Cooking Award and still have the trophy! So why would a *shortening* get me interested in nutrition, anyway? Because I asked one simple question: How is it made?" She learned that Crisco was a man-made product that shifted natural liquid plant oil into a solid that doesn't really exist in nature. "My response was, If it doesn't exist in nature, how does my body know what to *do* with it? But no one then could really answer my question. That's how my career got started."

The group paid rapt attention to the down-to-earth Beve. "My goal is to bring people back to the joy of eating. The best medicine for you is good food. I have eight hundred patients, and when I see most of them, they're wiped out." Her youngest patient is three years old; her oldest, ninety-one. She orders labs to find nutritional issues such as those involving blood sugar, vitamin D, or potassium. A couple of people nodded. Terri noted that she'd heard about vitamin D on *Oprah*. "It's funny, this kind of stuff has to get on *Oprah* or *Dr. Oz* before people start to believe it, doesn't it?"

Some of Beve's information was new to me. "If you consume coffee, you should wait an hour before you eat anything because the caffeine will stall your body from getting nutrients from the food," she said. "Increasing fiber is one of the best things you can do in your diet. If you eat pasta, make it one hundred percent whole grain. Fiber helps drop your sugar. I have one client whose weight can fluctuate by sixty pounds just based on how much rice he eats."

Most people have cravings due to deficiencies. "If you increase protein in your diet, cravings for carbohydrates and sweets go away. It doesn't matter if the protein comes from meat, fish, or beans." For people who eat meat, she suggests consuming half as much, but spending the same amount of money to buy better quality. Grass-fed beef doesn't hike up cholesterol or estrogen levels and includes more omega-3 fatty acids than traditional beef. "If you normally use a pound of ground beef in spaghetti or eat an eight-ounce steak, halve the amount and buy grass-fed beef instead."

She advocated reading labels on everything. "A 'health nut muffin' sold at a coffee shop near my office had more sugar than cake does," she said. But the name would lead one to believe that it's healthy. "You want muffins? Make your own and cut down the sugar. Learn to make your own salad dressings, too."

"We did that! I make vinaigrette all the time now," Gen piped up. "It's so easy."

Beve nodded. "Yes, it is. By learning to make some simple things you'd normally buy prepared, you'll be amazed at how easily you can avoid ingredients like high-fructose corn syrup, cornstarch, the hydrogenated oils, sodium, that sort of thing. We consume way too much soy in our diet, especially soybean oil."

Dri took a lot of notes. She had been practicing every lesson at home. Weight had been an issue for her for years, and part of her interest in cooking was to simply eat a healthier diet. "I'm finding that as I make more of my own food, I don't want some of the things that I used to eat. I mean, I look at boxes of pasta or rice dishes and I think that doesn't even appeal to me anymore."

Terri nodded. "The thing with me, though, is that I would probably not be good at memorizing a lot of rules, or I don't want to change what I'm eating too much. I mean, after listening to all this, I'm thinking that fast food, for sure, simply has to go."

Beve's basic rules were simple. "My clients can eat almost anything as long as a serving exceeds three grams of fiber and has less than six grams of sugar and more than six grams of protein. That pretty much eliminates ninety percent of the prepared stuff you find in the supermarket."

Most convenience foods fall short of the fiber requirement not only due to the nature of processing but also because the ideal shelf-stable foods lack fiber. Their softer state makes them easier to freeze and ship, as well as faster to consume. Plus fiber fills. That's not good for manufacturers who want you to eat a lot. That's their profit margin.

I had seen a presentation called "Sugar: The Bitter Truth" by Robert H. Lustig. He argues that sugar in any form is bad news. "When god made the poison, he packaged it with the antidote. Sugarcane is a stick. You can't even chew it," he said.

When I mentioned that to Beve, she agreed that everyone consumes too much sugar, often without knowing it. "Food labels don't help." Sugar is listed in grams on nutrition labels, and there's no "daily requirement" for sugar. "Why not? You don't really need fructose. You can get all the sugar you need from carbohydrates, dairy, and fruit. The last thing you need is sugar added to food. But if you're going to eat something like cake, make it from scratch, not a box." Her reasoning, in part, is that you'll see the sugar you're creaming into the butter. "Most sugar is so hidden that you never know it's there."

Lisa had been sitting next to me. She got up and started looking at the labels on various items in the kitchen. She quietly came back, sat down, and whispered, "How much sugar is in a gram, anyway?" I didn't know. I later checked. Four grams equals a teaspoon of sugar, so a tablespoon is twelve grams. As I began to routinely note the sugar on every can, jar, or bottle I picked up, I was surprised to find the sugars lurking in foods I didn't necessarily consider sweetened, such as granola bars, yogurt, or even ketchup; a tablespoon of the latter contains a full teaspoon of sugar.

Beve fielded a hail of questions. Are frozen fruits and vegetables a good choice? "Sure," Beve answered. "Sometimes frozen vegetables are actually better than fresh vegetables, as they haven't been shipped a long distance and may have more nutrients still intact."

What about fat? "Fat isn't necessarily bad. Some fats are good. I think everyone could use eating half an avocado every day," she said. "Trans fats, anything that's hydrogenated, that's not good. But you're better off eating a little fat than eating a lot of something that's nonfat. Often nonfat stuff has additional sugar in it."

Her final conclusion: It's your life. No one will judge you for ordering in a pizza every so often or if you have the occasional hit of ramen noodles for lunch. "But when it comes right down to it, Michael

Pollan had it right. Don't eat anything that your grandmother wouldn't recognize as food, or at least don't eat it all the time," Beve said. "Just eat simply. If you cook more and you think about it, even just get in the habit of reading labels, you're more than halfway there."

~~~~~~

᥍ Mike's Yellow Cake

Most off-the-shelf cake mixes are filled with excessive sugars, hydrogenated oils, and other additives. Considering that a boxed cake requires getting out a mixer or beater to add at least three ingredients, consider trying one from scratch. You can use a mesh or small-holed colander to sift the flour if you don't have a sifter. You just want to get rid of lumps and add some air. It's best to measure the flour after you've sifted it. Cake flour will yield the best results, but all-purpose flour will work if you don't have it, or make your own as noted below. Just be aware that plain all-purpose flour will result in a denser, flatter, and pale-colored cake. This is based on a recipe from the folks at Wilton, the baking and cake decorating goods company.

3 cups sifted cake flour (300 grams), or $2\frac{1}{2}$ cups sifted all-purpose
    flour (300 grams)
$2\frac{1}{4}$ teaspoons baking powder
$\frac{1}{2}$ teaspoon salt
$1\frac{3}{4}$ cups sugar
6 tablespoons unsalted, softened butter ($\frac{2}{3}$ cup or 150 grams)
$1\frac{1}{2}$ teaspoons vanilla
2 eggs
$1\frac{1}{3}$ cups milk

❧ Preheat the oven to 350°F. Grease the bottoms of two 8-inch round cake pans; line the bottoms with wax paper or parchment paper. Sift together the flour, baking powder, and salt; set aside.

❧ With an electric mixer on medium-high speed, beat the sugar and butter together until they become light and fluffy, at least 5 minutes.

Add the vanilla, then beat in the eggs one at a time until thoroughly incorporated, about 4 minutes.

✤ Next, add one-third of the flour mixture, then half the milk, then more flour mixture, then the rest of the milk, and end with the rest of the flour mixture, beating well after each addition. When it's all combined, beat for one more minute.

✤ Spread the batter evenly into the prepared pans. Bake for 25 to 35 minutes, until a wooden pick inserted in the center comes out clean. Cool for at least 10 minutes before removing from the pans. Cool completely before frosting.

Note

You can make your own version of cake flour by sifting $\frac{3}{4}$ cup all-purpose flour (84 grams) with 2 tablespoons cornstarch (15 grams) for each cup of cake flour called for in a recipe.

~~~~~~

⮳ Creamy Chocolate Frosting

Making your own frosting eliminates heavy doses of corn syrup and partially hydrogenated oils, which form the bulk of most canned frostings. If this gets too slippery for frosting a cake, toss it in the fridge for a few minutes to let it thicken. Don't skip the sifting of the sugar and cocoa as that would change the texture of the frosting. Don't bother using fancy cocoa powders or blends here; plain cocoa powder such as Hershey's will provide the best outcome.

$2\frac{3}{4}$ cup confectioners' sugar
6 tablespoons cocoa powder
6 tablespoons butter, softened
5 tablespoons evaporated or 2 percent milk
1 teaspoon vanilla extract

✤ Sift together the confectioners' sugar and cocoa; set aside.

❧ Using a mixer or a beater, cream the butter until smooth. Gradually shake in the sugar-cocoa mixture, alternating with the milk. When all is combined thoroughly, add the vanilla. Beat until light and fluffy. Add more milk or cocoa powder if needed to adjust consistency and to taste.

CHAPTER 12

෬෩

Waste Not, Want Not

෬ LESSON HIGHLIGHTS:
Using Your Leftovers Can Save Money and Help the World

For the four years I lived in London, I held a traditional Thanksgiving dinner. Most people outside North America seem confused by the whole concept. An English friend once asked, "So what does Thanksgiving have to do with the Fourth of July again?" It may take the isolation of expatriation to appreciate the curious nature of Thanksgiving. We commemorate a holiday prompted by the most puritanical of Christians with one of the seven deadly sins, gluttony.

The reason for the original Thanksgiving, at least the one attributed to the Pilgrims,* was to celebrate bounty in a time otherwise gripped by hunger, since the Puritans spent the bulk of their time and resources figuring out how to avoid starving to death.

Many things interest me about Thanksgiving. It's one of the rare opportunities when most people give genuine thought to meal planning, cook a whole animal, make a lot of food from scratch, and celebrate the use of leftovers. Part of the experience of the holiday is the nature of the feast, each person assigned a role, from setting the table to mashing potatoes to crafting a pie.

Of course, that's before everyone falls asleep in a tryptophan haze in front of the television. As my husband likes to point out, the

---

*There are other claims to the "original" Thanksgiving, both in Canada and by the Spanish in St. Augustine, Florida.

occasional Cowboys and Redskins football games scheduled on the day demonstrate just how far we've drifted from the whole concept of that first Thanksgiving with our Native American hosts.

Even as they bemoan food prices, American consumers are generally unaware that they spend less of their wages on food than any other country in the world; just under 10 percent of their paychecks.* Compare that to 1900, when 40 percent of wages went toward food. Around 1960, the first time the amount spent on food was no longer the biggest expenditure, the figure was about 25 percent. The declining cost comes with the rise of industrialization of farming practices and the shift of everything we eat—from pigs to cows to orange juice—into mass-produced merchandise.

Perhaps it's the lack of investment that leads to a cavalier attitude toward food. We may give thanks for our bounty once a year, but then as a country we collectively waste about 40 percent of the food produced for consumption the rest of the time. Anthropologist Timothy Jones spent more than a decade studying food waste. His research finds that some crops sit abandoned or unharvested in the fields where they're grown. Supermarkets or suppliers discard another few percent dismissed as too imperfect for retail. The rest—about 25 to 30 percent—we throw away at home. That food goes into landfills to rot, where it emits clouds of methane, a greenhouse gas more toxic and damaging than carbon monoxide.

"By treating edibles as a disposable commodity, we teach our children not to value food," says Jonathan Bloom, author of the book *American Wasteland: How America Throws Away Nearly Half of Its Food (and What We Can Do About It)*. He puts the figure on what we waste at more than $100 billion annually. This jived with what I found in the interviews with the volunteers and the kitchen visits and what I observed in my own house and in the homes of friends. A few of the volunteers agreed to keep a journal of what they bought,

*The U.S. Department of Labor reports that in 2008, the average American spent 5.6 percent of his or her wages on food eaten at home and 4 percent on food eaten in restaurants or fast-food joints, or a bit more than 9.6 percent total.

ate, and threw out for two weeks. The result? They reported less waste due to the guilt they felt knowing they had to write it down, but even then, an average of 18 percent of their grocery bills went into the trash.

But why do we waste so much? Both Jones and Bloom offer some interesting insights.

First, people often shop for the life they aspire to, not their real one. Everyone knows that they're supposed to eat fruit and vegetables, so we stock up on perishables. Since most people don't plan meals for the week, those beets or greens that looked so great at the farmers' market sit untouched as we end up eating convenience foods. With proper planning, buying in bulk or loading up on two-for-one deals can be a genuine money saver; without a plan, it's just a recipe to double or triple the amount of food tossed away.

Dr. Trubek from the University of Vermont has studied the activities of home cooks for years. To her, the greatest lack of skill when it comes to cooking isn't the inability to wield a knife. "Planning menus is the greatest skill that we've collectively lost," she said. "That, and what to do with leftovers." Fortunately, I found two people to help out with both subjects.

As part of my search for volunteers, I had been a guest on a radio show with celebrity chefs Tom Douglas and Thierry Rautureau. A week after the show, Chef Thierry e-mailed me. "I'm curious about your plan. Would you like some help?" As I noted earlier, Thierry hosted a regular radio segment called *What's in the Fridge?* Callers would dial in and discuss the contents of·their kitchen, and Chef Thierry would offer suggestions. Thierry had walked callers through using everything from slivers of avocado to too much zucchini to half a turkey. If anyone could inspire someone to use leftovers, he was the man.

Chef Thierry walked into our kitchen in shorts, a tasteful tropical shirt, and flip-flops, his expensive chef's jacket flung over his shoulder.

"I am here!" he announced with a flourish, smiling and extending his arm in a wide embrace. Thierry has the classic dark coloring of a Frenchman and immediately owns a room. "*Mes chéris,* do you have anything for a cocktail? Tonight is my night off."

That week, people were crazy from the heat. The temperature spiked up to 103 degrees—a record. Lisa went to five places looking for ice and found a lone bag stranded at the bottom of an ice case at a gas station. We chiseled an area out of the packed stand-up freezer for our sacred bag. We presented him with a bowl of it and led him over to the fridge. Jeff and Mike moved around the table and chairs to set up an ersatz demo area as Thierry demonstrated his first use of leftovers, a pitcher of cocktails from remnant vodka, vermouth, and limes. He held up his glass and smacked his lips after tasting his creation. "Ah! *Fantastique!* Now I can talk leftovers!"

For him, teaching people not to waste food is personal. He grew up on a small farm in the Muscadet region of France in an area where cows and chickens outnumbered people. His family cooked only what they grew, and as the oldest child, Thierry routinely took on the task of helping with dinner. His family ate meat only once a week, usually on Sundays. He remembers many lean times. At age fourteen, he started an apprenticeship with a local restaurant, training that eventually took him throughout France, to Chicago, and ultimately to Seattle. One of the best meals I've had in my entire life was at his restaurant Rover's. The simple roasted squab sat in a warm bath of seafood *nage,* a kind of light broth. I qualify that meal as a near sexual experience; it was embarrassing to eat in front of the two people with me at the table. This kind of reaction may account for the popularity of his restaurants.

With a celebrity chef as a teacher, the volunteers turned up in force, a few bringing along friends or family members. As the crowd spilled in, Thierry put his chef's jacket over his shirt and downed his drink. "Ah, the chef must stay hydrated," he said as he poured another.

I welcomed everyone in. "No diapers today, you are just going to watch." Everyone took a seat.

"But I want Chef Thierry to see my knife," Sabra said, disappointment in her voice, as she sat down next to Gen.

"Oh, speaking of that, I got a new knife," Gen said. "And I just bought a whole chicken yesterday. It was so much cheaper than buying the chicken breasts already separated. My boyfriend was pretty confused about how I am going to turn this whole chicken into fajitas, but he shall soon see how it's done."

Dri piped in. "Oh, I buy them all the time now. I'm getting so fast at it. I mean, they're not the most beautiful pieces of chicken, but they taste the same, right?"

"I roasted a chicken, too," Shannon added. "And I have to say that I've rarely done that because I was so scared of undercooking it. We have two meat thermometers and neither seemed to work. One said it was 130 degrees and the other one said it was 230 degrees. I was like, What's going on with this chicken? So I pulled the legs away to check on the juices and pierced the thigh to tell if it was done. My husband was like, 'How did you know to do that?' It was like a Jedi trick or something."

"Hey, have any of you made the bread?" Trish asked. Jodi, Shannon, Dri, and Cheryl said they had at least once. "Mine didn't turn out. I wonder if my yeast was bad." As they started to discuss their various bread experiences, Chef Thierry clapped his hands at the demonstration table. Almost immediately, sweat beaded on his neck. It felt about a thousand degrees in the kitchen.

"I'm not going to turn on the stove since it's a record heat day here, yes?" said Thierry, the seasoned charmer. "So *What's in the Fridge?* is based on a very simple idea that happens in every home, even mine." People buy ingredients for a recipe but don't use them all. Or they're left with bits of random food. It's easy to throw those out.

"In America, we have a full fridge and it's so full that we can't even close the door. People look inside at this stuffed fridge and think, There's nothing to eat! I always wonder, What are you waiting for? A hand to hold out a sandwich for you? But one of the most important things to learn in life is to nourish yourself and those around

you. I've been doing it for thirty-five years, which is amazing considering that I am only thirty-nine years old!"

I mentioned to him that I had just taken part in a challenge posted
by a food writer friend, Kim O'Donnel, as part of the national movement called "Eating Down the Fridge." The idea is to avoid buying
groceries for a week, and instead try to use the remnant food instead.

"I love that!" Thierry approved. He suggested putting a favorite
photo in the back of the fridge and freezer. "You'll want to see it, and
if you can't, there's something wrong. Your fridge shouldn't be that
full."

Using up older products first is known as rotation in restaurants.
Home cooks need to learn it, he said. "Buy one pepper, not three.
Buy three potatoes, not three pounds. You'll have less waste and it
will help you as a cook.

"If you have less food in your fridge it will actually push you to
cook better. You will have to make something different. It will force
substitutions. You think, I don't have a green pepper but, oh, wait,
I have a zucchini, so I will try that. It's a good thing. That's how you
learn."

People give up on food too easily. They throw out a whole apple
due to one dent that could easily be cut away. "That zucchini that
looks a little soft today? It's like anything, like paying bills. The more
you avoid it, the worse it gets. It will never look any better. It will
just look worse in a week when you get around to throwing it out."

Thierry has some fundamental strategies. "Soup is a gift for leftovers. In the summer, I love to make cold soups; in the winter, I make
hot soups." He will unload all the unused vegetables from his fridge.
"Get half an onion, caramelize it, add your leftover vegetables, some
water or stock; it does not take long to make." Salads are big with
him. "It is easy, and it's almost like not really cooking." With that,
we went to the fridge.

Everyone shifted off their seats to the set of handsome upright
commercial fridges. By this point, we had accumulated leftovers from
all the various classes. We had also asked people to bring in leftovers.

Sabra brought in the remnants of a cheeseburger and fries; someone else brought in a hard-boiled egg; another, leftover chicken salad.

"Wow, this is so well stocked, we will eat like *cochon* tonight," Thierry said, tossing out the French word for "pig" as he pawed through the bounty, which included mushrooms, basil, garlic, eggs, lemon halves, bell peppers, a red onion, and various cheeses. "Wow, this is fun, but this is probably a lot more food than you have at home. Most of you have things more like that," he said, picking up the bit of chicken salad. "Oh, look, here's some zucchini."

Some volunteers traded glances. "We've cut up a *lot* of zucchini," Terri said.

Jeff set down a big bowl for Thierry to collect his choices from the fridge. He started dropping the produce into it. Then he came to some cream left over from last month. "Oh, this doesn't go into dinner. This should go into a museum!" he said.

He stumbled onto tomatoes. "Oh, no, tomatoes in the fridge." Uh-oh, I put those in there. "Never do this, do you know why?" he asked the group.

Trish raised her hand. "Because it kills the flavor?"

Thierry pointed at her and then slapped his hands together in affirmation. "Yes! Lemons shouldn't really go in the fridge either."

He concentrated again on the fridge and took out a nearly empty jar of mustard. He turned to the group. "Love it. This is great. You get to the bottom of a jar of mustard, you add some lemon"—he picked up half a lemon from the bowl—"and then some olive oil and shake it up. Voilà, you have vinaigrette. Or just add some vinegar and canola oil. Use what's in your house; that's the name of the game."

"We learned to make vinaigrette, but I love the tip about the mustard jar," Shannon said. "You could do that with the end of the jam in a jar, too."

"Or the end of a bottle of olive oil, since there's always some on the sides," Dri added.

I conjured up many options: the bottom of a jar of pesto, soy sauce, balsamic vinegar, or sesame oil. "That's a great tip, Chef," I said.

He stumbled onto a bouquet of parsley. "Greens, store them like flowers, the stems in some water. And a batch of parsley like this?" He held up a bunch of the green stuff. "It is a massive amount for a couple of people. Make a kind of pesto sauce with it. Chop it up in a food processor with olive oil, garlic, perhaps walnuts. Freeze it in ice cube trays. It will be a frozen cube of green. You can then take some hot, drained pasta and toss in a cube of the pesto, or you can add it to the top of steamed or roasted vegetables. You will look like Martha Stewart!"

"That could be a great flavoring for chicken," Dri observed.

His inventory complete, he brought his choices back to the demonstration table and everyone sat down again. Lisa circulated more ice water. The traffic was loud outside, so we closed the door so that Thierry could be heard, but the heat became unbearable. Thierry waved for us to open the door and just talked louder.

"It's so tempting to overbuy, but discipline yourself," he said. "Don't buy enough fruit for the next two months. Buy it just for the next two days. Just because you can buy something doesn't mean you should. That half flat of raspberries? Yes, it looks great. But that's six pints, it's a lot. You need a Plan A *and* a Plan B *and* a Plan C on what to do with that much. We've lost the art of preserving and of canning, the whole idea of harvest," he said. "There is seasonality to food, but we don't feel it. There was a tradition to get as much as you could from the harvest and save it for the year."

I thought about that point. We live in a time when you can get peaches in January in Cleveland thanks to an international transportation system that can ship food long distances. In America, food comes from sunnier states such as California and Florida, Mexico, or Central or South America. In Europe, the food comes from Spain, Turkey, or various African countries.

Thierry advised that if you buy too much, you can do home IQF, which stands for "individually quick frozen." Spread berries or vegetables on a tray, freeze them, and when frozen, put them into a plastic bag. "In January, you can pull out a handful onto your pancakes and it's summer again." He took a sip of his cold drink and mopped his face with a diaper.

All the volunteers had small legal pads. He noticed. "I see you writing. Here's an assignment. Go home. Open your fridge. Take everything out. Toss out only the truly bad expired stuff. Then come up with a plan to use what's left."

This is especially true with spices, he said. "Most people have a museum of spices. If you have spices that are more than two years old, toss them out. Find a place that sells spices in bulk and buy one ounce of all the spices you think you'll use. After a year, see how much you've used. When you have fresh spices, you'll notice. Everything will taste so much better. You will taste cinnamon, not dust."

Then Chef made a salad. He started to discuss onions. "I like to caramelize them; it adds so much flavor." He picked up a knife and got ready to chop. "Do you all know how to chop an onion? Does anyone want to come up and chop with me?"

Sabra bolted her hand in the air. "We're professionals at that," she declared. She jumped up to cut with the chef. Thierry chopped his onion, a fluid motion. Sabra then chopped hers quickly and confidently. Thierry raised his eyebrows. "Ah, you do know how to chop an onion. I am impressed."

Chef showed Sabra how to skin a bell pepper, a tricky technique that involved sliding the knife under the pepper. Sabra did it. She raised her hands over her head in victory. Gen and Shannon high-fived her as Sabra returned to her seat. "You all are very good. You must have a good teacher," he said, and winked at me.

Not to be outshone by a twenty-three-year-old prodigy, Chef finely sliced a tomato into paper-thin slices and then curved them into a circle, a classic French technique. He briefly sautéed the onions, adding strips of the peeled red pepper. He placed them artfully into the center of the sliced tomato and topped the dish with a drizzle of balsamic vinegar, chopped basil, and a sprinkle of grated Parmigiano-Reggiano. Finally, he topped it off with two anchovies.

"It is nice to really think about different ways to make salad. You do not necessarily need lettuce, see? It doesn't take too many components to make it work. It's funny, most people are afraid of messing up their kitchens by cooking. I want to ask, How do you feel about your bedroom?" he said, raising an eyebrow.

Then he presented his dish. It was beautiful, with the deep red of the tomatoes set against the green of the basil and zucchini and the velvety caramelized onions.

"Trust yourself. Yes, I am a chef, but I am like all of you. I just want something good to eat after a long day working," he said. "I believe all of you can do it. Prove me right." With that, the chef took a bow, tipped his hat, and the crowd applauded. "You know what I have for dinner some nights? Fresh bread, jam, and hot chocolate. You don't have to cook every night. Just eat real food."

Then he looked at his glass. "Oh, no, this is empty. Is there any more . . . water?" With that, I understood why he wanted a *clear* cocktail.

I knew that Chef Thierry would be a hard act to follow. But the way to avoid a lot of leftovers in the first place is to plan meals. So the next week another guest speaker came to talk to the group. Jenny, the supermarket chef, waddled into the kitchen eight months pregnant. A fair-skinned blonde who was likely a waif in her less exaggerated state, she looked tired when she arrived. "I'm so excited to teach tonight, but do you have a stool? I can't stand up for more than eight minutes."

Jenny started her culinary career working in restaurants (at one time for Chef Tom Douglas, in fact). But she decided that she wanted to make more of an impact on how people cook at home. Her present position was as a chef with a high-end grocery where she interacted daily with shoppers and home cooks. Most people acquire their food through supermarkets and Jenny knows how markets work.

"Strategists figure out how to use every single inch of a supermarket to get the most profit out of it," she said. "Nothing is left to chance."

Few of us realize that we shoppers are mice in a complex retail maze. Supermarkets spend a vast amount of money to figure out how shoppers behave. Every detail is purposeful, from the music they play to the size of the font declaring sales. For instance, you probably notice that it's chilly in a supermarket. I used to think that was because the chill helped to preserve the food. In fact, cold triggers hunger. If you're hungry, you'll buy more. The first thing that you run into in a supermarket is the produce section. The tactile experience of touching food and the bright colors get you in the mood for shopping. The milk, flour, and cereal are invariably spaced far apart. Why? Supermarkets are designed to slow you down. The longer you spend in the maze of a store trying to find staples, the more likely you'll buy something on impulse. Food manufacturers pay for premium shelf placement at eye level, or, in the cereal aisle, at the eye level of children.

"God, that explains why I hate the cereal aisle!" Shannon said. "I dread it. My kids will come up to me and say, 'Why can't we have this cereal, Mommy, it's got Cinderella on it? Most of the time, I will be like, Where did you get that? I didn't even see it."

"Manufacturers also pay for premium space at the ends of aisles, known as the end caps," Jenny said. "Sometimes this stuff is on sale, sometimes not. A lot of times the best deal is not on the end cap but around the corner in the aisle."

Terri nodded and took notes. She had said during her kitchen visit that she loathed shopping. "I have never felt like a very savvy shopper," she said. "I always want to get in and get out and I could never figure out why it took so long or why sometimes I would pick up stuff that I thought was on sale, like on the end stands, and then it wasn't."

Like Thierry, Jenny pulled leftover items out of the fridge. While Thierry was classically trained via the rigors of the French apprentice system, Jenny had earned her degree from a well-respected program at a local community college. Yet much of their messages were the same.

"If you want to save money and eat well, worry less about buying in bulk or what's on sale," Jenny started. "The number one way to save money on your grocery bill is to not waste food. You can buy in bulk, within reason, on nonperishables, but for the fresh stuff, just buy less and shop more often."

Smart shoppers plan meals and use thorough lists. They also stock up on basic staples. The meal plan doesn't have to be a strict "tuna casserole on Tuesday," but a looser structure that simply means planning five or six meals for the week.

"There's nothing wrong with eating the same things routinely. The goal is to feed yourself and the people around you with real food. Cook on the weekends and use leftovers during the week. If you'll eat the leftovers, cook twice as much as you'll eat and put the rest aside for lunches. Or cook twice the amount you'll eat and feed your neighbors once a week and have them do the same for you."

"For nights you have no plan, I tell shoppers to figure out a few simple strategies that are quick and use up the bits of food you've got in your fridge. Some require very little cooking. I have some strategies that I call 'Desperation Dinners.'"

The first involved a whole wheat flatbread. "You can do this with naan or tortillas, too." From our leftovers, she added a handful of mozzarella, cut-up tomatoes, some garbanzo beans, some chopped red onion, half a red pepper, and then she cracked an egg in the middle. "I am a trained chef, but you know what I cook with most on weekdays? Our toaster oven."

She slid the flatbread and egg into the kitchen's toaster oven. She made three different versions using the leftovers: a bit of ham, sliced Parmesan, chopped leeks, zucchini, sliced mushrooms. On each she cracked an egg and then chucked it into the toaster oven. When they emerged, the egg whites and yolks cooked, she topped them with a handful of arugula lightly dressed in olive oil. "It's an easy way to use up bits of greens, and kids like anything that looks like a pizza. Tortillas or flatbreads keep well, or you can always freeze them and then quickly thaw for a few seconds in the microwave."

Next she demonstrated "Desperation Pasta." She seasoned the water with salt and pepper. As the pasta started to cook, she cut a few florets of broccoli off the stem and crafted strips of carrots with a vegetable peeler. "I like to do this with carrots. They cook quickly, and they add some nice color." She dropped both into the water as the pasta finished cooking. After two minutes, she drained the pasta and dropped it into a bowl and tossed it with a handful of greens and grated cheese. "Now I'm just going to top it with some olive oil, some vinegar, and taste to see if it needs more salt and pepper. Vinegar is wildly overlooked. It's great to add flavor, and it has no calories, plus it has great shelf life. Really wakes up food."

She explained the concept of dinners as "layers." Her daughter will eat the first layer, say, plain pasta with grated cheese and maybe some broccoli. For Jenny and her husband, she'll "finish" the dish with pine nuts, chopped chilies, greens, sautéed shrimp, and so on. "If your kids are fussy, you don't have to make a completely different dish. Just evolve it into something more suited for adult tastes."

The class asked about gadgets. She doesn't use many. "A microplaner is great. You can use it to grate cheese, garlic, gingerroot, just a ton of stuff." We handed out slices of her Desperation Pizzas and Pasta. While everyone ate, she discussed more shopping tactics. Make a list of foods with strong flavors that store well in your pantry—things like capers, artichoke hearts, beans, dried mushrooms, and olives, that sort of thing. Buy basics in bulk, and buy fresh sparingly until you routinely use *all* of your produce, and then add more. "For produce, I look for what's fresh, in season, and hopefully on sale. We buy a whole chicken every time we shop. Sometimes I break it down but usually I just roast it for dinner that night. I have learned endless uses for it. Salads, pasta, burritos, chicken potpie, chicken salad, risotto. The list goes on. Then I make chicken stock, which also has endless uses."

"Oh, and a basil plant is a great investment," she said. "Any herbs that you buy regularly, consider keeping those plants in your kitchen window. You can get an herb plant at a nursery for the same price as a package of herbs at a grocery and just use what you need."

Like Thierry, she advocated trying to force using the last elements in the fridge. "Try this: Open your fridge. Take out three ingredients that sound like they go together. Put them into the search engine of a recipe site that you trust. If it turns out terrible, well, it's just one meal."

Jenny summed up the evening with one message. "You have to define what value is to you in your food. Is it cheap? Or are you going to get a lot of enjoyment from it? Maybe I'll splurge on some great flank steak, but then we'll get three meals from it. But the key thing is to think of food as money. You wouldn't toss a five-dollar bill in the garbage can, would you? If you throw a head of lettuce and some dead cucumbers in the trash, it's exactly the same thing. It adds up."

Shannon took a lot of notes. She had told us that she spent about seven hundred dollars a month on food, which turned out to be average for a family of four, according to the USDA. But she was always looking for ways to extend her budget. "Everything that we've been learning in class has been so helpful, but thinking about this whole leftover piece is a big thing for me. I've never been one of those people who could open the fridge and figure out stuff to make from it. I think that's how stuff goes bad, by not knowing what to do with it. This is all super helpful."

Trish had been trying to plan more meals, but she had recently figured out the problem. "My husband likes to be spontaneous. I'll have dinner halfway done, and then we'll go to yoga. Afterward, he'll say, 'Let's go out.' But I have dinner half-finished at home. So that's still a challenge for me." On the positive side, they rarely throw away food thanks to his fearless approach to sell-by dates. "Oh, he'll eat everything, even stuff with mold on it!"

The morning after Jenny's class, I took everything out of my fridge, from the condiments to the last remnants of vegetables from the crisper. I remembered the heavy use of Post-it notes throughout the commercial kitchen. I estimated the cost of every item and tagged each with a price on a Post-it. In the course of two weeks, if I had to throw an item away, I'd take the Post-it note and stick it to an area inside one of my cabinet doors.

Almost immediately, tossing something signaled defeat by surrender. My mind-set changed: Oh, no, I don't want to put that Post-it for this bell pepper on my door. Hmmm, what can I do with it? At the end of two weeks, I'd thrown out about sixteen dollars in food, less than usual but still nothing to make me proud. Among the culprits: remnants of hummus of unknown origin, the estimated cost of leftover bits from dinners, the end of a bag of red grapes, a smudge of mesclun salad left in the container, a nearly full package of sour cream, half a lime that turned brown, leftover chicken salad, half a sandwich brought home from a restaurant that got pushed behind our bread dough, and crumbled bleu cheese that had taken on a disturbing consistency. But the exercise forced me to use some items that I might have tossed: bits of bread pulverized into bread crumbs, the last of a jar of horseradish added to mayo for a spread for sandwiches, black bananas puréed into a kind of ice cream, limp carrots and green onions forced into duty in stock, wizened apples cut up and baked and topped with brown sugar on top of oatmeal, and half an avocado whipped with olive oil and sparkling water for a kind of dressing. One came directly from Jenny, her ersatz "pizza," with the last half handful of just-starting-to-wilt spinach.

During the process, I started to read *More-with-Less Cookbook* by the late Doris Janzen Longacre, a classic cookbook developed in the early 1970s with the Mennonite Central Committee that's still in use twenty-five years later. Longacre preached avoiding heavily processed foods, eating simple meals and more whole grains, and relying less on meat. She advocated shortening the shopping list and developing a stable of recipes on which to rely rather than trying to reinvent the culinary wheel for every single meal. In an opening scene, she describes a four-color advertising pitch she received in the mail for a new recipe-card set that promised to "make cooking easier and more exciting than ever before!" The ad stunned her sensibilities. "The pitch indicates again how we try to turn eating into a super-experience," she wrote.

It reminded me of an old issue of a food magazine that had offered a week of "fast meals." The lineup included a shrimp curry, Moroccan spiced lamb chops, a Mediterranean fish sauté, a beef stir-fry, and seared scallops with braised cabbage. The shopping list next to it contained more than fifty ingredients. Sure, some people might have some of the ingredients on hand as staples, but I examined the recipes closer. If you made all those dishes, among the leftovers you'd be left with half a head of cabbage, half a can of coconut milk, the remainder of bunches of cilantro, parsley, and basil, among other things. So what exactly to do with all of those extra remnants of food?

When I thought about Longacre's views, why would I take on a set of menus that would leave me with so much? Does anyone need lamb, scallops, beef, fish, and shrimp all in the space of five days?

Chef Thierry, Jenny, and Longacre all had a point. While exploring my crisper drawer, I found a nearly full two-pound bag of organic carrots tagged with a four-dollar Post-it. Half an onion beckoned. Rosemary sprigs sat waiting on my counter. Rosemary and carrots together? I would never have thought of that combination if I had not been forced to figure out how to use them up. The result was a savory yet sweet chilled soup. I didn't know what the volunteers had learned through these classes, but I had learned something important. We all can do more with less.

൭ Velvety Chilled Rosemary Carrot Soup

This savory and sweet soup can be served at any temperature, but it's excellent chilled. Immersion, or "stick," blenders are great for soup because you can plunge them directly into the pot. Hot soup can create a vacuum in conventional blenders, so if you use one, let the soup chill slightly first, and then take the cap off and cover with a towel. Running soups through a food mill is a low-tech option. If you have none of the above, simply mash the softened vegetables with a fork or potato masher; it will lend a rustic feel to the finished product. Add the rosemary, branch and all, but be sure to remove it before pureeing.

2 tablespoons olive oil
1 medium onion, chopped (about 1½ cups)
2 leeks (white and light green parts), chopped
1 pound carrots, diced
Several fresh rosemary sprigs
1 bay leaf
2 quarts chicken or vegetable stock
Coarse salt and freshly ground black pepper
Pinch of cayenne (optional)
⅓ cup quality plain yogurt (optional)
Croutons (optional)

❧ Heat the olive oil in a 4-quart or larger saucepan. Add the onion and leeks and sauté until softened. Add the carrots, rosemary sprigs, bay leaf, stock, a couple of pinches of coarse salt, a few grinds of coarse pepper, and a pinch of cayenne if using. Bring to a boil, then cover and reduce the heat to simmer until the carrots soften, about 1 hour.

❧ Remove from the heat. Discard the rosemary and the bay leaf. Puree until smooth. Add additional water if necessary. Return to the pot. Check the seasonings, adding salt, black pepper, and cayenne to taste. Serve warm or cooled. Garnish with a scoop of yogurt or croutons if desired.

CHAPTER 13

⊗⊛

The Power of Soup

⊗ LESSON HIGHLIGHTS:
It Turns Out That *Supper* and *Soup*
Come from the Same Place

My mother always said that if you can boil water, you can make soup. Chef Thierry had remarked that it's a gift for leftovers. From the beginning, I planned a class on stocks and soups as the last class, knowing that we'd end with a fridge full of leftovers.

As the volunteers filed in to claim a diaper and an apron, they all fretted about the night being the last. "It's going to be so strange not to see everyone each week," Gen said. I asked what people had been up to in their kitchens.

"You know, I've been thinking a lot about what the nutritionist said," Dri said. "It's funny, we hear so much about how fats are bad, but then she talked about the difference between good fats and bad fats, and how olive and coconut oil are good, but, then, palm oil isn't so good. So I went through everything in my cupboards and I looked at all of the labels." She considered the impact of feeding bad fats not only to herself but to her nieces and nephews who visit regularly. She was surprised by what she found in her wares, already edited significantly as part of her recent move. "Really, after the Alfredo versus Alfredo night, I just kind of decided to ditch most of that stuff anyway. I've just decided that I simply will not eat out of a box anymore."

The comment spurred a lot of conversation. "I never thought I'd

227

be like that but I'm getting there," Jodi said. "I went to make pancakes the other day and I looked at the label. It was basically just flour, hydrogenated oil, corn syrup, and baking soda. I thought, Do I really want to feed this stuff to my son? I looked up a pancake recipe in a cookbook and thought, That's it?" She had whipped up the batter and then mashed in an overripe banana. Her face took on an obvious look of pride when she reported that her son loved them. "He was like, 'Mommy, these are the greatest pancakes!'"

Cheryl was baby-free again this week. Of all the classes, she confessed that this was a big one for her. When we visited her kitchen, she had made a can of soup for lunch. "I buy a ton of soup," she admitted. The organic kinds can be expensive and often still come packed with salt. "I want to master soup so that I can cut down on how much I buy. After all these cooking classes, it feels a little lame to be opening a can."

Few nutriments date back as far as soup, which likely debuted shortly after cavemen discovered the joys of boiling water. The word *soup* stems from the same Germanic word that led to the English word for "supper," writes Alan Davidson in *The Penguin Guide to Food*. "From that came a noun, *suppa*, which passed into the Old French as *soupe*. This meant 'piece of bread soaked in liquid' . . . which ultimately led to the word 'sop.'" So the words for *supper, soup,* and *sopping* up the soup with bread all derived from the same source.

By the late 1600s, soup was so beloved, people didn't want to leave home without it, resulting in the development of "portable soup," which was meat stock boiled so long it reduced to a thick paste that was dried and cut into strips. The strips were then reconstituted with hot water. Davidson quotes a portable soup enthusiast from 1736 who referred to it as "veal glue." Mind you, those were words used by someone who *liked it*. The term *restaurant* stems from the French verb for "to restore," a reference to the shops that sold soup in the late nineteenth century. To complete the cycle in something of an ironic twist, modern restaurants make "soup du jour" from leftovers of their nonsoup menus items. I knew that Lisa had a story about the trauma of soup du jour and asked her share it.

"My very first job cooking, I spent a year making soup," Lisa started. She reported to work on the lunch shift with a chef who had worked in the industry for nearly forty years. She was impressed by his seemingly laissez-faire attitude toward soup du jour. Broccoli looked a little shaky? He'd whip up cream of broccoli soup. Too much cabbage? He'd ask Lisa to shred it and then add some ham, white beans, and carrots. The owners fired the chef without warning a few days after she started. In her first week out of culinary school, she found herself managing a lunch shift for a sixty-four-seat restaurant all by herself.

"It felt like being thrown out of a plane with a scribbled five-point list on how to complete a parachute jump," Lisa said. In addition to a hundred other tasks that she had to complete the morning she first worked alone, she had to come up with the soup du jour. In the walk-in, she found a Thai curry base used for a seafood dish. She thinned it with chicken stock. A revelation! Sauce is thick soup!

Although she got a handle on the rest of the job after she figured out that there would be no replacement for the axed chef, she fretted about the soup. It kept her awake at night. "The very nature of it, that it can be *anything*, just freaked me out," she told the group. You could feel her tension in the room. Lisa studied culinary school textbooks and looked up recipes trying to combat her soup angst. "But then I would get to the kitchen and find that I didn't have all the ingredients, so I'd panic."

Then a friend gave her *The Daily Soup Cookbook* by Leslie Kaul and Bob Spiegel. This simple book offers straightforward instructions on two hundred soup recipes organized by ingredient or theme, such as tomatoes, beans, or gumbo. She showed off her battered copy to the class.

"I would pile up my dying ingredients on a counter, and then flip through this book to find recipes that would fit. I could make something like minestrone or a tortilla lime soup, but not exactly. I would have hamburger and not sausage, or sausage but not chicken." At first, this struck her as the culinary equivalent of forcing a square set of ingredients into a round hole. But she discovered that no matter what she changed, as long as the flavors seemed to go together, the soup always turned out anyway.

The soup du jour changed her perspective as a cook. "All those substitutions taught me that I do not have to be a slave to a recipe, or even to convention," she said. "It also taught me something critical. You don't have to buy ingredients for soup."

With that, we all ransacked the fridge, pulling out vegetables and the remnants of a chicken I'd roasted the day before. "Soups generally follow the same formula," I began. "You sauté some aromatics, usually chopped garlic or leeks, and then you add in vegetables, meat, or poultry that needs some time to cook. Add in stock or water. That's a good time to add a bit of salt, some herbs and spices. Simmer for at least an hour. Give your soup some time to develop." Foods that don't take much time to cook, such as shellfish or pasta, go in at the end. "Then taste it. Add salt or whatever it might need to pep up the flavor. That could be lemon, vinegar, maybe minced garlic or fresh herbs." Garnishes such as croutons or grated cheese are great but unnecessary.

We started two pots, then split up the volunteers into teams and let them figure out a soup from the leftovers. One team settled on chicken noodle soup, the other on a variation of minestrone. Each built an initial layer of flavor by sautéing onions and leeks. Team Chicken added carrots, celery, fresh corn, and a fistful of fresh thyme and parsley tied together, along with the remains of the roasted chicken. Team Minestrone added zucchini, green bell pepper, cauliflower, garlic, red pepper flakes, a can of tomatoes, and the rind of some Parmigiano-Reggiano.

"You can also just start any pot of soup with half a roast chicken, whether you've bought it or you've made it, and go from there. It's an easy shortcut," Lisa said. "If you keep your pantry stocked with some basics it's super easy to pull together a soup with minimal effort.

I usually have canned tomatoes on hand, coconut milk, curry paste, rice, some type of pasta, dried beans, bacon, fresh herbs, stock, onions, carrots, celery, some dried chili pods. That's about it, that's most of my pantry. Everything else is accessories."

Often, the difference between boring soup and fabulous soup is just time. Soup almost always has to simmer for at least an hour, usually two. It takes time to draw all the flavors out of the components. "Trying to boil it like mad for a half hour is not going to trick the laws of cooking into thinking it's simmered for two hours," Lisa said.

We left each pot to simmer as we turned our attention to the notion of stocks.

As if on cue, Ted sauntered into the kitchen. "I heard there was some stock action going on in here," he said. Ted is a stock aficionado; he once penned a two-thousand-word missive on the subject. "Thought I'd just drop by and have a look."

I waved him in. "So, stock is the extra bonus from a roast chicken," I started. "You can just simmer the bones with some vegetables. One chicken can generate a couple of quarts of stock. Considering that you pay two or three dollars for a quart of chicken stock, it's worth it not to throw them away. When it comes to the vegetables for stock, some of them can be odds and ends or trimmings you might normally throw away, like the hard heel of celery, scraps of onion, and the tough green tops of leeks. Those can all go into stock."

"So it's basically free," Sabra commented. "That's cool."

The roasted chicken version is an easy shortcut, but applies the same principles of all stock. "Now we're going to start with some bones."

Over the weekend, I had rounded up plastic bags marked "For chicken stock" and "For beef stock" from my freezer. I never let a bone go, whether it comes from a chicken I've broken down, hot wings that I made at home, or even leftovers from restaurants.

Not long before the class, we ate at the Space Needle Restaurant with friends from out of town. Mike and his friend Bill ordered the day's special, a twenty-five-ounce steak that had a *Flintstones*-style bone jutting from the meat. The server looked at me like I was a crazy woman when I told him I wanted to take home the bones, but he good-naturedly wrapped them up in a takeout bag. As we waited for the elevator, the Italian maître d' asked what was in the bag. His face lit up. "Ah, now, that's a smart cook! I never understand why people leave without them! My nana would kill for bones like that."

I'd roasted all the bones and made most of them into stock. I kept a small pan of each set of bones to show off the result of roasting. The chicken bones had a crisp quality and a mahogany color in some places where the bone was exposed, and wept brown puddles of caramelized goodness onto the pan. The beef bones looked dried and nearly charred, like trees in a forest recently ravaged by fire.

I had Ted take over the explanation. For chicken, beef, veal, or other meat-based stock, the method remains the same. "You can just simmer chicken in water with the vegetables. That's known as white stock," Ted said. "But you'll get more flavor if you roast the bones first. You want your oven nice and hot, around 400 degrees. The goal is to caramelize the bones a bit. About a half hour or forty-five minutes is usually enough. When you can really start to smell them, that's when you're getting somewhere."

I waved everyone over to the big stove. "Okay, here are the two pots of stock that I made from the rest of the bones. They've been simmering about two hours. I want you to smell it and taste it."

Lisa handed everyone a spoon. Each person dutifully sniffed the gurgling liquids, then dipped her spoon in and sipped a taste. They looked thoughtfully at one another. "It reminds me of the stock tasting," Cheryl said. "It's more meaty and chickeny."

"So you take the browned bones, put them in a pot, and cover them with cold water. It's great to add some water to the roasting pans while they're hot and scrape up any browned bits left in them," Ted said. "It will clean your pans and boost the flavor of your stock. Add vegetables, typically onion, carrot, and celery. The usual ratio is one pound of vegetables for every three pounds of bones. Add a bay leaf, some thyme, parsley. Some people like to add whole pep-percorns and some garlic."

The point is to simmer them for as long as it takes for "the bones to give their all," as Julia Child once wrote. For chicken, that's usually two to four hours; for beef, about double that.

Ted pulled a ladle from among the coterie of utensils and demonstrated a key technique. First he skimmed off a slight oil slick on the top of the stock, and then tackled an island of bubbling foam. "Skimming simply means to do a seek-and-destroy of any foam or fat on the surface," Ted said. "It makes a world of difference to both stock and soup. It keeps it from being greasy, for one thing."

Ted had a few other points on meat-based stocks. "Try not to boil it or it will turn cloudy. What you want to do is get it superhot and then reduce the heat until you get the occasional, or 'lazy,' bubble. Don't add salt. As the water evaporates, the salt flavor will concentrate and it can be too salty."

Since Lisa had brought in her soup book for show-and-tell, I opened a copy of *Vegetarian Cooking for Everyone* by Deborah Madison. During my fling with vegetarianism, I started to make vegetable stocks, a habit that I keep up. "They're built the same way. Roast the vegetables and then simmer for about a half hour. This book has a great section on vegetable stocks." I flipped through the section. "There's a whole breakdown of vegetables to use by season, stocks for stir-fries and curries, mushroom stock, and even tomato-style stock. You just want to avoid strong flavors such as cabbage, beets, broccoli, or, as she puts it, 'funky or spoiled' vegetables that you wouldn't eat."

Next, we moved on to fish stock. In French, it's known as "fish fumet," a common foundation in chowders and seafood dishes. I had bought two pounds of fish bones for a dollar from my regular fish-monger, an assortment of fragile skeletons and thick pieces of white bones from larger fish.

"A lot of recipes will call for clam juice, but what the food writer really wants you to use is fish stock." Personally, I loathe clam juice. Most supermarket varieties are simply too brackish. "Even the cheap stuff is almost three bucks for eight ounces, so you're paying twelve dollars for a quart. You want white fish without too strong a flavor. No mackerel, no salmon." I combined some onion, celery, half a lemon, a bay leaf, a few sprigs of parsley, and the fish bones in a pot with cold water.

"You can do the same thing with shrimp, crab, or lobster shells, too. I sometimes get Dungeness crab shells from my fish market. They're free and it's awesome in gumbo," I said.

Together, Ted and I strained the pot of gurgling chicken stock. "If you've got a big pot, don't try to pour it out. Remove the bones with tongs, and then ladle the liquid out." He ladled the stock through a mesh sieve lined with cheesecloth over a massive bowl. "This is traditional but a colander with a coffee filter works, too." After the chicken, he strained the fish fumet.

"I'm totally not digging that smell," Dri said of the fumet. "I mean, I guess it's good for chowder, but it's pretty fishy." Sabra nodded. She wasn't into it either.

A hot steaming pot of stock cools slowly and has a tendency to linger in what food safety types refer to as the "danger zone," or temperatures between 40 and 140 degrees. "You want to make sure your stock stays out of the danger zone by cooling it quickly," Ted said. "You can do a few things. Take the stock and put it into an ice bath in the sink and keep stirring. You can pour it into a shallow pan, like the bottom of broiler. Or you can wait until the stock cools below 180 degrees and then plop plastic bags filled with ice into the stock. Whatever, once it cools to room temperature or below, put it into the fridge right away."

The other option is the remarkably low-tech "cold porch" method, Lisa added. "In winter, I just put a big pan of stock outside uncovered and stir it every so often until it cools down."

Shannon signaled a time-out. "Okay, I'm a little confused. What's the difference between stock and broth?"

"Stock is made from bones, broth is not. Technically, there's no such thing as vegetable stock. But since people aren't sure, a lot of things are called stock interchangeably with broth."

"All these years, and I never knew that," Shannon said.

We went back to the soups. Team Chicken finished theirs by tossing in handfuls of pasta left over from the pasta class, shredded cooked chicken, and chopped fresh parsley and oregano. Team Minestrone added chopped tomatoes, a can of red beans, then garnished each bowl with grated Parmigiano-Reggiano and chopped basil.

The streetlights came on outside. Each person slurped the various soups. Lisa produced a bottle of cava from the fridge. With great drama, she launched the cork and we all toasted.

"Here's a toast to you," Dri said to Lisa, Ted, and me. We clinked glasses.

"Here's to all of you and your willingness to chop zucchini!" I said. Clink.

"To zucchini!" Sabra said. Clink.

"To diapers!" Shannon said. Clink.

Then the mood turned bittersweet as the volunteers reluctantly took off their aprons and dropped their diapers into the bag we hauled around for the dirty laundry.

After they left, Lisa, Ted, and I did a final cleanup in the kitchen. I stayed behind to mop. Alone in the kitchen, I dragged the bright yellow roller and swished the mottled gray-yarn mop across the black-and-white tile. I was deep into the Zen of the rhythmic motion when my phone rang.

"It's Eddie," my mother said.

My stepfather, Eddie, had suffered from an impressive string of maladies in the past dozen years. A recent surgery had left him weak, and since then he'd been falling. That morning, he collapsed and broke a chair. My mother tried for forty-five minutes to get him up. An ER doctor diagnosed him with pneumonia, a serious illness for a seventy-eight-year-old who already had enough health problems.

This time I heard something different in my mother's voice: sheer exhaustion. He'd barely slept for a week. I knew that as his caretaker, she hadn't either. "Mom, I'm coming home," I told her. She insisted that it wasn't necessary. I hung up and called Mike, then I finished mopping the floor. By the time I got home, Mike had booked me a ticket to leave the next afternoon.

We had set up a couple of makeup classes for the following week. I called Lisa. "Oh, no, should we reschedule?" she said.

"No, you're going to teach them," I said.

"I can't teach them by myself," she replied quickly. "Let's reschedule."

"Are you kidding? *I've* learned stuff from you. So of course you can. I have total faith in you."

In Florida, the relief on Mom's face said it all. She looked as if she'd aged years. Eddie's gaunt appearance threw me. A thin guy by nature, he'd lost twenty-five pounds. His cheeks had an unhealthy hollow. As I hugged him, I asked, "What can I do for you, Eddie?"

"Make me dinner?" he asked. "It's not like I travel now. The high-light of my day is hitting Walgreens for prescriptions. Food is all that I have to look forward to."

That week, my sister, Sandy, and I spent two full days making huge vats of food, from spaghetti with meatballs to beef stew to scal-loped potatoes. Fresh from the soup class, I cleared out my mother's fridge to make three different varieties, including chicken noodle, Eddie's favorite. Ever competitive, Sandy made Eddie's all-time favor-ite meal, a classic full-on Thanksgiving spread replete with turkey, mashed potatoes with gravy, and homemade stuffing. We diligently labeled and froze all of it into portions sized for two—enough for two months' worth of meals.

Doing this gave my exhausted mom a break from both shopping and cooking. She rested, and we took long walks on the beach together. The stockpile of varied foods kept Eddie interested in eat-ing. Each morning, she'd open the freezer and ask what he wanted. "How about we have the turkey gumbo for lunch and the cassoulet for dinner?" He gained back some weight and his condition improved.

Before leaving for the airport, he gave me a lingering hug as he thanked me for the meals. "I can tell with every bite that you love us."

As I sat on the plane back to Seattle, I thought about the power of cooking to nourish, to comfort, and to heal. It was the fourth time in one year that I had contributed meals to people's freezers in the midst of a crisis: Mike's sister had gone through chemotherapy for breast cancer, a friend's husband had had surgery to remove a brain tumor, and our friend Amy had suffered life-threatening complications after the birth of her son.

It's a simple act, but to bring someone chicken soup when they're sick is not just about a meal, it's a tangible and physical sign of caring. If you buy a chicken and make it from scratch, the message is completely different from bringing over a can. It says, "You're important, and I care about you enough to take the time to help restore you." Like laughter, soup is not the same when it's canned.

~~~~~~

⌘ Blissfully Simple Chicken Stock

Gather up all the bones from a roast chicken after you've wrested all possible use from the meat. Depending on how much water you add and how long it simmers, the yield will be six cups to three quarts.

Bones from 1 roast chicken
½ medium onion, quartered
1 celery stalk, roughly chopped
1 large carrot, chopped
Few sprigs of fresh thyme and/or parsley
1 garlic clove
1 bay leaf
4 to 5 quarts cold water

⚜ Put the chicken bones, onion, celery, carrot, fresh herbs, garlic clove, and bay leaf into a 5-quart or larger pot. Add 4 to 5 quarts of cold water. Bring just to a boil and then turn the heat down until it simmers. Let it simmer for at least 1 hour and up to 3 hours. Skim any foam or fat from the top with a spoon. Drain it in a colander or mesh sieve lined with cheesecloth or a coffee filter into a large bowl. Cool, then refrigerate or freeze until needed.

༄༅

CHAPTER 14

Kitchens, Revisited

LESSON HIGHLIGHTS:
What Effect Did the Classes Have on the Volunteers?

Not long after the last class in early September, an acquaintance shared a most discouraging quote. Her grandfather used to say that he'd "rather try to change someone's religion than change the way they eat."

"I'm only telling you this so you're not discouraged if your project didn't work," she said. I may have defriended her on Facebook.

Although the signs had seemed encouraging over the summer, that conversation dogged me. What if I had spent all this time and effort—not to mention the work of everyone else—yet it had no impact? I waited until after Thanksgiving to follow up. As we had the first time, we'd audit their cabinets and ask them to prepare a meal that they ate regularly. I wanted the distance of time to see what, if anything, had stuck.

SABRA

Six months after our first visit, a frigid November wind wailed outside as I stood in Sabra's warm kitchen with Lisa and Sabra's dad. He was just as curious as we were. Sabra had assembled a casserole in a new pan, one of many recent additions to her kitchen. "I got this idea from Stouffer's. It's a Cheddar and potato casserole with broccoli and bacon," she said, sliding the prepared dish into oven. "I can make twelve servings of this for the same price as a couple of dinners, it tastes way, way better, and I know what's in it."

I asked what her biggest takeaway was from the course. "Confidence," she replied quickly. "I can look at any recipe and know that I can make it now. I never thought that before." She picked up her chef's knife from the counter and handled it with reverence. "Learning knife skills changed everything. One reason I used to get intimidated by cooking was I'd see a bunch of stuff to cut up, but now I know that's not a big deal. I actually like that part."

From the minute we arrived, Sabra seemed eager to show off her freezer. "You ready?" she asked. We all nodded. With a flourish, she flung it open. "Notice there are *no* frozen meals in here," she said proudly. Two whole frozen turkeys took up the space once occupied by stacks of frozen dinners. "They're a Thanksgiving gift from my dad's business," she explained. "I haven't made them yet because I don't have a pan big enough, but I've asked for one for Christmas," she said, eyeing her dad sitting at the kitchen counter.

Rounding out the freezer were bags of tortellini, vegetables, and individual portions of various leftovers. "Those are lunch," she explained. "Oh, look!" She grabbed a plastic bag and shook it. "Chicken bones! For stock! I made some, but I'm out."

If the project had succeeded in nothing else, Sabra, the young woman who had served us frozen lasagna and White Trash Garlic Bread a mere six months ago, no longer wandered the frozen-foods aisle looking for dinner.

"While they're cheap, I just realized they aren't such a good deal after all," she said. "I find that if I cook a couple of times a week, then there's always something my boyfriend and I can eat, which is cool. It's just like convenience food, except you make it."

Avoiding frozen dinners wasn't the only shift in Sabra's habits. She found herself shopping more often, hitting a farm stand nearby for vegetables. Whenever she buys food, she always does so with at least two meals in mind. "I think we're spending about the same on groceries but less on food overall because we eat less takeout. We waste a lot less food, too."

Sabra used to eat Hamburger Helper every other week. She admitted that she hadn't made it since July, about midway through the project. Her remaining box of the stuff had been banished to a high shelf to make way for new additions to her modest pantry. "It's funny, a lot of things expire that I never thought about, like oils, flour, and spices." She had used up the rest of her expired flour, had replaced her dead spices, and now buys smaller doses of everything. "Now when I buy something like olive oil, I get the smaller size even though it's more expensive. But I know that it will stay good until I can use it all."

"Oh, and check it out!" She reached into the dairy drawer of her fridge to retrieve a paper package. She unwrapped a bit to expose the tip of a hard wedge of Parmigiano-Reggiano cheese. She hadn't seemed that engaged in the tasting class, but she reported that it had had a powerful effect on her. "The tastings made me really think about what I buy. People can say you should go and spend the extra money and get real cheese, but until you taste it for yourself, it's almost impossible to know that it's worth it."

Her fascination with McDonald's had subsided, too. "It's funny how if you eat well and then you go eat fast food, you can really feel it. It kind of sinks in my stomach, and I can hear my body saying *whoa whoa whoa,* what the . . . ? I don't want this." She held her stomach and groaned.

That comment, it must be noted, came from the woman who equated love with McDonald's and who told me that if cooking dinner would take more than twenty minutes, she'd go out for fast food.

"Oh, yeah, I know I said that. But a big thing I got out of it was that cooking is worth my time," she said. "Homemade stock is basically free and you can make so much stuff out of it. Although I cut myself twice in class when I first started learning to use a knife, it was so worth it," she said with a laugh. "The chicken class was important because I was afraid of chicken, that whole salmonella thing. And I'm going to be honest, I was kind of freaked out by cutting up the whole chicken at first. But that made me rethink food in a lot of ways. You're right, it's easier to remember that it was once, well, a chicken."

Yet for all these strides, some things she cannot let go of, White Trash Garlic Bread among them. "But that's more about the memory of that, since I ate it growing up with my mother. But I use the good cheese now, not the stuff from a can."

The other untouchable? Gold 'n Soft. "I can't give that up because butter still tastes funny to me," she admitted. "But I use less, probably because I use olive oil more now."

In a way, Sabra was railroaded into this project by her stepmother, Lisa. I would not have faulted her if she had attended, feigned polite enthusiasm, and resumed her life in the fast-food lane. Instead, she embraced it and made extraordinary changes. Given all that, how could anyone deny her a few tastes of her childhood? I certainly could not.

TRISH

When I first visited Trish, Mike filmed the proceedings. This time around, Lisa came along. Like me, she marveled at Trish's collection of immaculate white binders filled with recipes she'd been clipping for decades, each encased in its own plastic sheath.

She exuded a sense of calm on this visit. "So I don't think what I've bought or cooked has changed as much as something has changed in *me*," she started. "I'm more relaxed and I'm not so hard on myself."

She gave the recipes in the binders as an example. She pulled out one that said "appetizers" and started to flip through it. "I went to all this trouble to put these together, but then I really didn't make many of the recipes. I was so intimidated and worried that they wouldn't work out. So I used to just look at them. Now I'm actually *cooking* out of them. I make notes, and the ones that I don't like or don't work, I throw them away."

"So did you keep recipes that didn't work out before?" I asked. She nodded. "Why?"

"I thought there couldn't be anything wrong with the recipe and so whatever went wrong was my fault," she explained. This led her to a bigger realization. "I have this psychological thing that if I can do it then it must not be special or good. Plus, my mother didn't like to cook. She thought she was terrible at it and I absorbed that," she said. "Now I think I may not be the greatest cook, but I know that I *can* do it. I am not afraid of it."

Her mother was the one who owned the *I Hate to Cook Book,* a title that sold three million copies. The premise of the book was that women should get the whole cooking thing over with, thus avoiding any more drudgery in the kitchen than was absolutely necessary. This advice was couched in humorous terms by the author, Peg Bracken, who also advised women not to throw too much angst into meals either. Trish's mother managed to pass down the dislike of cooking, and not Bracken's ultimate message, which was that, in the end, cooking isn't that big of a deal. The irony was that of all the initial kitchen visits, Trish's ratatouille was probably the best food I ate, certainly the healthiest, and the only one made with whole foods. She slipped the binder back onto the shelf and we went into the kitchen.

She started to organize the makings of a vegetable and bean stew from *Feeding the Whole Family* by Cynthia Lair, which is, incidentally, one of my favorite cookbooks.

Trish set up her cutting board on the counter, carefully placing a wet paper towel underneath. She showed off her two new knives, a seven-inch chef's knife and a santoku, a Japanese-style design characterized by its curved spine and small indents in the blade. She set out her metal bowl for scraps. "There are little things, like using a bowl for scraps, that have made a big difference. My kitchen stays cleaner and I feel more organized."

She cut an onion perfectly. "I had a big aha over the onion," she said. "In the knife skills class, I thought, So that's the secret! She used to use a garlic press. "I stopped using that because now I like cutting, and that just dirties the garlic press." She turned to a six-quart stainless steel pot—another recent purchase—and tossed the vegetables into hot oil.

"Oh, and the other thing, I made stock." She opened the freezer and showed off a collection of carefully marked blue-lidded plastic containers. She pulled one out to show us.

"Wow, Trish, check you out!" I said.

She looked proud. After she tucked the container back in the freezer, she went to the stove and held up a small blue handmade glazed ceramic box with a lid. "I had wondered for years what to do with this. My son made it. Now I keep my coarse salt in it so I can pinch salt. That's another little thing. It seems silly, but trying to figure out a pinch with a shaker is hard!"

She ticked off items she'd tried since the summer. "I'm still terrible at cutting up chicken, but I love to do it." She regretted leaving the meat class early. "I should have stayed. I would have liked to learn more about braising." She had enjoyed learning to make the vinaigrette but rarely did it. "I don't know, buying it in the bottle is just so easy."

Of the other classes, she used the soup class the most. "I now have a sense of how to make soup from just about anything, and we love soup."

Once again, she set the table with beautiful dinnerware, a sculpted silver breadbasket in the center of the table, and immaculately ironed cloth napkins. The stew was light yet savory and brightened with the flavor of cilantro. It was the perfect lunch for a cold, rainy day. The timer dinged for the pear tart she had made for dessert. "When I made it the last time, I took it to my friend's house and she had a perfect silver oblong pan and it looked so pretty. Everyone said, 'Wow, Trish, you're so good in the kitchen.'

"And this may seem silly, but it was a big moment for me. I was proud of something that I cooked." Her eyes got a little misty at the memory. "No one expected that from me. I didn't expect it from myself. It is remarkable that at my age I can still change, and that I can still surprise myself."

JODI

When I met Jodi, she had found herself suddenly a stay-at-home mother after being laid off from her high-tech job. She had gone back to work again that autumn, juggling her home life with a three-year-old and trying to keep up with expectations in her new job. When I learned that she had gone back to work, I worried that whatever momentum Jodi had gained in the project might have dissipated.

As soon as I walked into her kitchen, I realized I didn't need to worry. Jodi could barely contain her excitement when we arrived. It was as if she had a secret that she just couldn't wait to share. It was a remarkable shift from the air of defeat and tentativeness I had felt on the day that she made Japanese curry from a cube.

By contrast, she was smiling and relaxed as she told us she was planning to roast a chicken. She showed off the simple roasting pan that she had bought for twenty dollars at a restaurant supply store. "Oh, yeah, I do this all the time now," she said about the chicken. "I've learned that as long as the chicken isn't too big, it takes right around an hour." She has made a hobby of finding uses for the leftovers. "I made chicken Alfredo and it was *so* good," she gushed. "I make the fresh tomato sauce so often that I think I'm going to have to take a break from it because my husband and son might be getting sick of it, but I still really like it."

She had Brussels sprouts that had somehow gotten overlooked at Thanksgiving. She'd never made them before, but she figured she'd give them a sauté. We could smell bread baking in the oven. Jodi opened her fridge door to reveal a plastic bin with dough nestled into the center. "I've used more flour in the last three or four months than I've ever used in my entire life! I got a couple of big plastic containers for white and whole wheat flour, and I'm refilling them all the time."

"I make a version that's kind of half wheat and half white now.

My son likes it and I like to make it. I find it rewarding to pull hot bread from the oven, and it's something that I can make after work at least a couple of times a week."

She proudly showed off her new copy of *Joy of Cooking.* "This summer completely changed the way that I think about cooking and nutrition, especially around processed foods, you know? I have tried a ton of recipes, which I would have *never* done before. Also, we buy way more organic now and I read the labels on everything. Don't get me wrong, I'm still not making mayonnaise from scratch or anything like that, but I've come a long way."

On my earlier visit, the small walk-in had been packed with cases of canned and boxed goods stacked in piles on the floor. Now it looked organized and functional, and notably absent were ultraprocessed foods, save for a few boxes of macaroni and cheese. "I tried to eat through a lot of things like canned tomatoes, but some of the stuff I cleared out and took to a food bank."

Her fridge was similarly less cluttered. In her fridge door was a jar of parsley pesto, a tip she had taken from Chef Thierry. She was still working on eating through the freezer.

Inventory over, she went back to her cutting board. She tenderly separated leaves from a few sprigs of rosemary, chopped garlic, and effortlessly seasoned her chicken as she talked. She seemed as if she had been doing it for years. Even so, she still feared falling into the gender role that had trapped her mother in what Jodi viewed as a life of voluntary servitude.

"I don't mind cooking, as long as my husband and I both agree that it's a partnership and it's not just *my* job," Jodi said. "I think that it should be about who gets home first rather than the assumption that I'm supposed to do it, even if, to be honest, I rather like to cook now."

Interestingly, her newfound interest in the kitchen both gave her equal footing and threatened the delicate balance of the power that had existed when her husband was the main cook in the family.

"We've had a couple of arguments about cooking, but that's

probably because I never used to have an opinion." She now rejected suggestions and debated technique. Recently, she made a dish that left a layer of food stuck to the bottom of a skillet. Her husband kept scrubbing and complaining. "I said, 'Hey, it's no big deal. Just deglaze it.' He was all 'What?' I said, 'Get the pan hot and add some liquid. It will come right off.'" He kept scrubbing and finally threw the pan in the sink in disgust. "I went to the stove, got it hot, and added water, and it was clean like that," she said, snapping her fingers. "Ha, so I knew that, and he didn't."

"So, this is funny," she said in an obvious move to change the conversation. "I have been trying to find a recipe for Japanese curry that doesn't use a cube. But all the Japanese people I asked say they use the dang box! I'd say, 'Hey, don't you know what's in that?'" She laughed. "So I asked a food writer friend who is Asian, and she thought it was a great question. So she's going to research it and I'm going to help with recipe testing."

So while she still makes golden curry, she's thinking about it more and making it less. "I know this sounds dumb, but I used to think that the stuff in a box was something you couldn't make. Now I know they all just mimic real foods, so if it's in a box, there's got to be a way to make it for real. If you go to a good restaurant in Japan, then they'll have this same curry and it's amazing. So I guess that's my holy grail now. One day I will learn how to make that same curry *without* the darn cube!"

DRI

Dri had moved from the hood into a comfortable condo in a leafy urban neighborhood. "The greatest thing? I'm just across the street from Mutual Seafood," she said, naming one of the city's most respected seafood outlets.

Dri seemed happy and relaxed. She also looked as if she'd lost a bit of weight. Compared to her former one-cook-is-too-many-sized kitchen, her new one seemed vast and luxurious with its open plan, dark maple wood cabinets, and stainless steel appliances. "It's great. I sometimes wake up in the morning and think, Wow, I live here. I feel like such a grown-up."

She had a basket on her counter filled with the kinds of stuff that she had discussed abandoning in the final class: dehydrated soup mixes, pasta side dishes, broccoli soup mix, and corn muffins among the lot. She blushed, a bit embarrassed.

"So this is awkward," she said. "I did a favor for my friend and as a thank-you gift she gave me this lovely basket with all this packaged stuff." She could not stifle her laughter. "It was such a nice idea, but I thought, I just don't do that anymore. I guess for some people it's a treat, but now I know better."

Like a lot of people who live on their own, Dri reported that she found it hard to get motivated to cook for one. "The project amplified the importance of taking time to cook and actually to make it a priority," she said. "Plus it changed the way that I plan and stock my kitchen by about 175 million percent. I know that's a really big number, but it's true."

She opened a cabinet to show off a collection of oils and vinegars. "I got most of this stuff after our lesson in salad dressings." She'd stocked up on red wine, balsamic, and champagne vinegars, soy sauce, sesame oil, and a good extra-virgin olive oil. "One big takeaway was that you don't need to go out and buy something specific, but use what you've got. I can make an almost endless variation of dressings. I used to eat plain steamed vegetables, which are pretty blah and hard to get excited about. Now I think, Huh, what can I put together to make those actually taste *good*?"

The contents of Dri's French door–style stainless fridge resembled those of other volunteers, with a bouquet of greens in water and a plastic container with bread dough. "I don't shop for meals as much as I shop for basics, which I consider onions, carrots, celery, garlic, lemons, limes, and a few other ingredients. I always have those on hand now," she explained. "I feel like I can make most anything from these staples."

This is radically different from the way she used to shop. "I used to go to the grocery store or a farmers' market and I'd see all these various things and think, Oh, that looks good, this looks good. I'd buy a whole bunch of random stuff. But then I wouldn't really have anything in mind about what to do with it. That's where a lot of my food waste came from." Dri said she made many decisions with Thierry's voice in her head. "Now when I look at something highly perishable, I think, Okay, if I buy that, then what am I going to do with it in the next two days?"

As she chatted, Dri started dinner. She moved with calm purpose as she chopped vegetables for a curried cucumber salad with a new chef's knife and pulled a beautiful small loaf of bread from her oven. Where Dri had dubiously poked at her chicken only a few months earlier, that night she demonstrated how to "spatchcock," a technique in which the backbone is removed to butterfly a whole chicken so that it lies flat to cook faster and more evenly. "I learned this from *Cook's Illustrated*. The editors use poultry shears, which I don't own. It's a little tricky with a knife but it works."

She put her weight down on the backbone to break it. Using the tip of her chef's knife, she made a surgical-like outline around the length of the spine. With one big tug, she ripped out the backbone and set it aside. She turned the chicken over and placed her hands one over the other as if to perform CPR on the bird. Instead she put her weight down on the sternum to break it with a mighty crack. "Funny, I remember not being terribly thrilled by the sight of a chicken in that class," she said. "I guess it doesn't bother me now, huh?" She placed the chicken on a cushion of thinly sliced potatoes lining the bottom of a roasting pan, "to soak up the yummy sauce," she explained. She seasoned it simply with fresh thyme, olive oil, and salt and pepper before shoving it in the oven.

Dri cooks one big meal during the week and a pot of soup on Sunday. With leftovers, that covers meals for at least four days. Other nights, she makes a quick salad, sandwich, or pasta with staples she keeps on hand. "I still suffer from this issue of cooking for one and trying to get portions right. I try not to have *too many* leftovers. I don't mind them on day two, but on day four? I usually can't go there. Sometimes I just take all the leftovers out of my fridge and bring them to work. I'll say to somebody, 'Hey, you want some chicken? I brought you lunch.'"

I didn't realize in the first visit that behind her quirky, smiling exterior, Dri's innate desire to make a radical life shift ran deep. "When it came to how I approached food, I knew that I needed to change course, but I had no idea where to start."

ANDRA

Andra seemed in good spirits when we met her in December at her apartment in Sea-Tac. She looked more rested and her face seemed thinner. When I mentioned that I thought she looked like she'd lost weight, she laughed. "Oh, that's so nice of you to say! I can't say that I've lost a ton of weight but I definitely feel like I'm eating better."

I'm endlessly fascinated with her apartment. This time, I noticed that the entire length of the fridge was plastered with a mosaic of different magnets. A dress covered up a magnetic statue of David in the top right-hand corner; magnetic poetry spelled out "Yes, a shadow wakens."

After the project, Andra made a concerted effort to add more fruits and vegetables to her diet and to cook more. "As usual, money is tight, but it's getting better now because I'm working more. Of course, the holidays are always a bit of a drain financially." She relied on public transport instead of a car. "Sometimes I'm on ten buses in one day. It's exhausting, but that's my choice. I've started to take the new light rail train, which is nice. But some nights, I get home exhausted from all the travel."

Due to the maze of buses that makes up her daily commute, she now relied on sandwiches or other foods that are easy to eat en route. She avoided the inexpensive burger joints that she used to frequent for lunch. "Fast food is not a good value. I am hungry not long afterward and I don't feel good after eating it." She timed both to confirm that it took longer to stand in line to order than it took to make a sandwich and pack an apple at home. "It's less money, less time, and healthier. It just takes planning."

Andra missed more classes than any of the other volunteers. A shame, because as we talked, it was apparent that she took away a lot from the ones she did attend. As the others agreed, the knife skills class proved to be the most useful. Shortly after the last class, she made her first roast chicken. "It was just me and my cat, but she seemed to really like it!" Roasted chicken thighs and vegetables had become dinner staples, and she regularly made artisan bread. She sometimes cooked salmon in paper. In a pinch, she relied on scrambled eggs. "I've cooked for some of my friends and I have had no complaints."

At Thanksgiving, she made stuffing from scratch with her mother and helped cook the turkey. "She noticed my new chopping skills, and that felt good. I even made the vinaigrette for the salad." She was impressed by tasting different types of lettuce. "I confess that I buy bags of salad, but that's a big move for me. I wouldn't have bought greens before at all."

Her cupboards were more filled out this time, with whole wheat pasta and cans of tomatoes, beans, and soups. She selected one of the small plastic bags of herbs she'd purchased in bulk to use in the eggs she was making for lunch. "I think about what your chef said, that if you don't have anything else, you can make an omelet. I make scrambled eggs more often, but an omelet feels more like a meal." We watched her crack the eggs into a bowl, quickly whisk the yolks together with salt, pepper, and a bit of thyme, and then pour them into a pan. She added a bit of grated cheese to the center, and then slid the omelet to fold it onto a plate. It was perfect.

It struck me that her omelet was a world away from the hyperprocessed pizza bites that she had made the first time I visited. I asked her about the contrast as she cut the edge of her eggs with a fork. "I don't know if I would buy those now," she said. "I think more about value rather than just cost." A big bag of greens costs the same as a fast-food dinner, she observed. She searched out places to buy vegetables less expensively than in a conventional supermarket, such as a local farm stand. "I've got limited money for my food, so I need to get the most out of it that I can.

"Now that I can cook better, I don't have to settle for crappy food. It's been ages since I ordered a pizza, and those guys used to know my voice on the phone."

TERRI

Terri had finally tossed her four-year-old frozen turkey dinner. "I didn't want you to come back and find that it was still there!" she said with a nervous laugh. Her fridge was still relatively bare. "I've gotten rid of all the science experiments," she admitted. Little else had changed in her cabinets. "I find that I'm going grocery shopping more often, which is funny since I actually hate grocery shopping," she said. "But I also don't want to waste food, so I usually just buy enough for a day or two and that's why I don't have a big stock of it here."

She had signed up as a client with Beve, the nutritionist. Her counter was lined with brand-new bottles of vitamins she'd been assigned to take after Beve had Terri's medical doctor run various tests. Like most people who live above the thirty-seventh parallel, Terri was wildly deficient in vitamin D; the sun is too weak most of the year for most people to produce it naturally. She had shifted to eating shredded wheat for breakfast to up her fiber intake and relied on scrambled eggs at lunch to help increase her protein.

On my first visit, she had made whole wheat pasta with a bit of olive oil. She'd advanced to adding the fresh tomato sauce from class, something she made at least twice a week. "I'll be honest. I don't mind eating the same thing all the time. I kind of like routines," she said. "It's also something that I don't really have to plan for. I always keep whole wheat pasta, tomatoes, and garlic around."

Terri was the only one who didn't chop an onion as demonstrated in class. Instead, she cut off the ends, quartered them and dropped them into a food processor, and gave them a quick whirl. "I know, I know, I'm cheating," she apologized. "I find myself reverting back to old habits."

Well, not all of them. Terri used to eat fast food for dinner up to four times a week; now it was down to less than once every couple of weeks. She had cut back on another indulgence, regular visits to Starbucks for breakfast or lunch, although that had as much to do with money as with nutrition.

Of all the people in the study, self-employed Terri had the most enduring sense of "time poverty." I heard a lot about "time" in the first round of visits with the volunteers. In the second round, the issue was noticeably less significant. When I later reviewed the videos, Terri mentioned the word *time* on twenty-two occasions in both her first and second kitchen visits. Like the White Rabbit, she seemed invariably late and rushed, even as she mentioned that her tour business more or less ground to a halt during the off-season.

"I'm glad to know about how to cut up a chicken, although I don't think I will do it myself," she said. "It was just a little too . . ." She struggled for a word. "I guess that I'm just squeamish, and it doesn't help that I am not that crazy about chicken in the first place."

Of all the classes, she liked the meat class with Robin best; it involved cutting up red meat and pork, but that bothered her less. "Learning to make rubs was helpful because pork chops are one of my standards, although I haven't made a rub yet. I liked the soup class and I plan to try that one day. The vinaigrette lesson was useful in terms of thinking about flavor combinations, but I don't make salads at home, I only eat them when I go out. As you can see, I don't keep a lot of food in my fridge, so leftovers aren't that big of a deal for me."

But she explained that this didn't mean that for her the project wasn't successful.

"It did help me to realize that I should think more about what I eat, but not necessarily worry about what I cook." Terri had slashed her fast-food runs from twenty to two per month. By doing so, she had eliminated 195,000 mostly empty calories in the course of a year, the equivalent of 550 hours on a treadmill. She explained that while some people can change their habits overnight, she learned while overcoming alcoholism that time and routine are critical for her. "When I try to change everything at once, that never works. I feel like I have started to develop a foundation and I have to be happy with where I'm going."

Given all that, so what if she used her food processor to cut onions to make something healthier at home? More power to her.

CHERYL

At Cheryl's, the Christmas tree fell down on her four-year-old son. He had pulled on an ornament, sending the tree straight down. He started wailing.

"Oh, no!" Lisa and I raced over to rescue him. As we righted the tree, Cheryl grabbed her son. She conducted a quick inventory for injury before clutching him to her chest tightly. Then she held him out at arm's length. "I told you to stop playing with the tree!" she rebuked. "I want you to sit on the couch and read your books while Mommy finishes her visit." Her son grabbed two picture books off the coffee table and dutifully climbed up onto the brown leather sofa.

On our first visit, Cheryl had opened a can of organic soup for lunch. This time, she made a pot from scratch, a fragrant curry-scented number with coconut milk and vegetables. "It's really easy," she said. "I make one pot and then my son and I eat it for a couple of days for lunch. My husband's in construction, so he takes it in his thermos. I freeze the rest in small portions for lunches later."

We watched her efficiently chop an onion, carrots, and celery for her soup. Baby Liam scooted around the kitchen floor at her feet. She had recently had all her kitchen knives sharpened. "It makes a huge difference having a super sharp knife. I can cruise through chopping." She tossed the vegetables into her pot and started to simmer them.

Her husband hunts and brings home a motley assortment of

game. She used to struggle about how to prepare it. "I used to think, What do I do with a pheasant?" she said. "Then I learned to braise! Now a lot of my cooking is braising, braising, braising. I have to say that my braised pheasant is a big hit."

She picked up Liam, who had grown noticeably bigger, and balanced him heavily on her slight hip. "The class definitely changed some fundamental basics about how I cook," she said. "I make more sauces, soups, and meals from scratch. I am more confident in the kitchen because I just have more faith in my skills. I think the class not only helped me learn new things but also taught me not to be afraid of cooking and trying new things on my own."

Cheryl had been fairly label conscious and the class had just made her even more so. "For instance, I rarely buy bread." She opened her fridge to reveal two containers of bread dough, one white and one whole wheat. "My husband is the official baker in the family. He experiments with all kinds of versions. You know, I've gotten to the point that I just want to know what's in everything that I feed my family now."

SHANNON

Shannon is endlessly up for a challenge. "It's funny, I made some applesauce. I had all these apples," she said, holding her arms out wide to indicate a massive crate of apples. "Weirdly, it was really fun. I was totally cruising through chopping them." She smiled broadly. "My hand was a little sore after doing it, but I totally dug the Zen of getting into it."

By this point, the volunteers had some consensus on the efficacy of classes. Knife skills, the chicken class, stock, soup, no-knead bread, and learning to cook fish in parchment came out as strong themes. Shannon was no different. But I was interested in her take-aways. She was the mother of two young children and someone who carefully watched her food budget.

Some things she'd been less hip to. "I've made my own stock and

I really like it, but sometimes I just can't get there," she said. "It's hard to compare my own stock against supermarket stock because it's just so different. But if I buy it, I totally check the sodium. I get it as close to unsalted as I can. I found a brand that has only three grams of sodium that I like."

One class that she doesn't remember fondly was the tasting class. In retrospect, eager to offer a lot of options, I may have presented *too* many and pushed a couple of volunteers into sensory exhaustion. Nine types of salt were probably six too many. "I remember leaving that class feeling that I had been physically beaten." She liked the later classes in which we did a single tasting at the beginning of class. "Don't get me wrong, I liked comparing tastes of things that I actually cook with, such as pasta and canned tomatoes and chicken stock. It was just too much at one time." Even so, she was the first student to announce she had tossed her iodized salt. She had seen a notice online for the comparative beef tasting at a Red Velvet Dinner. "That's something I'd be interested in, the whole grass-fed versus corn-fed, or the taste of organic chickens versus the kind from the meat department."

As far as the fish class, the emphasis on hitting a separate store didn't factor into the complexities of being a mother and a cook. "While I'd love to go to a fish market, the reality is that at the end of the day I have only so many trips in me. I've got to guide a baby and a young child and sometimes it's all I can do to just get milk. So I buy fish from the higher-end supermarket where I know they have good fish and I buy some of my other stuff there, too. Honestly, the reason why I like the parchment is because it always turns out. I can prep it in advance while they're napping and there are no dishes."

Who could argue with Shannon? She had the information and weighed her options based on a frank and realistic set of expectations for her life right now. For instance, nurturing a pot of stock for hours wasn't a priority, but she didn't want to add the liquid equivalent of a salt lick to her food. So her decision to seek out unsalted chicken stock seemed like a completely reasonable solution. I'm sure the list went on.

That has not kept her from exploring new culinary territory, in part based on the confidence and information she gained from the classes. "I've always been kind of scared of my Crock-Pot. I don't really understand it," she said. But she had dragged it out of a closet and dropped a couple of lamb shanks into it recently. "When I came back in the meat was separated from the bones and I thought, Yes, that's right, that's what Robin said was supposed to happen. It tasted really awesome."

In June, Shannon noted that she felt uncomfortable cooking without a recipe. So it was a surprise when she shared the provenance of her lunch. "I had a lamb ragout in a restaurant when we were on vacation," she started. "It was so yummy! Oh, my God, it was so good! So then I wondered how I could re-create it. I looked online and found some recipes for ragout, but they all used ground lamb, which wasn't what they used. But I realized, Oh, that's just a braise. So I got a lamb shoulder and I cut it up into pieces and braised it. For the polenta, I made it from cornmeal and threw some cheese into it to make it gooey and yummy and it all worked."

Her family approved. "We were like, 'Oh, yum!' The funny thing about that story is that before class, I just don't think I would have ever thought to tackle something like that. Now, I can. I feel like I deserve a pat on the back for that one."

At that moment, I realized that not only had Shannon passed Cooking Basics 101 with flying colors, she was probably ready for a 301 class.

GENEVIEVE

Due to moving schedules and life in general, it took us months to catch up with Genevieve. She had been living with three roommates in a comfortable rental house when we met her, but she had since moved into a new condo with her boyfriend, John. The sleek kitchen boasted dark cherrywood cabinets, gray slate floor tile, a black man-made quartz countertop, and stainless steel appliances. "It's funny, part of what we liked about this place was the cabinets, but it turns out some are super shallow." She demonstrated by showing that a canister she uses for tea barely fits inside. "Oh, well, they look nice."

The shallow cabinets included a healthy roundup: wheat pasta, cans of tomatoes, artichokes, and olives, brown rice, and a collection of oils and vinegars. "It turns out that I really like vinegar," she said. "I was kind of surprised. Now I'm all over them. My latest favorite is tarragon. It is super tasty."

In her fridge was a spectrum of colored vegetables, a wrapped packet of fish, some greens, organic milk, white wine, prepackaged Jell-O pudding, and leftover butternut squash soup from the weekend. She kept cilantro in a small glass of water like flowers, as Thierry had suggested. In her cheese drawer was a wedge of real Parmigiano-Reggiano. Among the items she kept in her freezer were frozen strawberries, pot stickers, and a couple of frozen pizzas, plus some butter because she doesn't use it often.

"One thing that's I've changed is my buying habits. I don't buy premade packages of stuff, like those frozen pasta dinners with the sauce. I used to get those a lot. But now I realize that it's no comparison to what I can make fresh, plus the list of ingredients kind of turned me off. I find it hard to order pasta in a restaurant. I think, Twenty dollars? I could totally make this for three."

She and John hit a farm stand a couple of times a week rather than stocking up at the grocery store and sought out a stand-alone butcher and fishmonger. "I rely less on getting my food from one place." Shopping together, they both try to rotate the goods in their fridge to avoid food waste. "A couple of times a week I do a sweep of the fridge for what needs to be used. Whether it's leftover chicken or vegetables or herbs, I'll just chop them up and add them to a salad and then make vinaigrette. Sometimes that's dinner."

On her counter rests a small bowl filled with avocados and

tomatoes. Beve, the nutritionist, had made a comment that everyone could eat more avocados, a source of healthy fat. So Gen had learned to make guacamole. John chimed in. "I have to say, her guac is great."

During our first visit, Gen combined a bag of prepared cabbage slaw with a jar of teriyaki sauce. On the follow-up visit, she made wild-caught Alaskan salmon cooked in parchment paper and roasted asparagus. "I make this pretty often. I've even taught the paper trick to a couple of people. I remember when you asked how many portions a big chicken breast made, and then you weighed it and it was more than a pound, so it was really four servings. I use that as a reason to buy better meat or fish but eat less of it."

She reminded me of something that I'd said offhand in class. "You said, 'No one is going to make you pack your knives and go home if a dish doesn't turn out.' I think about that a lot. That kind of attitude makes me more confident, and that's why I enjoy it more. It allows me to try things without getting worked up about it." A week ago, she had been sautéing a piece of fish and decided to make a sauce with diced apple, rosemary, and white wine. "I thought, What the heck? I'll give that a try. You know what? It was really good."

DONNA

Of all the volunteers, I was most intrigued by Donna. I genuinely liked her and was sympathetic to the power struggle over food and cooking in her new marriage. We never managed a date for a second home visit. After a few months, I sensed that the project had had no lasting effect on her and she was simply too polite to let me down.

Finally, a year after the project ended, we caught up on the phone. "Honestly, I didn't change my lifestyle much right after the classes," she started, my initial suspicions confirmed. "But there's one phrase that repeats in my head, even to this day. When you were at my house, you said, 'Do you ever wonder what they do to foods to make them low-fat?' I guess I never cared before. Crappy food had always been a fact of life. But then I started questioning things, although not much else changed."

Then, a few months earlier, she had started to cook on Sundays. "I'm not sure how it started, but I just decided that Sunday was the only real time that I have to cook." She made three or four meals, and then wrapped them up in individual servings to eat for lunch or dinner throughout the week. She favored vegetable-centric dishes that pack well; vegetarian chili was a standard in her rotation. In the three months since she'd started, she'd lost ten pounds.

"After years of trying to find the 'secret' to battling my weight issues, I seem to have found it in cooking," she said. "I'm an emotional eater. Taking my food with me to work and eating the same things has helped me maintain that food is fuel and not luxury or reward."

She doesn't come home ravenous anymore, a good thing because her husband lost all interest in cooking, a major shift in the original context of their relationship. "He eats mostly frozen food now," she said. "I don't want that for myself but I don't want to fight him about it either. If he cooks, that's okay, but I don't rely on him to do it anymore," she said, adding that he's still about ninety pounds overweight. "Now if we eat something homemade, I make it. The thing is that he hasn't changed, I'm the one who has changed," she said. You could hear a surge of independence in her voice. "It's pretty exciting, really."

When we first met, her husband selected most of their groceries, but his shopping ethos troubled her. He'd buy five heads of lettuce at a warehouse store, only to throw away three. It conflicted with the values from her day job working with an African aid organization. Now she shops for her food, and he shops for his.

"So I still buy a lot at the warehouse store because they have good deals, but now I go with a friend from work. We shop together and then we split it. Doing that has helped me save money but waste less food. It's fun, too. My friend and I trade recipes and catch up." For fruits and vegetables, she hits a farm stand near her house two or three times a week. "I've been trying to eat organic, too. I am now okay with paying a little more to get something local or organic. My husband thinks I'm crazy but he supports me."

As Donna made the same recipes over and over again, she found herself experimenting with them. "I used to follow everything to the letter. Now I'm not a slave to a recipe. I trust my taste more, and I'm getting better at knowing when a dish needs something and what that might be."

As with the other volunteers, small bits of information had had an impact. "I didn't realize spices expired! I thought they lasted forever. I think it's crazy to make a pasta dish from a package. It's about the same amount of work and mine tastes so much better." She'd even made gnocchi from scratch, something I personally have yet to master. "I had a lot of potatoes and I thought that I could probably figure it out. I've done it a few times and I'm getting really good at it now."

Not long ago, she made her mother-in-law's classic white rolls. The first time she tried them, they turned out well. When Donna made them at her mother's house, they burned. "In the past, I would have thought it was my fault. See? This is proof that I can't cook. But this time I thought, Oh, well, I can make these, it's her oven, and this isn't about my ability. It's a bigger shift in my own self-worth."

She credits a chicken with some of her confidence.

"I had wanted to roast a chicken, but I always felt intimidated." A few months ago, she had bought her first whole chicken. She delighted in the sense of victory when it turned out perfectly. Now roast chicken is one of her staples. "A week ago, my friend came over and she said, 'Wow, look at you, you're an amazing cook.' And I thought, What? It's just a roast chicken." Then she remembered that not that long ago that was a big deal.

"So I've encouraged people around me to cook. I know that it makes such a difference. Small changes put together can be big enough to change your whole life," she said. "I have a friend who always bought her vegetables precut. When I asked why, she said she was scared of knives. I was, too, before this started. So I showed her how it's done, so she could get past her fear."

This, she said, was the greatest lesson. "You get so afraid of things and then you do them and think, What was I so afraid of? You just have to do it."

How had I changed? My spice drawer is immaculate, thanks to the Great Spice Cleanout of 2009. Our freezer is lined with pasture-raised beef, pork, and chicken, a nod to the various classes on the subject and, in a way, a circle back to my early life on the farm in Michigan. I make soup at least once a week now to clean out my fridge. As Thierry suggested, we have a photo in the back of our fridge, an image of Mike and me embracing in Paris, taken by Holly during the AAA tour.

I often think of that speech I gave at the Cordon Bleu graduation. In a blur of anxiety and grief, I urged the graduates to find something they were passionate about and just go for it. What I didn't realize then was that I needed that advice as much as anyone in the audience, and I learned as much as or more than any of the volunteers over the course of the project, including unexpected things I didn't even know needed to change.

Not long after the project ended, Mike announced that he was going to make Alfredo sauce. I hovered. "Maybe you should add some garlic," I started. "You might not want to stir it so much." Then, "Oh, hey, you know, you could add some of the chicken stock in the fridge. It's a different way to do it, but . . ."

Mike handed me the spatula. "Fine, you finish it the way you want it."

"But I was just trying to be helpful," I told him.

"This is why I don't like to cook with you in the kitchen," he said heatedly. "You know why I always make Thai food? You never try to correct me on it." I knew how he felt. It replayed a similar scene from earlier in the summer.

When we moved back to the United States in 2005, I hadn't owned a car for six years. Mike would sit in the passenger seat and offer me "helpful" tips. "Kat, there's a pedestrian over there." Then, "Oh, you'll probably want to slow down, there's a sharp turn coming up." Or, if he felt that I was going too slowly, "You know the speed limit is forty-five here, right?"

It made me so nervous, I'd second-guess myself. Even if he didn't say a word, I felt him silently critiquing my every move. Only weeks before the Alfredo episode, I had pulled over, unbuckled my seat belt, and said, "Fine, you drive." His shock at my response was the same as mine to his irritated resignation about the pasta.

In the midst of a project designed to encourage people to cook, it seemed I thwarted the person closest to me. I learned to back off, to let him explore his own tastes and give him the reign of the kitchen now and then. As a result, he flourished as a cook. Now we routinely cook together.

But that's the thing about teaching. You find lessons you never expected beyond the ones you've taught. I'm grateful for that existential crisis onstage in Paris. Sometimes we need a good shake-up to remind us of who and where we are in life and to prompt us to change courses. Am I a chef? Not really, but how well does a single word define us? Julia Child never needed or wanted the title of chef. I write, I cook, I teach. I know that I'm the sum of those passions.

With that, I'm off to take a class on canning with Shannon. She recently earned her "Master Canner" designation. Last summer, Shannon didn't know how to hold a knife. Tomorrow, she will teach me how to preserve pears. It's the most fitting close to the circle that I can imagine. We live, we learn, we teach one another. Isn't that the way it should be?

Extra Recipes

෨෨

In this section, you'll find a few other recipes taught in or developed as a result of the project. Most are meant to replicate items frequently purchased. Go ahead, give them a try.

෨ Baked Chicken Nuggets

My sister and I started making this alternative to the ubiquitous ultra-processed fried chicken nuggets for my niece Sarah a decade ago. Store-bought bread crumbs can be stale and loaded with sodium, so try making your own. Toast two slices of bread, let them cool, and process them into crumbs in a small food processor. You can also use panko, Japanese bread crumbs, or toss in ground cornflakes for extra crunch. Cooking the chicken on a cooling rack allows the dry heat to crisp both sides, but if you don't have one, simply coat a parchment or foil-lined cookie sheet with cooking spray, and turn the chicken pieces over after ten minutes. Try to use real cheese rather than a canned variety; it will make a big difference in flavor.

MAKES ABOUT 2 DOZEN NUGGETS

$1\frac{1}{2}$ pounds skinless, boneless chicken breasts or tenders
1 cup bread crumbs
$\frac{1}{3}$ cup grated Parmesan cheese
$\frac{1}{2}$ teaspoon kosher salt

1 teaspoon dried thyme or mixed herbs
Pinch of cayenne (optional)
Freshly ground black pepper
1 egg
¼ cup skim milk, yogurt, or buttermilk
Cooking spray

❧ Preheat the oven to 400°F. Place a cooling rack in the center of a cookie sheet. Set aside.

❧ Cut the chicken breasts into 1½-inch pieces. In a shallow bowl or a large plastic bag, mix together the bread crumbs, cheese, salt, dried herbs, cayenne (if using), and a few grinds of black pepper. Combine the egg and milk in a small bowl. Dip the chicken into the milk mixture and then coat it well with the bread crumb mixture, either in a bowl or by tossing it inside the bag. Place the coated chicken pieces on the cooling rack and put the cookie sheet into the oven. Depending on your oven and the size and thickness of the chicken, the pieces will take 15 to 20 minutes until firm and cooked through. Spritz the chicken lightly with cooking spray and then place the cookie sheet under the broiler for 1 to 2 minutes, until browned, if desired.

ᔅ Cream of Mushroom Soup

Many "cream of" condensed soups are little more than simple white sauces easily replicated at home. The result tastes better and contains far less sodium, preservatives, and fat than you'll find in the canned variety. You can use any variety of dried mushroom that fits your budget and taste, but avoid shiitake, as its pronounced flavor may throw off many recipes. For best value, buy mushrooms in bulk; you can find them online and in warehouse stores. Mushroom bouillon can be found in health-food stores, Italian food specialty stores, or online.

YIELDS ROUGHLY THE EQUIVALENT OF AN 11-OUNCE CAN

$\frac{1}{8}$ ounce dried mushrooms (about 1 tablespoon)
8 ounces hot water
$1\frac{1}{2}$ tablespoons butter
$1\frac{1}{2}$ tablespoons flour
$\frac{1}{2}$ cup cold milk
$\frac{1}{4}$ teaspoon mushroom or beef bouillon
Salt and freshly ground black pepper

❦ In a bowl, steep the dried mushrooms in the hot water until they soften according to the package directions. Remove the mushrooms with a fork, reserving the dark liquid, or "tea." Chop them finely, and set aside.

❦ Heat the butter in a small saucepan over medium-high heat. Once it's melted, add the flour. Whisk continuously as the mixture bubbles for about 2 minutes, until it smells like popcorn, then remove the pan from the heat. Whisk in the cold milk until blended. Return to the heat and add the steeping liquid, the chopped mushrooms, and the bouillon. Add a pinch or two of salt and a few grinds of coarse-ground pepper. Bring to a light, bubbly boil and then simmer for about 5 minutes over medium-low heat, until it thickens. Taste, and add more salt and pepper if desired.

Variation: Cream of Chicken

❦ Use 8 ounces of chicken stock in place of the dried mushrooms and water and $\frac{1}{4}$ teaspoon chicken bouillon in place of the mushroom or beef varieties.

❧ Easy Spaghetti Sauce

Less expensive, tastier, and healthier than most jars of pasta sauce, this can be made in roughly the time it takes to boil pasta and toss a quick

salad. As a bonus, you can add fresh or leftover vegetables or other fla-
vorings. This also makes a terrific pizza sauce.

SERVES 4 WITH PASTA

4 tablespoons olive oil
$\frac{1}{2}$ onion, finely chopped (about $\frac{3}{4}$ cup)
$1\frac{1}{2}$ teaspoons dried mixed Italian herbs
3 garlic cloves, chopped
One 14-ounce can tomato sauce
Pinch of red pepper flakes (optional)
$\frac{1}{2}$ cup water
1 bay leaf
Coarse salt and freshly ground black pepper
1 tablespoon balsamic vinegar (optional)

❧ In a saucepan over medium heat, warm the oil, then cook the
onion and herbs until tender. Add the garlic, stir, and cook for 1 minute. Add the tomato sauce, red pepper flakes, water, and bay leaf, plus
a couple of pinches of coarse salt and a few cranks of black pepper.
Bring just to a boil, and then immediately lower the heat to a simmer.
Cook, uncovered, on low heat for 15 minutes. Add the vinegar, if
using, and cook an additional 2 minutes. Taste and adjust the seasonings. Remove the bay leaf before serving.

Consider adding the following:
About $\frac{1}{2}$ cup green and/or black olives with the onions for a
   puttanesca-style sauce
Handful of finely chopped mushrooms with the onions
Red wine in place of the water just before simmering for a
   cabernet-style sauce
 A tablespoon or two of chopped fresh herbs, such as basil, oreg-
   ano, or parsley, at the very end of cooking
About $\frac{1}{4}$ pound cooked hamburger or cubed chicken with the
   onions

3 tablespoons vodka and $\frac{1}{4}$ cup cream 5 minutes before the end of
  cooking

~~~~~~

❀ Pomodoro (Fresh Tomato Sauce)

*Be sure to have the pasta cooking and all the ingredients ready before
starting the sauce; this is ready more quickly than you'd expect. Flavorful fresh tomatoes make all the difference here; cherry tomatoes work
especially well and they're available year-round. Just cut them in half.
Carefully scoop out a bit of the pasta water to finish the sauce.*

MAKES ENOUGH FOR ABOUT 4 SIDE PORTIONS OR 2 MAIN-DISH SERVINGS

8 ounces dried pasta, such as penne or linguine, or 12 ounces
  fresh pasta
Coarse salt
1 tablespoon olive oil
2 to 3 garlic cloves, minced
About 12 ounces tomatoes, chopped
$\frac{1}{4}$ cup Parmesan cheese, grated
Pinch or two of hot pepper flakes
Handful of chopped parsley or basil
Freshly ground black pepper to taste

❧ Boil water for the pasta. Add at least 1 tablespoon of salt to the
water; it should taste slightly salty. Cook the pasta according to the
package directions; reserve about $\frac{1}{2}$ cup of pasta water after cooking.

❧ Meanwhile, add the olive oil to a sauté pan over medium-high
heat. Add the garlic and cook for 1 minute; be sure not to burn it or
you'll need to start over. Add the tomatoes and any other vegetables (see below), and cook until the vegetables are softened, about 3
to 5 minutes for tomatoes on their own, longer if you add other
vegetables.

❧ Add the reserved pasta water and cook until the sauce is reduced
slightly and the rest of the ingredients begin to break down, about

another 2 to 3 minutes. Remove from the heat, add the cheese, red pepper flakes and parsley or basil (if using), several cranks of fresh black pepper, and salt if needed.

Consider adding the following:

Splash of cream at the end of cooking for a more creamy texture
Handful of additional chopped vegetables, such as zucchini, artichokes, olives, and/or asparagus, to extend the sauce and offer additional flavor
Shrimp or diced cooked chicken with the tomatoes (Shrimp can be added raw, but be sure to cook them thoroughly; they should turn white throughout and curl up tightly.)

ᐳ *Potage Parmentier* (Leek and Potato Soup)

This is inexpensive French soul food. If leeks aren't available, try sweet onions. Makes about four to six servings.

3 medium leeks
2 tablespoons butter
1 pound potatoes, peeled and diced
1 bay leaf and $\frac{1}{2}$ teaspoon dried thyme, or a bouquet garni
2 quarts water or chicken or vegetable stock
$\frac{1}{4}$ cup whipping cream, or 2 tablespoons butter, softened
Coarse salt and freshly ground black pepper
Cayenne to taste (optional)
3 tablespoons minced parsley or chives

❧ Prepare the leeks by discarding the roots and the tough green upper stalks. Slice, then rinse them in water to remove any residual dirt. In a 4-quart or larger saucepan, melt 2 tablespoons of butter, then sauté the leeks for about 5 minutes, until they are softened and translucent. Add the potatoes, bay leaf and thyme or bouquet garni and water or stock. Simmer for about 40 minutes, until the vegetables are tender.

⚜ Remove from the heat. Discard the bay leaf. Break down the vegetables with a fork or a potato masher, or puree in a blender. Return to the heat. Add the whipping cream or 2 tablespoons butter. Taste. Add salt and pepper if needed, and a bit of cayenne if desired. Garnish with chopped parsley or chives and a couple of cranks of black pepper.

A "Cheat Sheet" to Flavor Profiles

What makes something taste Italian or Cajun or Moroccan? Whether crafting vinaigrette, seasoning chicken, or developing a soup, understanding the flavors of ingredients that help to define various cuisines can be deeply useful.

Every cuisine has its regional variations; Basque cuisine is vastly different from the classic dishes from Provence, but they're both French. So consider this a shorthand reference to a few culinary stereotypes. Don't overdo it. Try incorporating two to four ingredients from a cuisine group to tilt a flavor profile in that general direction.

Cajun/Creole
dark roux, onions, celery, green pepper, tomatoes, parsley, cayenne, Cajun spice blends, blackening seasonings, lemon, scallions, andouille sausage, crab, shrimp

French
butter, shallots, onions, celery, carrots, thyme, tarragon, herbs de Provence, bay leaves, chives, chervil, capers, red and white wine, truffle, soft cheeses, Dijon mustard, mushrooms, cream

Indian
tandoori spices, garam masala, curry, yogurt, coconut milk, basmati rice, tamarind, cardamom, cumin, coriander, cilantro, fennel, garlic, saffron, fenugreek, dried chilies

Italian
garlic, onions, celery, basil, pesto, prosciutto, Parmigiano-Reggiano cheese, mozzarella cheese, pine nuts, tomatoes, artichokes, olives, olive oil, oregano, lemon, fennel, flat-leaf parsley, red pepper flakes, rosemary, white beans, balsamic vinegar

Japanese
miso, sesame oil, sesame seeds, rice vinegar, sake, soy sauce, wasabi, ginger

Mediterranean/Greek
oregano, lemon, olives, tuna, rosemary, bay leaves, thyme, olive oil, lamb, garlic, feta cheese, tomatoes, red onions, fish, shellfish

Mexican/Tex-Mex
cumin, chili powder, hot sauce, green peppers, oregano, lime, garlic, onions, celery, cilantro, tomatoes, scallions, black beans, Cheddar cheese, avocado

North African
mint, lemon, harissa, saffron, turmeric, parsley, cilantro, honey, olives, almonds, dates, raisins, chickpeas, eggplant, green bell peppers, carrots, lentils, onion, ground ginger, paprika, cumin, cayenne, figs

Central/South Asian
ginger, garlic, scallions, shallots, lemongrass, Thai basil, cilantro, fish sauce, shrimp paste, soy sauce, coconut milk, sesame seeds, sesame oil, rice or sweet wine vinegar, cilantro, lime, oyster sauce, galangal, hot chili peppers

Acknowledgments

ᔕᔓ

ᔕᔓ First, here's a nod to the crew at Viking Penguin, including my wonderful editors, Stephen Morrison and Rebecca Hunt, publicist Lindsay Prevette, editor Beena Kamlani and copy editor Randee Marullo. I'm thankful for the wisdom and support of agent Larry Weissman through this project.

Nine volunteers opened up their hearts, kitchens, and lives, and for that I will be eternally grateful. I'm beholden to the volunteer teachers, chefs Thierry Rautureau, Robin Leventhal, Lauri Carter, and Jenny Nichols, plus nutritionist Beve Kindblade. Life wouldn't be the same without my chef friend Ted Lawrence.

I couldn't have done this project without my friend Lisa Simpson, who soldiered with me through kitchens and chickens and taught me a lot along the way. I'm indebted to pals Maggie Savarino and Jeff Manness for lending their remarkable talents and energy.

Many people lent their time offering feedback on this work while it was in progress, among them Deirdre Timmons, Laura Evelev, Cherie Jacobs Featheringill, Lee Mohr, Jackie Donnelly Baisa, Cindy Kane, and Philip Lee. Shalini Gujavarty came on board as my assistant during the writing of the book and contributed research, recipe testing, and beyond. Jamaica Jones did a bang-up job double-checking my research. My resident knife expert, Bill Magee, kept my blades sharp and my cutlery facts straight. My Le Cordon Bleu classmate Anne-Catherine Kruger led me to the catering kitchen owned by Kristine Pottle. I'm grateful to Zoë François and Jeff Hertzberg for their terrific no-knead bread recipe.

I recruited more than 150 recipe testers to try out and provide feedback for recipes in this book. The most active included Adrian Amo, Lauren Robinson, Marie Asselin, Susan Baird, Jane Bonacci, Libby Brill, Eric Compton, Deb Coupland-Porter, Glenn Dettwiler, Jessica Friedman, Michele Gartner, Lisa Glatt, Alka Goyal, Seika Gray, Scott Harbour, Eric Himan, Julie Hinson, Lindsey Hunt, Lee Mohr, Dayna Quick, Maria Raynal, David Rojas, David St. Clair, Jenise Silva, Shannon Valderas, Michael Wagner, Brenna Wilson, and Diana Wisen.

I relied heavily on my education from the chefs at Le Cordon Bleu in Paris, and I know now that I'll be forever indebted to that famed institution. I'm grateful to the many people in the food-writing community who contributed directly or indirectly to this project and whose work and research inspires me, including Ken Abala, Pam Anderson, Jonathan Bloom, Dina Cheney, Amanda Hesser, Lia Huber, Deborah Madison, Marion Nestle, Michael Pollan, Michael Ruhlman, Jamie Oliver, Ruth Reichl, Rick Rodgers, Jon Rowley, Kim Severson, Laura Shapiro, Frances Short, Andy F. Smith, Virginia Willis and among many others. The late Julia Child never fails to motivate me.

Petra Martin developed the Whidbey Island Writing Refuge, a quiet place in the woods where I wrote portions of the book. David John and Linea Anderson lent me the use of their sailboat. Both spaces were in addition to my usual shelter at the Richard Hugo House.

I'm thankful to the woman in the supermarket for having the faith to let a stranger help her out with a chicken. I hope someday she knows how that afternoon changed my life.

Finally, my deepest, heartfelt appreciation goes to Mike Klozar, partner in everything, writing coach, editor, technical guru, idea man, husband, and love of my life. There aren't enough words in any language to thank you.

Selected Bibliography
❧❦

Blaylock, Russell L. *Excitotoxins: The Taste That Kills*. Abingdon, England: Health Press, 1996.

Brackman, Pat. *The Compleat I Hate to Cook Book*. New York: Bantam, 1988.

Cheney, Dina. *Tasting Club: Gathering Together to Share and Savor Your Favorite Tastes*. New York: DK Publishing, 2006.

Child, Julia. *The French Chef Cookbook*. New York: Knopf, 2002.

Child, Julia, Simone Beck, and Louise Bertholle. *Mastering the Art of French Cooking*. New York: Knopf, 1961.

David, Elizabeth. *An Omelette and a Glass of Wine*. Guilford, CT: Globe Pequot, 1997.

Davidson, Alan. *The Penguin Companion to Food*. Harmondsworth, UK: Penguin Books Ltd., 2002.

The End of the Line. Director, Rupert Murray; producer, Arcane Pictures. Dogwood Pictures, 2009.

Ettingliner, Steve. *Twinkies Deconstructed*. New York: Hudson Street Press, 2002.

Fisher, M. F. K. *Serve It Forth (Art of Eating)*. New York: North Point Press, 1989.

"Food 52" Kitchen Tour with Amanda Hesser. Producer, Food 52.com, 2009. http://vimeo.com/5133553.

Food, Inc. Director and producer, Robert Kenner. Magnolia Pictures, 2009.

Gladwell, Malcolm. *Outliers*. New York: Little, Brown, 2008.

Gladwell, Malcolm. *The Tipping Point*. New York: Little, Brown, 2002.

Jacob, Dianne. *Will Write for Food*. New York: Da Capo Press, 2010.

Kallam, Tawra Jean, and Jill Cooper. *Dining on a Dime*. Temple, TX: T & L Group, 2004.

Katz, David L., and Catherine S. Katz. *The Flavor Point Diet: The Delicious, Breakthrough Plan to Turn Off Your Hunger and Lose the Weight for Good*. New York: Rodale, 2005.

Keller, Thomas, and Deborah Jones. *The French Laundry Cookbook*. New York: Workman Publishing, 1999.

Kessler, David. *The End of Overeating*. New York: Rodale, 2009.

King Corn. Director and producer, Aaron Woolf. Mosaic Films Inc., 2007.

Kriger, Ellie. *The Food You Crave*. Newtown, CT: Taunton, 2008.

Kurlansky, Mark. *Salt: A World History*. New York: Penguin, 2003.

Millstone, Erik. *The Atlas of Food: Who Eats What, Where, and Why*. Berkeley, CA: University of California Press, 2008.

Mitchell, Margaret. *Gone with the Wind*. New York: Scribner, 1936.

Moulton, Sarah. *Sarah Moulton's Everyday Family Dinners*. New York: Simon & Schuster, 2010.

My Big Fat Greek Wedding. Director, Joel Zwick. Gold Circle Films, 2002.

Oliver, Jamie. *Jamie's Food Revolution*. New York: Hyperion, 2009.

Patel, Raj. *Stuffed and Starved: Markets, Power and the Hidden Battle for the World's Food System*. London: Portobello Books, 2007.

Peterson, James. *Splendid Soups*. New York: Bantam, 1993.

Pollan, Michael. *In Defense of Food: An Eater's Manifesto*. New York: Penguin Books Ltd., 2008.

Pollan, Michael. "Out of the Kitchen, Onto the Couch." *New York Times Magazine*, July 29, 2009: MM26.

Reichl, Ruth. "The New Culinary Order." Keynote, IACP Annual Conference, April 22, 2010.

Ruhlman, Michael. *The Elements of Cooking*. New York: Scribner, 2007.

Sanders, Laura. "Binging Rats Get Hooked on Junk Food." *Discovery News* 21 (Oct 2009).

Shapiro, Laura. *Something from the Oven: Reinventing Dinner in 1950s America*. New York: Viking Penguin, 2004.

Short, Frances. *Kitchen Secrets: The Meaning of Cooking in Everyday Life.* Oxford, UK: Berg Publishers, 2006.

Smith, Andrew F., *Eating History: Thirty Turning Points in the Making of American Cuisine.* New York: Columbia University Press, 2009.

Smith, Andrew F. *Souper Tomatoes: The Story of America's Favorite Food.* New Brunswick, NJ: Rutgers University Press, 2000.

Staten, Vince. *Can You Trust a Tomato in January?* New York: Touchstone, 1994.

Weber, Karl. *Food, Inc: How Industrial Food Is Making Us Sicker, Fatter, and Poorer—and What You Can Do About It.* New York: Public Affairs, 2009.

Wilder, Laura Ingalls. *Little House on the Prairie.* New York: HarperCollins, 1971.

Recommended Reading
࿐

General Cookbooks

Bittman, Mark. *How to Cook Everything: 2,000 Simple Recipes for Great Food.* Hoboken, NJ: Wiley, 2008.

Child, Julia. *The Way to Cook.* New York: Knopf, 1989.

Better Homes & Gardens, *Better Homes and Gardens New Cook Book.* 15th ed. New York: Wiley, 2010.

Rombauer, Irma S., et al. *Joy of Cooking.* New York: Scribner, various editions.

On Learning to Cook Intuitively

Anderson, Pam. *How to Cook Without a Book: Recipes and Techniques Every Cook Should Know by Heart.* New York: Broadway Books, 2000.

Page, Karen, and Andrew Dornenburg. *The Flavor Bible.* New York: Hachette USA, 2008.

Ruhlman, Michael. *Ratio: The Simple Codes Behind the Craft of Everyday Cooking.* New York: Scribner, 2009.

Reinventing Family Dinners

David, Laurie, and Kristin Uhrenholdt, et al. *The Family Dinner: Great Ways to Connect with Your Kids One Meal at a Time.* New York: Grand Central Food & Style, 2010.

Lair, Cynthia. *Feeding the Whole Family*. Seattle, WA: Sasquatch Books, 2008.

References for Every Kitchen

Herbst, Sharon Tyler, and Ron Herbst. *The New Food Lover's Companion*. 4th ed. New York: Barron's Educational Series, 2007.

Joachim, David. *The Food Substitutions Bible: More than 5,000 Substitutions for Ingredients, Equipment and Techniques*. Toronto, ON: Robert Rose, 2010.

QA International, *The Visual Food Lover's Guide*. New York: Wiley, 2009.

Cooking for One

Yonan, Joe. *Serve Yourself: Nightly Adventures in Cooking for One*. Berkeley, CA: Ten Speed Press, 2011.

Knife Skills

Ward, Chad. *An Edge in the Kitchen: The Ultimate Guide to Kitchen Knives—How to Buy Them, Keep Them Razor Sharp, and Use Them Like a Pro*. New York: William Morrow Cookbooks, 2008.

No-Knead Bread

Hertzberg, Jeff, and Zoë François. *Artisan Bread in Five Minutes a Day*. New York: St. Martin's Press, 2007.

Baggett, Nancy. *Kneadlessly Simple: Fabulous, Fuss-Free, No-Knead Breads*. New York: Wiley, 2009.

Strategies to Save Money on Groceries

Dacyzyn, Amy. *The Tightwad Gazette*. New York: Villard, 1992.

Longacre, Doris Janzen. *More-with-Less Cookbook*. Scottsdale, PA: Herald Press, 2000.

Pennington, Amy. *Urban Pantry: Tips and Recipes for a Thrifty, Sustainable and Seasonal Kitchen*. Seattle, WA: Skipstone Press, 2010.

Soup

Kaul, Leslie, Bob Spiegel, et al. *The Daily Soup Cookbook*. New York: Hyperion, 1999.

Blake, Susannah. *500 Soups: The Only Soup Compendium You'll Ever Need*. Portland, ME: Sellers, 2007.

Modern Food Issues

Bloom, Jonathan. *American Wasteland: How America Throws Away Nearly Half of Its Food (and What We Can Do About It)*. Cambridge, MA: Da Capo Press, 2010.

Fussell, Betty. *The Story of Corn*. Albuquerque, NM: University of Mexico Press, 2004.

Nestle, Marion. *What to Eat*. New York: North Point Press, 2006.

Pollan, Michael. *The Omnivore's Dilemma: A Natural History of Four Meals*. New York: Penguin Books, 2006.

Understanding Nutrition Labels

Farlow, Christina Hoza. *Food Additives: Shopper's Guide to What's Safe & What's Not*. Lafayette, LA: KISS for Health Publishing, 2007.

Vegetarian Cooking

Dragonwagon, Crescent. *The Passionate Vegetarian*. New York: Workman Publishing, 2002.

Madison, Deborah. *Vegetarian Cooking for Everyone*. New York: Clarkson Potter, 2007.

O'Donnel, Kim. *The Meat Lover's Meatless Cookbook*. Cambridge, MA: Da Capo Press, 2010.

Index of Recipes
༄༅